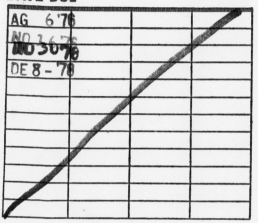

FOREIGN POLICY AND THE AMERICAN SPIRIT

FOREIGN POLICY *and*

the AMERICAN SPIRIT

Essays by DEXTER PERKINS

John L. Senior Professor in American Civilization
Cornell University

Edited by GLYNDON G. VAN DEUSEN

and RICHARD C. WADE

KENNIKAT PRESS
Port Washington, N. Y./London

FOREIGN POLICY AND THE AMERICAN SPIRIT

Manufactured by Taylor Publishing Company   Dallas, Texas

Preface

THE editors of this book had hoped to select a group of essays which would suggest the many facets of Professor Perkins' extraordinary career. This proved to be impossible, for his interests are so wide and varied that no one volume, whether large or small, could begin to encompass all of them. However, in the past decade Professor Perkins has been especially concerned with two ideas about diplomatic history. One is the notion that there *is* a uniquely American approach to foreign affairs; and the other is that "revisionist" writing on the two world wars of this century, though stimulating, is essentially "history by hypothesis" and, as such, often misleading and dangerous. We have brought together seven articles, some previously published, to illustrate these arguments. For those who know Professor Perkins, no appreciation would be adequate if it did not also include a few popular lectures given to nonprofessional audiences. We present four of them here, hoping they will convey something of the warmth, wit, and wisdom which have made Dexter Perkins the most sought-after speaker in Rochester and Ithaca. The volume concludes with Professor Perkins' Presidential Address to the American Historical Association given on December 29, 1956.

In assembling these essays and papers, we have had the generous assistance of Miss Marjorie Gilles, Professor Perkins' secretary, and Mrs. Beatrice Burch, secretary of the History Department of the University of Rochester. We wish also to acknowledge the kindness of the following for permission to reprint several articles by Professor Perkins: Massachusetts Historical Society, Princeton University Press, Union College, *The American Historical Review*, *The Journal of Modern History*, *The Virginia Quarterly Review*, *The Yale Review*.

GLYNDON G. VAN DEUSEN
RICHARD C. WADE

The University of Rochester
March, 1957

Contents

A Biographical Sketch of
Dexter Perkins by the Editors

DEXTER PERKINS was born in Boston, Massachusetts, June 20, 1889. He was educated at the Boston Latin School, at the Sanford School of Redding Ridge, Connecticut, and, inevitably, at Harvard, where, in the midst of brilliant accomplishments, he received his A.B. in 1909 and his Ph.D. in history in 1914. Then the fledgling instructor made his way to the University of Cincinnati.

One year later Instructor Perkins was called to Rochester on the recommendation of Laurence Packard, a close friend and former brother-in-arms at the Harvard Graduate School. At Rochester, Packard and Perkins soon became names to conjure with. President Rush Rhees could congratulate himself upon having created, in a department with already distinguished traditions, the beginnings of a new galaxy of historians.

Assistant Professor Perkins promptly fell in love with one of his most brilliant pupils, Wilma Lois Lord, and, as the culmination of a romance that made history on the campus, married her on May 4, 1918. Then, for it was in the great days of the Allied and Associated Powers' answer to the German *Friedensturm*, he hied himself off to war as a private in the United States Army.

Private Perkins became Captain Perkins before the war was over. He then served for a few months with the historical section of General Headquarters at Chaumont and saw at first hand some of the proceedings of the Versailles Peace Conference. The fall of 1919 found him back in Rochester, where he had been elevated during his absence to the rank of Junior Professor.

The war had quickened the nation's interest in history, and to this Rochester was no exception. Professor Perkins' fund of historical knowledge, his breadth of view, his idealism, his capacity for brilliant generalization, became proverbial on the campus and attracted increasing attention in the town. Those who sat at his feet as he marched up and down before a class, twirling his Phi Beta Kappa key around his index finger and commenting incisively upon the historical developments that had led to the existent state of the nation, counted themselves as fortunate to have such a brilliant teacher. And when, in 1925, Laurence Packard left Rochester for Amherst, it was a foregone conclusion that Perkins would succeed him as Chairman of the Department of History and Government and Watson Professor of History.

The confidence of President Rhees in his new chairman was amply justified, for the popularity and influence of young Professor Perkins (he was in his middle thirties) steadily grew. Adept in personal relationships, blessed with an inexhaustible vitality and with an equally inexhaustible fund of enthusiasm, impatient of detail but with a singular capacity for the larger view, he was often, as Winston Churchill said of Harry Hopkins, "Lord Root of the Matter." His advice had weight both with campus radicals and with University trustees.

The chairmanship of a department is all too often regarded as a haven after the storm and stress of productive scholarship are passed. This was not so with Dexter Perkins. In 1927, within two years after his elevation to the chairmanship, he published his first book, *The Monroe Doctrine, 1823–1826*, a revision of his doctoral dissertation. This was followed, at five-year intervals, by two additional volumes which carried the story of the doctrine to the year 1907. *Hands Off: The History of the Monroe Doctrine*, a brilliant survey which carries the story of the evolution of this great national policy down into the present era, appeared in 1941. Three years later, *America and Two Wars* explored the circumstances under which the United States became involved in the titanic struggles of the twentieth century. *The United States and the Caribbean, The Evolution of American Foreign Policy*, and *The American Approach to Foreign Policy* were published during the next eight years. In 1955 appeared *The History of the Monroe Doctrine*, an up-to-date edition of *Hands Off;* in 1956, *Charles Evans Hughes and American Democratic Statesmanship;* and in 1957, *The New Age of Franklin Roosevelt*. While these books were being published, numerous articles and speeches, ranging from reflections on the love of knowledge to critical commentaries on the conduct of American foreign policy, historically considered, appeared in a wide variety of learned periodicals. These publications established Professor Perkins' national and international reputation as a scholar of the first rank.

As his reputation grew, honors and responsibilities multiplied. He was made Secretary of the American Historical Association in 1928, serving in that capacity until 1939. In 1936 he was made city historian of Rochester, in which position he laid the basis for the notable research and publication in Rochester history so ably continued by the present incumbent of the office, Dr. Blake McKelvey. In 1937 Professor Perkins was appointed a lecturer on foreign policy for the Commonwealth Fund at University College, London. At the close of the Second World War, he acted as official historian for the Overseas Branch of the Office of War Information at the United Nations Conference in San Francisco. That fall he went again to England, this time to serve as the first Pitt Professor of American History and Institutions at Cambridge University. Thus he became the first in a succession of distinguished American scholars who have represented American culture at one of England's most distinguished centers of learning.

The close of the Second World War marked an expansion of the area of Professor Perkins' activities, both within and without the University of Rochester. As Chairman of the History Department, which was separated from Government in 1933, he developed the University's first program of graduate study at the Ph.D. level in the Arts, giving that program, not only a sound scholarly basis, but also an emphasis on teacher training which brought it at once to the favorable attention of educators throughout the country. He was a leading spirit in the founding of the Rochester Association for the United Nations in 1946, acting as its President for three years and as Chairman of its Board for three years more and playing a major part in establishing the RAUN as the most powerful local organization in the United States of all those which function under the aegis of the American Association for the United Nations. Somehow he found time to lecture every year on American foreign policy at the National War College, to become deeply interested in the Salzburg Seminar in American Studies, to represent American academic life at Uppsala University in the spring of 1949. In 1950 he added to his other duties the position of President of the Salzburg Seminar. There, with distinguished success, as administrator and lecturer, he has promoted among Europeans that understanding of America's culture which is the Seminar's great contribution to international understanding.

The recognition of Professor Perkins' qualities kept pace with his achievements. He became a member of the Harvard Board of Overseers and Chairman of the Harvard Foundation for Advanced Study and Research. He served in 1952–1954 as Moderator of the Unitarian Churches of the United States and Canada. Union College granted him an LL.D. in 1951, Harvard a Litt.D. in 1953, and the University of Rochester an LL.D. in 1956. In this same year he became President of the American Historical Association.

In 1954, after thirty-nine years of service, Professor Perkins became Emeritus Professor of History at the University of Rochester. As he laid down his duties at the institution which he had served so well, he was called to and accepted the post of John L. Senior Professor in American Civilization at Cornell University. There he lectures on American diplomatic history and each year gives a series of public lectures. The lamp of learning in his hand shines as brightly above Cayuga's waters as it was wont to shine on the banks of the Genesee.

The secret of a man's success can never be defined with anything approaching exactitude, but the qualities which make for that success are more easily discernible. Professor Perkins' enormous vitality, his quickness of comprehension, his instinct for moderation, his capacity for combining that wisdom which is the end product of great learning with the practicality which is the product of much experience—all help to explain his career. Added to these qualities are others still more intimate and endearing. His wit flashes. He loves a ready jest, a happy turn of phrase, just as he loves bridge, croquet, and scrabble. He has a keen appreciation of the ridiculous, the comic aspects of life, but more outstanding is his talent for inspiring affection.

Professor Perkins' capacity for living and enjoying the strenuous life has been one of his greatest characteristics. It is in recognition of a rare spirit, as well as in recognition of his scholarly attainments, that the editors of this volume offer it as an expression of their affection and esteem.

G. G. V. D.
R. C. W.

I ~

THE AMERICAN APPROACH
TO FOREIGN POLICY

I ~

What Is Distinctively American about the Foreign Policy of the United States?*

FIRST of all, and above all, we must emphasize the extraordinary degree to which American foreign policy is derived from public opinion, rather than from the secret deliberations of the diplomats. Of course there is some control of diplomatic action in virtually every democratic nation today. But in no other country is the tradition of popular participation in these matters so long or so strong as it is here.

It is important to note, in connection with this matter, that for a very substantial part of its history the United States never had a professional diplomatic class. In the nineteenth century there were one or two individuals, like Hunter and Adee, who served the State Department for a very long time and were in a sense specialists. But neither our Secretaries of State nor our diplomatic representatives abroad, in this period, were technicians. Most of the former, down to the time of John Hay at any

* Paper delivered at a meeting of the American Historical Association, December, 1952.

rate, were politicians, sometimes very successful and eminent politicians. And even in the twentieth century the same general practice has been followed. Since the turn of the century, we have had three Secretaries—Hay, Lansing, and Marshall—who were in a sense technicians, but all the rest of the Secretaries have conformed to the usual pattern. As for our representatives abroad, the situation has not been quite the same. In the nineteenth century there were few men indeed in our foreign service who had had specialized training for their posts. But the number has, of course, much increased in the last fifty years and no doubt will continue to increase in the future. Undeniably the role of the professional has increased and is increasing. But it may be questioned whether the power of *ultimate* decision is very often in their hands. I have recently read and reviewed the remarkable work of Mr. Joseph C. Grew which deals with a diplomatic experience extending over a period of some forty years. What is most impressive about his narrative is his frank stressing of the way in which he was frequently excluded from the final choices of policy. No doubt, in the finding of the facts and in the presentation of the facts, the professionals play an important and a very useful role. But the last word, under our system, is pronounced by politicians—either by a politician in the State Department or by the President of the United States. These men seek to reflect and usually do reflect the public temper and the public aspirations and fears.

The role of the public in American foreign policy has, almost from the beginning, been an unusually large one. Our constitutional forms, the necessity of the ratification of treaties by the Senate, and the necessity for the approval of all appropriations of money by the House of Representatives contributed from the beginning to the formation of a popular diplomacy. True, so far as the Senate was concerned, there was assumed to be at the outset a rule of secrecy. But this rule was violated almost at once. It is one of the most familiar facts in our diplomatic history that the terms of the Jay treaty were made known by an opposition Senator before the Senate itself voted for ratification. In scanning the pages of *Niles' Register,* I discovered some years ago that many of the most important compacts in the history of the United States were correctly analyzed in the press while they were still under consideration in our august, but not exactly secretive, Upper House. In the twentieth century the practice of public discussion became increasingly common. The treaty of Versailles was, of course, fully debated; and in 1924 the Senate voted to consider all treaties in open session, unless some special consideration dictated another course. This new practice has been generally, though not universally, adhered to in the last twenty-eight years.

Nor is it only in the Senate that discussion of foreign affairs is almost coeval with government under the Constitution. The Jay treaty, or rather the bill appropriating funds for its implementation, was the subject of a long and brilliant debate in the House of Representatives. The diplomacy of the Adams and Jefferson administrations was examined at length in the Lower House. And the precedents there set have been followed again and again. It would, indeed, be tedious to labor the point.

There are other ways in which the public nature of our diplomacy can be well illustrated. The two most famous diplomatic documents in the first fifty years of American history under the Constitution were addressed, not to any foreign state, but to the American people. I allude, of course, to the Farewell Address and the Monroe Doctrine. And again and again since this early period, the same technique has been employed. President Roosevelt committed the country to a policy of aid to the foes of Hitler in his speech at Charlottesville in 1940. President Truman committed the country to a still broader program of resistance to totalitarianism in the famous message of March 12, 1947.

For a substantial period, moreover, we have published contemporaneously, and not after the event, important parts of our diplomatic correspondence. The stand of the United States in the submarine controversy with Germany was made known to the American public from the beginning in the notes of Woodrow Wilson. The negotiations preceding the armistice of 1918 were similarly handled. Since the Second World War a vast amount of material has been made available to our people in the midst of diplomatic controversy.

It is easy to understand why all this has been so. The American people have had a strong sense of their own importance and have believed with intensity in the right of self-government. The right of self-government includes, inevitably, the right to be informed. Where they have really cared about a matter, they have insisted that they be provided with the data to make a judgment upon it. The American press, the most active and energetic in the world, has sensed the fact and acted accordingly. It is important, however, not only to examine the causes for this peculiarly open diplomacy, but to see how it works in practice. There is no doubt in my mind that it has given a special flavor to the foreign policy of the United States, sometimes for good, sometimes perhaps with less advantage to the public interest. One of its consequences has been a strong element of partisanship in the conduct of our foreign relations. It is natural enough that this should be so. There are bound to be differences of opinion upon questions of foreign affairs, and it is not strange that our ambitious and realistic politicians should capitalize on these differences. They have acted on this principle from the beginnings of the government. The divisions of the Washington administration, the opposition of the Federalists to the acquisition of Louisiana and to the Jeffersonian embargo, the clamor of the Whigs at the Jacksonian diplomatic challenge to France, the opposition to the Mexican War, the Republican attitude toward the treaty of Versailles, the attitude of many members of the same party toward Franklin Roosevelt's European policy—these are only some conspicuous examples of a general fact. Most of us have been inclined to see some evidences of a similar temper in our own time.

It seems probable that the element of partisanship is diminishing. Our Latin American policy has been almost exempt from partisan controversy for the last twenty years, and the agreements which have implemented it have rarely met with much opposition in the Senate and have sometimes been passed unanimously. Our policy with regard to Europe has been marked with more consistency than most Europeans realize. There was not much difference in attitude between Willkie and Roosevelt in 1940, or between Dewey and Roosevelt in 1944. The Marshall Plan was enacted by a Congress in which the Republicans had a majority. The Atlantic Pact was ratified by an overwhelming majority. The dispatch of General Eisenhower to Europe in 1951 was approved by 69 to 21. The European Defense Treaty was accepted last summer with only ten Senators in opposition. Even in the Orient the differences have been somewhat less significant than the heated language of extremists suggests. There was little denunciation of President Truman's decision in June of 1950 to go into Korea. There was no body of sentiment strong enough to force the administration's hand after the dismissal of General MacArthur. The difference between the point of view of General Eisenhower and that of Governor Stevenson with regard to future policy in the Orient was never sharply defined in the campaign this fall, though the two candidates were far apart in their retrospective view of American action.

Nonetheless, there is no doubt that American politicians still engage in discussion of foreign affairs in a tone that is much misunderstood abroad and that our more irresponsible demagogues practice a degree of license which hardly has a parallel (except of course among the Communists) in any other country. This is the price we pay for the discussion of the issues in an open forum.

There is another characteristic of American diplomacy which is directly traceable to our habits of public discussion: it is singularly free from deals of the kind which have so often been typical of European action and which have so frequently been made at the expense of third parties. The American people are a highly moralistic people (of this more anon), and they shrink from the cynical practices that have often cropped up in the Old World. Jefferson tried to make a deal with France to put pressure on Spain for the cession of the Floridas and got roundly denounced by John Randolph for his pains. The Taft-Katsura and the Root-Takahira agreements were, in effect, recognition of Japanese interests in Korea and Manchuria in exchange for a pledge with regard to the Philippines. The Yalta agreement was, of course, a deal, though it is fair to remember that the Chinese Nationalist regime was not wholly dissatisfied with its terms. That it has come in for such widespread denunciation is entirely typical of the American attitude toward such agreements in general.

This does not mean that the United States is necessarily in the position where it cannot bargain on a decent basis or that it is forced by public opinion to demand all and concede nothing in a diplomatic negotiation. It has backed down more than once. In 1844 the campaign cry of the Democracy was "fifty-four forty or fight," but we compromised on the forty-ninth parallel. In 1895 Grover Cleveland demanded that Great Britain arbitrate the Guiana boundary dispute with Venezuela, but the terms of submission gave to the British a large part of what they had been demanding. Although President Franklin D. Roosevelt talked of unconditional surrender, it was possible to assure the Japanese in 1945 that they would not be deprived of their Emperor. Even in the violent climate of 1950 and 1951, the Truman administration, though exposed to constant attacks for its "weakness," was able to make many concessions in the negotiations with the Communists in Korea, until it came to the issue of the prisoners of war. We have not been as inflexible as we are sometimes accused of being by Europeans.

Nonetheless, there is a danger that a diplomacy influenced by public sentiment may be less pliant than that of the professional diplomats. The record of the United States does not demonstrate this; but the special circumstances of our own time, the very sharpness of the contrast between democracy and totalitarianism, suggest that we may here encounter a real danger. To embroider this point, however, would lead us into the field of prophecy, not of history.

Another characteristic of American diplomatic history is the importance that has been attached to general principles. This, too, springs from the popular character of American diplomacy. The mass of men have neither the knowledge nor the inclination to understand a complex diplomatic problem in all its various ramifications. They can judge only in the large, fixing the mood and general objectives; and policy, to be made intelligible to them, must be stated in broad terms. It is a sound instinct that has made the greatest of American statesmen do this very thing. Washington, of course, did this, in the Farewell Address; Monroe did it in the famous message of 1823; so, too, did his successors in the evolution of the celebrated doctrine; so, too, did Woodrow Wilson in his great war speeches; so, too, did Harry Truman in the pronouncement of March, 1947. American foreign relations are shot through with general ideas. These general ideas are usually affected with a moral content. That democracy is the best form of government and is of universal application, that aggression is immoral, and the notion that nations must act on ethical principle are among the most usual of these ideas. Indeed it is doubtful whether the statesmen of any other country are so given to moral homilies as our own. Read the correspondence of Cordell Hull with Admiral Nomura and you will see a prime—indeed, an unrivaled—example of this kind of thing; but there are many others. The strongly moralistic emphasis in American diplomacy is somewhat irksome to Europeans, who often put it down as hypocrisy. But it is really nothing of the kind. It is a reflection of a kind of naïveté that exists in the general public and that springs from an imperfect understanding of the play of forces which determines the intercourse of nations.

In dwelling on this point, on the importance of large ideas, I do not wish to be understood as saying that the American people have often become slaves to general theories. On the contrary, their natural impulse to generalize has been offset, time and again, by the strongly pragmatic streak in the national character. Monroe defied Europe in the name of general principle in 1823, but when asked to make an alliance by one of the South American states, he not only declined but made it clear that he would not act without Great Britain. Polk was wise enough to declare that the Monroe Doctrine applied with greatly increased force to the North American continent, but to turn his gaze away from the Anglo-French blockade of the Argentine. The Monroe Doctrine, in fact, was really applied only in the area of the Caribbean, where it was closely associated with the security interests of the United States. And it was conveniently transformed when expediency suggested that a unilateral pronouncement carried with it a kind of arrogant assumption of superiority distasteful to the states of Latin America. In the same way the attachment of the United States to democracy has not prevented it from dealing with other governments of quite a different stripe when its interests have demanded such action. It cheered Kossuth but kept out of the European revolutions of the forties; it enjoyed good relations with an imperial China and imperial Russia; it has always been ready to deal with dictatorships in the New World, dictatorships of the personal type; and it seems to see no obstacle today to closer relations with Yugoslavia or with Spain. Nor, to take a third illustration of its attitude toward general principles, does it today interpret collective security in a fixed way. The Latin-American engagements implementing the Charter of the United Nations call for one kind of action; the Atlantic Pact for another; the Pacific Pact for yet another. The empirical spirit is usually there to temper the generalizations—this is by no means to say that the generalizations have no influence on policy.

Another element in American foreign policy, profoundly related to the national temperament and to the play of public opinion, is the strongly pacific bent in the American philosophy. No one in his senses could accuse the Americans of being a militarist people. Of course they have had their moments of jingoism; they were spoiling for war with Spain in the late nineties. But they have not as a rule glorified war, and they have been peculiarly susceptible to the dream of peace.

Let us look at each side of the coin, as I have just presented it. One of the remarkable evidences of the nonmilitaristic temper is the way in which the Americans have tended to think ill of their wars after these wars have happened. Every struggle in which the United States has engaged has had its revisionist historians. The War of 1812, we are told, was not a war to resist Britain on the sea, but a war with an imperialist impulse behind it; the war with Mexico was a war of aggression; the war of 1898, so we are assured, might have been avoided if President McKinley had stressed more fully the scope of Spanish concession; our entry into the war of 1917 was due to our partiality for the Allies, to the inept diplomacy of the Wilson administration, to the pressure of commercial and financial interest, and to the wicked machinations of British propaganda; the war of 1941 was a deep-laid plot on the part of Franklin D. Roosevelt, who deliberately plunged the country into an unnecessary conflict. I am not endorsing these views, you understand; indeed I dissent from most of them. But the fact that they exist, and carry some weight, is a most interesting commentary on the American spirit.

There are many other signs of the peace-loving spirit in the history of American foreign relations. There is, for example, the emphasis again and again placed on alternatives to war. There is the legal approach, for example, which is rather distinctively American and which is associated with our constitutional forms at home. The concrete example of this approach lies in American advocacy of a world court. It is true that there was much opposition to this idea, as well as advocacy of it. But in few other countries was the juridical settlement of international disputes taken as seriously as it is in the United States. Another evidence of the same temper is to be found in the Kellogg-Briand pact. I do not believe that a proposal to outlaw war by promises, a general engagement to do so, could possibly have emanated from any European chancellery. Yet it came naturally to the Americans, and the pact itself was ratified with scarcely a dissenting vote. Other examples are easy to cite: the emphasis placed on the Covenant of the League in 1919 and on the Charter of the United Nations in 1945. We must not judge the League in the light of the opposition it aroused. We must think of it in its world setting and remember its American origin. And it seems likely that the League's successor has nowhere warmer support than in the United States.

The matters I have been discussing have to do with peace viewed from the institutional or legal side. But one of the most striking evidences of the peace-loving spirit in this country lies in the rapid demobilization which has followed quickly on victory in our two great wars of the twentieth century. A more sophisticated people, or a more brutal one, would have recognized immediately the vast bargaining power that we possessed in the victorious legions of 1918 and 1945. Yet we quickly threw much of that bargaining power away; and though voices are raised in lamentation today by our numerous retrospective critics, there were few to oppose the action which we took at the time.

Closely connected with the pacific spirit is the American attitude toward imperialism. Of course we have had imperialistic
impulses—for example, the impulse to extend our political power
over alien peoples. But our imperialism has always been imperialism with an uneasy conscience. It has always been associated
with the notion that some day we will grant self-rule to those
whom we have dominated. And during the last twenty years we
have not only abandoned the policy of intervention in the affairs
of New World states, but have, by two solemn protocols, bound
ourselves not to intervene. I know of no such act of abnegation
on the part of any other nation.

Because this is our point of view, we take a critical attitude
of the imperialism of others. We pressed for concessions on the
part of the British to India and of the Dutch to Indonesia; we
pressed for concession on the part of the French in Tunisia. We
associate ourselves with anti-imperialist policies in the Near East.
And in this the diplomats undeniably have the support of majority opinion.

Before I leave the question of imperialism, I want to inject
one special word. Despite our policies with regard to Latin
America, the word imperialism is constantly on the lips of our
enemies; and since they cannot fairly say that we are governing
anyone else directly, they like to speak of economic imperialism.
I want to raise the question whether any such term has exact
content *and meaning.* Without political control can a country
be truly imperialistic? Of course economic strength confers bargaining power and influence. But it does not confer domination.
And imperialism means domination. I find it a little difficult to
see how real imperialism can function without active political
intervention.

On the other hand, we must not imagine, of course, that all
is sweetness and light in the foreign policy of the United States,
historically considered, or that we have always been moved by
pacific instincts. The combative spirit has more than once ex-

pressed itself in American diplomacy, notably in the forties and fifties, in the period just preceding the Spanish-American War; and certainly the war temper grew between 1915 and 1917 and between 1939 and 1941.

The pacific spirit and the anti-imperialistic spirit have not been the only expressions of the foreign policy of the United States. It is worth noting that, historically speaking, the Americans have often given a very wide definition to the concept of security. This wide definition was never more evident than in the famous message of 1823, in which President Monroe declared that any intervention on the part of European powers in the New World would be dangerous to our peace and safety. In the first quarter of the twentieth century the Philippines came within our defense zone, and they have remained there ever since. The national definition of a security interest was again enlarged in the period of the First World War, when to many persons the collapse of British naval power and the victory of Germany were thought to present a definite challenge to the United States. And the broad definition of American security has never been better illustrated than in the enunciation of the Truman Doctrine, which proclaims the purpose of the United States to assist all peoples threatened by alien control. Such statements as those of Monroe and Truman are characteristic of American foreign attitudes, in the breadth of their generalization, in the instinct for bold and sweeping assertion. But characteristic, too, is the American instinct for the practical, the retreat from theory when retreat becomes convenient or necessary. This has been very well illustrated of late in the policy asserted with regard to Korea. We began by invoking the doctrine of collective security in favor of the South Korean Republic, in our eyes the legal government of Korea. But we quickly modified any purpose of unifying all the country and entered into negotiations for an armistice which would have left Korea divided. We negotiated with the aggressor, of course, on the condition that he cease from aggression, but without thought of further punishment. Do not misunderstand me; I am not saying that this policy was wrong. I merely illustrate the manner in which theory and practice unite in the development of American foreign policy.

· This union of opposites is, it seems to me, a very genuine source of strength. A diplomacy that rests upon the people must speak to the people. It can speak best in large and sweeping generalizations, which appeal to the heart as well as to the head, which can be understood—or perhaps I should say felt—by the great body of the voters. But the doctrinaire pursuit of a broad objective may very easily conflict with the practical realities of the moment, may sacrifice the national interest—whatever that illusive phrase may mean. In the United States the people have rarely objected to the modification of theory in the face of unpleasant facts. They have rarely insisted upon policies which were, in their upshot, disastrous for the United States (though of course our revisionist historians might challenge this observation). On the whole, such a diplomacy as ours is sufficiently realistic to deal with the actual world and sufficiently idealistic to derive great strength from its idealism. It makes mistakes—who does not?—but compare those mistakes with the mistakes of the dictators, with the insensate ambition of Adolf Hitler, with the cruel vanity of Mussolini, perhaps even with the calculating and sinister ambitions of Moscow. On this last, of course, we have not the true historical perspective today, and we may not have it for a long time to come. But in one fact we can take some pride. Our diplomacy is not only well adapted to, indeed the expression of, our national temperament, but it reflects the desire for a wider union of peoples. It serves America in a broader context than that of isolationism. It appeals to American idealism, but it is based on the genuine need we have today for a wide association of peoples in the face of the monster of the Kremlin.

2 ～

The American Attitude towards War[*]

OVER the age in which we live there hangs the shadow of a war of destruction—a war more far-reaching and disastrous in its consequences than any that has been fought on this planet. It does not lie within the province of the historian to say whether at some foreseeable time such a war will break out. But it does lie within his province objectively to appraise the contemporary situation in the light of the past, and to try to determine through an examination of the circumstances in which the United States has hitherto gone to war, and through an analysis of the national attitudes and beliefs, what are the circumstances in which it might be drawn into war in the future.

In an international struggle the people of the United States have, in the past, six times taken up arms: first, in 1798, when they waged an informal war on the sea with France; second, in 1812, when they locked horns with Great Britain; third, when they carried hostilities against Mexico; fourth, when they liberated Cuba—and, incidentally, acquired the Philippines, Guam, and Puerto Rico; and, fifth and sixth, when they became

[*] Reprinted by permission from *The Yale Review*, Winter, 1949.

involved in the great world conflicts of our time. What is to be learned from an examination of this record? What does it suggest with regard to the future?

In the first place, it is clear that the Americans have not needed to be invaded to be provoked into war. It is true that the sneak attack of the Japanese on Pearl Harbor precipitated the actual taking up of arms in 1941; but it is also clear that this country was on the verge of a clash with Germany and Japan when that event occurred. With the Reich we were at that moment engaged in a quasi-war on the seas; with Japan we had already broken off commercial relations, and were giving positive aid to a Chinese government which was resisting Japanese aggression. There may be some naïve persons who, in judging the conflict with Mexico, still put faith in President Polk's remarkable statement, in justification of hostilities, that American blood had been shed upon American soil, but our diplomatic historians have time and again pointed out, first, that it is doubtful whether the territory on which the first clash of arms occurred was really American, and, second, and more important, that Polk had made up his mind for war before the clash occurred. Broadly speaking, then, we must rule out the hypothesis that only actual aggression on our home land can lead to war.

There is also another conclusion which can be briefly stated. It does not seem probable that our entrance into an international conflict will be caused solely by an "incident." The record of the years indicates that while a single dramatic event may, of course, intensify popular passion, there is always a train of circumstances behind the actual taking up of arms. In 1798, for example, the American people were no doubt affronted by the rough treatment accorded their representatives in Paris, when the French government attempted to extort from the delegates of the United States a forced loan and a bribe as the price of the cessation of French aggression upon American commerce at sea; but this aggression had already been going on under trying con-

ditions for some time, and had produced in this country an irritation to which the rebuff of the so-called XYZ mission only
added. Again, the most famous episode in Anglo-American relations in the troubled period of the second Jefferson and the two
Madison Administrations was, beyond question, the assault of
the British frigate *Leopold* on the American war vessel *Chesa-
peake;* but it was not until five years after this event that the
United States took up arms. The war with Mexico, as has been
said, was not produced by the Mexican crossing of the Rio
Grande and the skirmish of Mexican forces with those of General Taylor. It is perhaps more difficult to rule out of account
in such dogmatic fashion the sinking of the *Maine* in Havana
harbor, in 1898, as a factor of the first importance in our engag-
ing in hostilities with Spain. But for some time before this happened the American people were being lashed into a mood of
profound indignation with Spanish misgovernment and brutality
in Cuba, and into an equally profound sympathy with the struggle of the Cubans for independence. Coming down to the two
world wars, it is significant that the sinking of the *Lusitania*,
while it provided the issue which led to the eventual entry of
the United States into the struggle against Germany, preceded
by nearly two years (May 7, 1915—April 6, 1917) the actual
declaration of hostilities, and that the sinking of the *Athenia*, at
the beginning of the period 1939–1945, produced hardly more
than a ripple on the surface of American opinion. It is dangerous,
of course, to speak with dogmatism in the complex field of human affairs, but it seems correct to say on the basis of our history
that while a dramatic incident may heighten the popular indignation that leads towards war, there must be for Americans
a longer train of causes actually to produce an armed conflict.
In one mood, an incident will have little or no effect; in another
it may add fuel to an already rising flame; but it can never be
regarded in and of itself as the explanation of an American resort to arms.

There is another generalization closely connected with this. As a rule, the American people have been rather slow to anger. The outrageous treatment of American commerce by the French which led to the explosion of 1798 began at least as early as the winter of 1796; the indignities to which American trade and the American person were subjected by Great Britain long preceded 1812; the Cuban conflict and insurrection which finally led to intervention in 1898 had begun in 1895; the aggressions of Germany to which America raised objection were, as we have just seen, of long standing in 1917; and the menace raised by Hitlerian and Japanese ambition was well recognized several years before the attack on Pearl Harbor. Even in the case of the struggle with Mexico, President Polk made what must, by the candid historian, be regarded as a *bona fide* effort to reach a settlement with the government at Mexico City before resorting to war. It is in a gathering irritation rather than in some sudden outburst of feeling that the basis of American action is to be found.

To say this is, of course, only to say that the action of the United States in international affairs is deeply influenced by its democratic forms. No prudent statesman in a democracy will force the issue until public opinion has been pretty clearly crystallized; he must and should wait upon its gathering force. And since it is the essence of the democratic principle that dissent can and should express itself, the integration of the people's will is bound to be a longer and more complex process than it is in a totalitarian state. We can, with caution, even go a little further, and say that it is probable that the first occasion of direct challenge is not likely to cause an actual outbreak of conflict; and that for better or worse, a democratic nation will always have a little of the water of appeasement in its blood.

A war for the United States, then, is not likely either to wait upon the actual physical invasion of American territory, or to result from a mere incident instigated by a hostile power. Is it likely, on the other hand, to be the product of American imperialism, of an impulse to conquer and dominate others?

In the sense in which it was true of Hitlerian Germany, I do not think it can be said that the United States is revealed by history to be an imperialistic nation, or, at any rate, that it is now imperialistic in this sense. Yet, even though the national mood today bears out such a generalization, as I shall attempt to show, there is more in the American past than meets the average American eye, and this may suggest that the people of the United States are not entirely free from the age-old passion to enlarge the national domain by force. Let us analyze the record in this regard.

There is, first of all, our series of wars with the Indians. To these most of us, even if we think we know quite a bit about American history, remain blandly indifferent. Yet the number of these struggles is considerable, and it is to them, in substantial degree, that we owe the gradual clearing of the continent. To say nothing of the colonial wars, there was Mad Anthony Wayne's victory over the redskins of the Northwest; there was Andrew Jackson's defeat of the southern Indians in the battle of Horseshoe Bend; there was the Black Hawk War, in which Abraham Lincoln played an inconspicuous part; there were the many campaigns against the Indians of the plains, and the dramatic conflict that ended with the massacre of General Custer and his men. All this may not count as aggression to the American mind; the Indian wars, indeed, are hardly remembered by many of our citizens, and are part of the family tradition of very few; compared with most conflicts involving movements of expansion, they caused relatively little loss of life, and even moralistic Americans would not wish to undo their results, or even to spend much time in regretting them. None the less, the fact that America's expansive energies involved only the dispossession of a relatively small number of persons of another race is due to chance rather than to virtue.

The record by no means stops here. On occasion, Americans have been spared the necessity of physical conquest by the easier process of expansion into other people's territory—and then revolution. It was by this indirect technique, for example, that we secured the region known as West Florida in 1810; American settlers moved over into the domains of Spain, and at a convenient moment staged a revolt, and set up an independent state. Before this state was fairly established, President Madison occupied the region, and thus, without much trouble, what might have been attained by conquest, became an innocent move to extend protection to our own kin, who had freed themselves from Spanish tyranny. The same technique, more cautiously and decently applied, brought us Texas. Again American settlement was followed by revolution; and the revolutionists set up a government, and in due course this new State was incorporated in the Union. If we had not acquired California by other means the chances are that a similar expedient might have brought us that rich and fertile region.

Twice, moreover, we have acquired territory by direct conquest. Historians differ as to the degree of culpability that attaches to President Polk for the waging of the Mexican War; it is generally recognized today that the Mexicans were themselves spoiling for a fight, and that Polk made an honest effort to come to a peaceable understanding with them; but it is also pretty generally agreed that with more forbearance on his part, war might have been avoided. And when it came, the promptitude with which California was occupied is only one of many evidences of the cupidity that lay behind the war itself.

In 1898 the United States took up arms against Spain. It was a war of liberation, of course, intended to free the Cubans from the tyrant's yoke. Yet the first important battle of the war was fought in Manila Bay, and led to the acquisition of the Philippines; and somehow or other when the brief conflict was ended, we found ourselves in possession of Puerto Rico and Guam as well, and had managed to annex Hawaii and establish ourselves in Samoa.

Nor was this the end of the story. For in the decades following the war of 1898, we acquired a distinct interest in the regulation of the little states of the Caribbean. We established a virtual protectorate over Panama in 1903. We intervened in Nicaragua in 1912; in Haiti in 1915; in the Dominican Republic in 1916. And, although these interventions were temporary, they were roundly denounced at the time in many of the countries of Latin America as nothing more nor less than "imperialism." It is possible, therefore, for cynical foreigners to see the history of the United States as by no means free from the acquisitive impulses, and to suggest that possibly the same impulses that were here expressed will, in due course, occur again. Is it so certain, they ask, that the United States will never again engage in a war of conquest or attempt to extend its physical control over other lands?

Of course, no historian is going to give a categorical answer to this question. Yet the history of the United States does distinctly suggest that the imperialistic impulse, which occurs in the development of every great nation, has run with our own a different course from what is assumed by our foreign critics. It has been strangely mingled with a respect for the democratic process that, in and of itself, makes conquest a little absurd. It is, indeed, the case that a good many of the acquisitions of the United States have come about only after substantial political opposition, and that always the strong respect of the American people for the principle of self-government had made itself felt in connection with the final decision. There was opposition to the annexation of Texas; there was strong opposition to the Mexican War; in the latter case President Polk himself drew back from the proposals of the more ardent expansionists for the annexation of all of Mexico, or even of northern Mexico itself. True, these earlier movements of opposition were connected with the slavery question; but half a century later, no such domestic issue entered into the equation when it came to the peace treaty wtih Spain. The opponents of the acquisition of the Philippines (and they were in not a few instances influential members of the party in power) were actuated by a strong dislike for the whole principle of imperialism; they believed that the words of the Declaration of Independence meant what they said; they went back to the fundamental principle that governments derive their just powers from the consent of the governed. They did not at first prevail; but they won a good deal of their contention in the long run. For the American policy became the policy of rapid preparation of the Philippines, and of Puerto Rico as well, for self-government; and today the United States has conceded complete independence to the first of these territories, and wide self-rule to the other.

Still more striking has been the reaction to the interventions in the Caribbean. A case could be made out for the political control by some strong government of such unruly little states as Haiti or the Dominican Republic, or Nicaragua in the second decade of the century. But American reaction against the occupation of these republics began with the end of the First World War. No one of these episodes lasted as much as two decades. The longest, that of Haiti, was only eighteen years. And the shortest, that of the Dominican Republic, was only about eight.

In this same period of the interventions, there was offered to the United States such a temptation as has rarely been put before a great power. Mexico with its great potential resources was a prey to violent internal disorders in the years after 1910. There were powerful American interests there ready to stop at no expedient to bring about aggressive American action. Yet no such action ever took place. With a forbearance that is almost un-paralleled, the government at Washington withheld its hand,

and even when the Mexican revolution had triumphed, and at times challenged our own conception of property rights, the thought of physical coercion was put aside.

Moreover, in the last decade and a half, we have gone further than any great state has ever gone to tie our hands in our relations with our neighbors. By the conventions of Montevideo and Buenos Aires we have stopped ourselves from interference in the domestic affairs of these states. And by a complicated series of arbitration treaties and conciliation treaties we have provided for the peaceful settlement of all disputes. More than this, we have in the convention of Chapultepec agreed to be bound by a two-thirds vote in defining an aggressor, as relates to the action of New World states against one another; and in this way again we have put a brake—an unprecedented brake—on our own unilateral action. Finally, it is to be observed that the most important of these engagements have been ratified by the unanimous action of the Senate—a rarity, as may well be imagined, in our international relations. This forswearing of imperialistic action in the New World may, therefore, be taken as reflecting a virtual consensus in the United States.

The strong desire of Americans to respect the democratic principle is now evident in our treatment of conquered Germany and Japan. The general set of our policy with regard to these countries is not to exploit them, or to maintain control over them; it is to prepare them for self-government. In Japan we have already set up representative institutions, and conceded considerable freedom to the native régime; in Germany our policy looks to a greater and greater degree of public participation by Germans, and to eventual self-rule. There is, nowhere, a demand to treat these countries as conquered provinces; we are spending money on them, not taking it out of them; and the general popular assumption is that the day will come when we shall withdraw, leaving them to their own devices.

All in all, then, the pattern of American political thinking and of American political action for the last fifty years does not suggest that the United States will embark upon any program which can be interpreted abroad as a program of conquest. True, the physical power of this country is apparent today in areas where it was much less conspicuous before; many of the island strongholds of the Pacific are in our hands; our fleet ranges the Mediterranean; our garrisons extend from Tokyo on the east to Berlin on the west. But the impulse to dominate by force of arms does not seem apparent.

Marxists, of course, will have their own opinion on all this. They can think of us in no terms but those of capitalist imperialism: the United States must, in the nature of the case, move towards the control of larger and larger markets, must extend its dominion further and further. But there is little in the history of the last fifty years to support the thesis of American capitalist imperialism; the physical area under the control of the American government (excepting occupied Germany and occupied Japan, in which we share with others the task of administration) is actually less today than it was fifty years ago. Contrary to Marxist assumption, it may well be that the expansion required by the nature of a capitalist society will take place in large degree vertically rather than horizontally, that is, by further technological advance in the United States rather than by an immense development outside its borders; and it is not clear that horizontal expansion, if it takes place, will raise any demand for new areas under the military control of the American government.

There are, however, countervailing considerations. Cynical domination of others does not seem to accord with the American character today. But the situation that now exists in Greece suggests a warning. Our presence there is, in my judgment, wholly defensible. The present government of Greece was chosen in a free election; in assisting it to stay in power by economic aid, yes, by military assistance as well, we are supporting the democratic principle, and leaving to the Greeks a freer choice over their own destinies than they would otherwise have. But it is a tricky business thus to assist others; and it can easily lead, in the name of democracy, to the perpetuation of régimes that have, in reality, lost their popular mandate and could be replaced in free elections. Furthermore, the implications of such actions are extremely far-reaching. Suppose, for example, that in due course Germany is evacuated by the victor states, and that a democratic régime is established there. Suppose that this régime is overthrown by one of a totalitarian cast. Might not the democratic principle itself then lead to intervention, and on towards an international war? The American people wish others to govern themselves, and they have frequently so demonstrated; but they wish others to govern themselves *in a democratic way*. Is not such an attitude one that can easily be the foundation for a democratic crusade that bears some family resemblance to imperialism?

Moreover, it is undeniable that there is a kind of rhythm in the history of American expansion. Sentiment for the acquisition of new territory certainly existed in 1798 when the Federalists had their eyes on the colonial territory of Spain, and, as Professor Pratt has sought to show in his "Expansionists of the War of 1812," at the time of our second war with Britain; it cropped up in a much more virulent form in the 1840's and 1850's, leading, not only to the war with Mexico, but also to such unofficial imperialism as William Walker's famous filibustering expedition into Nicaragua, and to constant Southern demands for the annexation of Cuba; and after a long period of quietude it was again apparent in the Nineties, in the movement for the acquisition of Hawaii, and in the agitation that preceded the war with Spain. Whether it is mere chance that all these upswings of a somewhat bumptious ambition followed a short time after a long period of depression, is a question that cannot be answered here; but it is at least possible that there is some connection between these two sets of phenomena, and it is impossible to rule out the thesis that at some time in the future, under the influence of economic difficulties at home, or in the more buoyant mood of recovery from these difficulties (as in 1845 and 1898), we might be tempted towards an aggressive policy abroad. At least, it may be said that one precaution against the development of jingoism in this country is to keep our economic house in some kind of good order.

Yet the wars of the United States, in general, have not been wars produced by the imperialist impulse in its naked form. Of the six international conflicts in which we have been engaged, four have been intimately connected with events in Europe and have, to a large extent at any rate, been brought about by hostilities which originated on the other side of the Atlantic. In the first two of these wars, one important factor was indignation at the violation of American neutral rights combined with resentment at the affronts to the dignity of the nation. This was, of course, particularly true of the informal war with France in 1798. The government of the Directory had acted ruthlessly against American shipping in the course of the general European war then raging. To make matters worse, it had first refused to receive an American envoy and then attempted to extort from the American negotiators who had been sent to Paris concessions in the way of a bribe and of a loan which they could not grant. The publication of their dispatches in Philadelphia produced a violent burst of indignation in the United States, and brought about war with France at sea. The War of 1812 has, as has already been stated, sometimes been assigned an imperialist origin. But resentment at the gross disregard of the rights of American seamen and at interruptions to American trade, were the declared motive of the conflict, and there would be few historians today who would entirely rule out this element in the situation. In 1917—despite the attempts of some students of diplomatic history to trace our entrance into the First World War to financial and commercial reasons—it is not to be denied that the actual *casus belli* was the German submarine warfare.

Wars for the defense of neutral rights are, from one point of view, an absurdity. It is not possible for a nation to secure respect for such rights by shifting from the position of a neutral to that of a belligerent. But the fact that three times the American people have, in a measure at any rate, been goaded into war by assault upon what they chose to regard as their dignity suggests that not merely national interest, coolly considered, but a profound emotional factor has often influenced their decision. Nations differently situated, especially small nations, have sometimes chosen in the midst of European convulsion a very different course. The Swedes, in particular, have more than once ridden out the storm without becoming actively involved, at the cost of a certain amount of national pride.

The chance of our participating in a new conflict as a result of a violation of neutral rights seems, however, remote today; for the balance of power in Europe has changed, and only one power of the first rank is left upon that continent. For this reason, the possibility of a new Armageddon depends less upon the outbreak of a purely European struggle than upon conflicts in the new set of forces that are now becoming apparent. The question is, therefore, to be raised whether other motives, besides wounded dignity, have played a part in our involvements in Europe, and whether these motives are still in existence today. The answer to this question must emphatically be given in the affirmative.

Those historians who think only in terms of some concrete national interest which is material in character miss a large part of the picture in their analysis of foreign policy. Ideas are a powerful directive of action. They are, perhaps, particularly powerful in a democratic state, where the mass of the voters find it easier to be guided by general principles than by any careful analysis of complex data. In every one of the European wars that have touched the United States, the influence of ideology is apparent, and perhaps it may be said to have reached its climax in the struggle just ended. To start at the beginning, the strong Federalist aversion · to the excesses of the French Revolution was a factor in sharpening the antagonism which led to conflict in 1798. The hereditary dislike of Britain was a factor in 1812. Looking at the matter objectively from the standpoint of affronts to American pride, there was as much reason in that year for this country to go to war with France as with England.

The psychological set of the American mind undeniably made war with Germany easier in 1917. From the beginning of that European struggle many of the most influential elements in American opinion were convinced that the war was a war of aggression on the part of the Reich; they were horrified by the invasion of Belgium; they were affronted by the strongly militarist bias of the German government, exaggeratedly described as autocracy. All these facts taken together undoubtedly helped to bring about the acceptance by the United States of the resort to arms. This phase of the matter may be usefully restated in slightly different terms. In 1914, in particular, there was evident from the beginning of the struggle a tendency to moralize the issues and to conceive of the European war as a conflict between good and evil. This tendency was still clearer in 1939 and 1940. The great mass of the American people detested or at least disliked the Hitlerian tyranny. They were shocked at Japan's cynical career of conquest in the Orient. And, ever since the battle over the League of Nations in 1920, there had been growing up in the United States a profound conviction that aggressive war was immoral. This conviction had been reflected in the Kellogg Pact of 1928, with its attempt to outlaw war; it was clearly evident in the popular reaction to the events that preceded the war of 1941. It was expressed as early as 1937 in the famous Roosevelt speech at Chicago proposing international "quarantine" of aggressors. Although, it is true, at that time there was still a strongly pacific spirit mixed with the moral condemnation of aggression, and although the President's utterance itself fell flat, it is also true that as time went on the popular feeling against Germany and Japan became deeper, and developed into a real antagonism in 1940 and 1941. The increasing sensitiveness of Americans to external aggression far beyond their borders is, indeed, evidenced by the contrast between 1914 and 1939.

In the First World War the American government began with neutrality and made an earnest effort to maintain that neutrality; it sought a settlement of the submarine issue, even after the sinking of the *Lusitania;* and, whatever President Wilson may have thought in private of the moral issues involved, his public speeches stressed the maintenance of American rights and not the moral conflict involved in the views of the two sets of belligerents, down to the actual entrance of the United States into the struggle. It was, besides, more than two and a half years before neutrality, at least in theory, was abandoned. Far different was the course of events in 1939. There was, from the beginning, no pretense on the part of the President or his advisers of moral neutrality; with the fall of France, after less than ten months of war, the Administration pledged itself to assist the democratic nations; the two great political parties were both committed to such a policy in the presidential campaign of 1940; and the enactment of Lend-lease in the late winter of 1941 was in effect a taking of sides in the struggle. During the same period, the extension of aid to China made it perfectly clear that the American government was not truly neutral in the war then being waged by Japan in China.

There can be no question that this sense of a profound ideological conflict, with the notion of evil genius largely transferred in our minds from Germany and Japan to Russia, has survived the war. It must be strong just in proportion as the faith in the democratic principle is strong. Were it to be as-

sumed as it well might be that democratic government is the
product of various concrete phenomena—of that vague thing
described as national temperament, of the wide distribution of
property, of a prosperity sufficiently constant to subject the nation to minor rather than major strains—the ideological conflict
with Russia would by that very fact be in some degree attenuated. But the constant harping upon a world conflict between democracy and Communism is obviously an explosive
force of very large dimensions.

There is another factor in the situation today that needs to
be taken into account. The moral antagonism that existed between militarist Germany or Japan and the United States, the
moral antagonism that exists between Russia and this country
today, is much intensified by the role of the contemporary press
and radio, and by the demand of these agencies, especially the
press, for the maximum publicity in international negotiation.
American journalism is based on the assumption that the public
ought to know as much as possible. In time of war, where the
national interest demanded, an honorable secrecy was indeed
practised, but in time of peace there are not likely to be many
restraints on the publication of any fact—or rumor—that is
interesting and exciting, even though such publication may, from
an objective standpoint, have undeniably serious consequences.
Conflict is in its essence newsworthy; agreement is far less newsworthy. It is the business of the newspaper man to report, of
course; but what he is apt to report or overemphasize is disagree-
ment. No doubt a democratic people get used to discounting the
rumors of war that constantly assail their ears and eyes; but only
a fanatical defender of the contemporary press would be likely
to maintain that such news stories act as an emollient in international relations.

Much the same thing is to be said with regard to open diplomacy. That the public should be informed of the broad lines
of policy in a democracy is, of course, true; but that newspaper

men should arrogate to themselves the right to be kept in touch with the details of negotiation is another matter. Negotiation involves compromise, and compromise is difficult if the two disputants find every concession that they make held up to view, to become the subject of controversy and perhaps condemnation, in the public prints. The total result of a given negotiation may be well worth while to both negotiators, and the broad judgment may be in favor of its acceptance; but, if every point yielded or won is to be blown up into a great issue, the wisdom of the whole may be obscured when it is finally disclosed.

Added to moral preoccupations, there are other elements which now have to be taken into the account in assessing the evolution of American opinion. The notions of security held by Americans today have developed into something very different from those of a hundred and twenty-five years ago. In the wars of 1798 and 1812, though the physical invasion of the United States, in one case, was set up as bogy by rabid Federalists, and, in the other, actually came to pass, we hear nothing of the argument that the integrity of the country was itself in danger. In 1917 there was certainly in the background of American thought the idea that for the Germans to secure control of the Atlantic would imperil the position of the United States. But not until the world war of 1939 did the idea that the American people were in actual danger of attack play an important part. It was stressed again and again by President Roosevelt, and indeed by many others. And, with the growth of air power, and the portentous reach of Hitlerian and Japanese ambition, who can say that this judgment was wrong? What constitutes security at a given moment is a metaphysical as well as a physical matter; but it is certainly reasonable to assume today that the occupation of western Europe by a totalitarian power, or the control of Germany by such a power, would constitute a direct menace to the safety of the United States. The range of American action has inevitably widened; sensitiveness to aggression has inevitably increased. Nor is it to be forgotten that President Truman placed our present action in Greece in part on grounds of security, and that it now seems logical and rational for an American fleet to patrol the Mediterranean. Putting the matter in another way, there are more trouble-points out of which a war might come than there have ever been for us before.

Nor must we forget that besides national security there is the notion of collective security. This idea is a twentieth-century creation, the product of the First World War. Its potency is difficult to measure. It was behind the Wilsonian conception of the League. It was, possibly in a somewhat naïve form, in the background of the famous effort of the Kellogg Pact to outlaw war. It was present in the policy of the Hoover Administration towards the Japanese occupation of Manchuria. It was implicit in some of the speeches of President Roosevelt. And it has a place in the Charter of the United Nations. Whether the American people are ready to appeal to force whenever aggression raises its head, and to act to the limit of their national power to repress such aggression, is by no means certain. The *threat* of punitive action might prove to be effective in preventing acts of violence by others; but it is also possible that the adherence to collective security might lead to war for the defense of a cherished principle, however remote the direct national interest involved. This is not to say that the notion is wrong. It is merely to say that in its practical working it *might* conceivably lead to a wider conflict than would otherwise take place.

This review of the national mood and of the national habits with regard to war offers others as well as ourselves definite clues as to our behavior in future periods of international strain or provocation that could end in armed conflict. It is important for all of us, if we are, as we must be, concerned with the present tension between the United States and the Soviet Union, to consider carefully what light these clues may throw on the future policy of our country.

Of course, we cannot with scientific accuracy deduce the future from the past; the problems are too complicated, and new and imponderable elements frequently enter into the equation. But certainly nothing that our survey reveals affords us the slightest reason for complacency or inconsequent optimism. On the other hand, it is important to inquire whether there are elements in the existing situation that entitle us to look upon the international scene with a qualified cheerfulness. I believe that there are such.

In the first place, the large-scale international wars in which the United States has engaged have been in part due to the fact that the enemies of America have counted upon the incapacity of the United States effectively to mobilize its people and resources. Both in 1917 and in 1940-41 the German government egregiously miscalculated in this regard. It drew, and perhaps was entitled to draw, some support for this miscalculation from the state of American opinion, from the strong peace sentiment manifested in the election of 1916, for example, and from the close vote by which the draft law was extended in 1941. While today some Americans still hold to the romantic notion that weakness and unpreparedness make negotiation easy, the existence of a peace-time draft is impressive evidence of a new evolution in American opinion. It is coming more and more to be recognized that power may act as a deterrent to aggression, and that very great power may act as a very great deterrent. The United States possesses that power today not only in the atomic bomb but in its advanced technology; and what American ingenuity may hereafter devise for a future struggle is so terrible to think of as to make a direct physical challenge to this nation less likely, perhaps, than ever before. This is, indeed, a grim way to look at the matter; but it is a better ground for hope than the belief that international antagonisms can be exorcised by vague appeals to good will.

Perhaps, as others have suggested, the very magnitude of the disaster of modern war will mean that the competition of ideologies will be fought by other methods than those of all-out military conflict. There are certainly clear evidences that Russian policy today seeks to attain its ends by intrigue, by infiltration, by the promotion of economic disorder, by a kind of psychological attrition, rather than by direct military action, and just because, as was so brilliantly pointed out in "Foreign Affairs" by Mr. X, the men in the Kremlin believe in the inevitable triumph of their side in the long run, they may be content for some time to rely upon these weapons. In the degree that this is so, the answer for us to such expedients lies in the preservation of our own economic health, in the extension of assistance to western Europe, in the attainment of economic reconstruction and economic advance, and in constant vigilance on the part of our military establishment and State Department. Complex as the problem is, the immense technological resources of the modern age give us reason to hope that the second half of the twentieth century may see such improvements in the standards of living in substantial areas as will make it possible for us to meet the challenge that comes from Moscow.

Furthermore, just as there has been a rhythm in our own foreign policy, so there may be a rhythm in that of the Soviet Union. Today the Kremlin appears extremely militant; but there must be at least a question whether in due course it will not be influenced by the immense need of quiet at home, by the pressure of the Russian masses for some improvement of their living standards, by the pursuit of that ideal of the good society which is by no means absent from the Communist ideology.

Finally, it is conceivable that some kind of *modus vivendi* can be worked out between the two rival systems, either directly or through the agency of the United Nations. There may be a policy of limited objectives in the field of international politics, as there often is in life in general. It is true that both the Russian and American systems are dynamic, and that any definite division of the world into rival spheres of influence is not only very difficult to arrive at in the first place (and sure to be denounced on both sides as appeasement), but that, even if it could be attained, there is no guarantee that it would stay put. Yet it is also true that neither the United States nor the U.S.S.R. is strong enough to give the law to the whole world, and that practical considerations of statesmanship may lead in time to some rough balance of interests, or better still to the development of some policy of common abstention from interference in the affairs of other states.

None of these things can be counted on in present circumstances, but each of them suggests the lines on which American foreign policy may move so long as armed clashes can be avoided. We must be strong; we must seek to preserve our economic health and assist world recovery; we must define our objectives in terms of reality rather than in terms so extended that our power for good is diffused, and wasted. And if we do all these things, while we must, indeed, face the future with a clear view of its possible perils, we need not quail before it.

3 ~

Open Diplomacy and Its Critics

ONE of the favorite American legends is that in the field of foreign affairs we are a simple, unsophisticated people regularly "done in" by wily and clever foreigners. How many times have we heard it said that we never entered into diplomatic negotiations with the British without our getting the short end of the stick, that we emerge discomfited from international conferences, that Woodrow Wilson, the Presbyterian scholar, had his leg pulled by unscrupulous Europeans at Paris in 1919, that Roosevelt was duped by Stalin at Yalta, that we have been outplayed in the last few years by the devious diplomats of the Kremlin? But these various assertions have rarely come from scholars; they have been rather the stock in trade of politicians, anxious to prove the case for isolationism or to discredit the party in power. Of late, however, more searching criticism has been directed against American diplomacy and has come from more respectable sources. Professor Hans Morgenthau's remarkable and valuable book, *In Defense of the National Interest*,[1] suggests that our foreign policy has too often been deflected from

[1] Hans J. Morgenthau, *In Defense of the National Interest* (New York, 1951).

37

desirable ends by ideological considerations, and this same thesis runs through George Kennan's provocative essays.[2] At the same time, publicists of great distinction have lamented the extraordinary publicity that attends the conduct of our foreign relations. Walter Lippmann has more than once embroidered this theme, and Richard H. Rovere and Arthur M. Schlesinger, Jr., in their work, *The General and the President*,[3] have pointed out the service performed for the Russians by the open hearings on the MacArthur controversy. In their commentary these various critics have touched on questions far more fundamental than those which used to be the object of popular criticism and on matters which ought deeply to concern every one of us. It is this question of ideology and of open diplomacy that I wish to examine.

There can be no doubt that ideological considerations sometimes play a part in our diplomatic action. That these considerations may blind a people or an administration to important practical considerations is also true. But was the diplomacy of the past directed exclusively by a cool calculation of self-interest or is the diplomacy of nondemocratic states so directed today? Were the wars of Louis XIV dictated by concern for the welfare of the French people, or even by the interest of the sovereign? Was the diplomacy of the Holy Alliance free from dogma? Were not the wars of nationality of the nineteenth century deeply dominated by an idea? In the world of only yesterday can it be said of the psychopath of Berchtesgaden that he judged with wisdom as to the interests of the German people? Have the plotters of the Kremlin wisely assessed the national interest of their people? Diplomats, like other human beings, are rarely objective; like other people they are moved by emotion and by general conceptions which may or may not be true; and their

[2] George F. Kennan, *American Diplomacy, 1900–1950* (Chicago, 1951).
[3] Richard H. Rovere and Arthur M. Schlesinger, Jr., *The General and the President* (New York, 1951).

judgments, like the mass judgments in a democratic state, are often liable to error.

Nonetheless, I think it must be admitted that the diplomacy of a democratic nation will be, or at any rate is likely to be, more affected by general ideas than that conducted by professionals, and for a very good reason. The mass of men are unschooled in the details of foreign policy; they have neither the time, the inclination, nor the special knowledge to study these questions in detail; they are, in the nature of the case, swayed by large generalizations which they do not stop to analyze. In the case of the United States, the following are amongst the most important: (1) the notion that democratic government is superior to all other forms of government and that the extension of democracy is in the order of nature; (2) the idea that the right of self-government belongs to every people; and (3) the feeling that aggression is inherently immoral. Every one of these ideas has had a powerful influence; the question is whether, in pursuing them, the American government, faithful to the prejudices of its constituency, has been unduly doctrinaire and unmindful of the possible unhappy consequences of too rigid an attachment to such ideas.

One thing, of course, has to be said at the outset. It is not possible for a popular regime to ignore the major preoccupations of the voters. It cannot contemptuously throw these theories into the ash can. It cannot proceed as if they did not exist. The critics of our diplomacy who constantly describe themselves as realists can claim little right to the name if they do not recognize this elementary fact. For better or worse, foreign policy in the United States, in its broad lines, is dependent upon the opinion of the masses. And the real question is how that opinion is reconciled with the interests of the nation, as seen from the point of view of special knowledge.

The contention of this article is that American policy in practice is remarkably successful in accomplishing this reconciliation. It has rarely been the slave to general principles; it has been guided and often fortified by them from the point of view of popular acceptance, but it has known how to abandon them in the face of the exigencies of a practical situation.

Take, first of all, of the major themes mentioned above, the notion that democratic government has a superior and supernal virtue. There is much in American history that illustrates the way in which that conception has influenced policy. There was strong popular sentiment, for example, in favor of the French in the wars of the Revolution. There was a widespread sympathy with the revolt of the Spanish colonies in the second decade of the nineteenth century, a sympathy expressed in the Monroe Doctrine. There was a warm feeling for the revolutionists of 1848. Yet in none of these instances did feeling really determine policy. The Washington administration turned away from France toward an understanding with Great Britain and was sustained by the Congress. When certain Latin-American states tried to turn the Monroe Doctrine into an alliance, the Monroe administration carefully retreated from the attitude of defiance that it had assumed toward monarchical Europe and even made further action in defense of the republics of the South dependent upon an understanding with Great Britain. The revolutionary upheavals of 1848 produced no rash action on the part of the American administrations of Polk or of Taylor. Nor was there any popular demand for such action. Democracy was all very well, but it was not to be made the object of an American crusade.

There are those who regard the war of 1917 as such a crusade and who deprecate the emphasis which Woodrow Wilson laid on making the world "safe for democracy." But the point hardly seems well taken. The President did not say that the victory of the United States would make the world democratic; he was laying down the arguable thesis that peace would be more secure in a world where arbitrary power at the service of military force had been crushed or put under control. Moreover, even if his emphasis is rejected, there may still have been good reasons for the American decision. Professor Morgenthau declares that Wilson made the right decision for the wrong reasons and defended it with the wrong arguments. This interesting observation suggests that American idealism and American interest in 1917 really went hand in hand. And if this be so, it seems that the criticism of the President loses much of its force. While it might have been wiser to place the war against Germany on other grounds—national security, for example—it was after all not altogether unfortunate that the United States entered the war under circumstances which combined an appeal to noble abstractions with concrete and fundamental interests.

To make another point, it can hardly be said that the United States has sacrificed its own interests in the world in order to spread democracy. Woodrow Wilson's policy toward Mexico, with its attempt to "teach the Latin-American republic to elect good men," was, in some of its incidents, conceivably, of doubtful wisdom; the efforts to install democratic regimes in the little republics of the Caribbean, in Nicaragua, in Haiti, and in the Dominican Republic can hardly be said to have been successful; the policy of withholding recognition from revolutionary governments in Latin America has usually been marked by failure; but in no one of these cases has any great damage been done to American interests. Moreover, strategic or economic considerations played a part in some of these cases, notably in the case of the interventions, and may be thought by some to justify the policy adopted.

Furthermore, the policies just mentioned are by no means typical of the long course of American diplomatic history. The United States has usually managed to accept and come to an understanding with regimes that are by no means democratic in spirit. In Latin America we deal constantly with governments that can hardly be said to be based on popular rule. We have tolerated such a dictatorship as that of Leonidas Trujillo in the Dominican Republic or the suaver and less complete absolutism of Somoza in Nicaragua; we have recognized a President like Batista, coming to power in Cuba by a military coup. Even with Péron, the most unlovely of the Latin-American *caudillos*, we pursued no persistent policy of hostility.

It is the same today with regard to Europe. We made a short-lived effort to show our displeasure with the fascist government that exists in Spain under General Franco; but it was not long before we reversed our policy, and we are now engaged in negotiations with Madrid, negotiations which, whether wise or foolish, at least demonstrate that we are not doctrinaire. More wisely, as it seems to me, we are cultivating a closer understanding with Yugoslavia, and in this case, too, we are dealing with a state whose political and economic philosophy has nothing in common with our own and which even bears a Communist label.

In the Orient there is a debatable question touching our policy towards Communist China. It is arguable that, if an ideological prejudice could have been set aside, early recognition at the outset of the regime in Peking might have prevented a close Chinese rapprochment with the Soviet Union. But it is also arguable that the British have gained very little from their own recognition policy and that, as in the case of Yugoslavia, a quarrel between Moscow and Peking is more likely to come about through errors on the part of the Kremlin than through any assiduous wooing on our part.

Taking the matter as a whole, it does not appear that the democratic dogma has reacted disastrously on American foreign policy, but rather that it has often been ignored or attenuated when motives of practical convenience dictated such action. This has certainly been true historically; it hardly appears less true today.

What of the collateral doctrine that nations have a right to their national independence? Has the United States adhered to this concept without deviation, or has it modified its point of view according to circumstances? If we turn our attention first to the past, it does not appear that we were the slaves of an idea in dealing with the peoples who came under our own sway after 1898. We did not grant any of them unqualified independence; even in the case of Cuba we attached strings to our grant of self-government and retained the right of intervention in the affairs of the island until the abrogation of the Platt amendment in 1934. The Philippines had to wait still longer for complete independence, and we still keep some ties with Guam and Puerto Rico, to say nothing of our new "trusteeships" in the Pacific. Nor are we the unqualified partisans of complete self-rule in the world of today. True, we were on the whole disposed to favor the independence of India, and we put heavy pressure on the Dutch in the case of Indonesia. But we are not taking so absolute a position in the case of the French protectorates in North Africa. We seem to be able to qualify our zeal where, in the interests of our own security, it seems wise to do so.

There may, it is true, exist a danger that the idea of national liberation will affect our future policy in some respects in a fashion not free from peril. When we find both the Democratic and Republican conventions calling for the restoration of the free nations of Eastern Europe, we cannot help asking whether this is mere bait for some of our foreign-born voters or whether it represents the beginnings of a policy that might lead to war. Implicit in such statements is the notion that we shall seek, not some kind of balance between ourselves and the Soviet Union, but a frank challenge with all its possible consequences. But it is a long way from such planks in party platforms to forthright action, and we do not need to prejudge the matter at the present time. Up to date, at any rate, our wars of liberations would be, by all but the revisionist historians, considered as coinciding with the real interests of the United States.

Amongst the dogmas which come under the fire of the contemporary critics of American foreign policy is the dogma of collective security, a dogma born of the American feeling that aggression is immoral. George Kennan suggests that there are many things wrong with this conception. He states that the application of the idea offers all sorts of peril; in particular, he stresses the dangers and embarrassments to which all coalitions are subject, the necessity for total victory which is implied in the moral condemnation of aggression, and the condign punishment of the aggressor. In answering these criticisms it is necessary to remember that the idea of collective security is still too young for us to judge it objectively and scientifically. Common action against a law-breaking state is a relatively new phenomenon in the intercourse of states. But how has that doctrine worked up to date, so far as it has been applied? It has certainly *not* been tied to total victory. In the test case of Korea, the "all-out" point of view of General MacArthur has been decisively repudiated, and the General himself has retreated to the refined offices of Remington Rand, more concerned with collective bargaining than with collective security. As for the working of coalitions, if one believes that all-out war would have been a blunder, then the co-operation of other nations in the Korean enterprise may have saved us from an error of colossal proportions.

Nor is it at all apparent that in Europe the notion of collective security has been applied in a fashion damaging to American interests. The existence of this idea, and the partial popular acceptance of it, has made easier the forging of a grand combination in opposition to Russian imperialism, and the American people, with their usual good sense, have preferred this idea to "going it alone." Moreover, their representatives have, with great wisdom, as it seems, fortified the Charter with a series of regional understandings that are based upon the interests of the states concerned. They have placed the concept of collective security not in a Utopian, but in a highly practical, concept. It may well be that they will continue to do so.

In one sense, however, it must be admitted, dogma has influenced, and influenced contrary to the nation's larger interest, the course of American policy. The favorite doctrine of the Americans is not any of those that have already been mentioned; it is the dogma that not force, but good will, is the true solvent of international difficulties. It is not necessary to repudiate out of hand the notion that a large and conciliatory spirit ought often to be demonstrated in the pursuit of the national interest broadly considered. But it is clear that the Americans have believed too much in the power of reason in international affairs. Woodrow Wilson believed in it too much in his negotiations with Germany; Charles Evans Hughes, perhaps, believed in it too much when he accepted the thesis that, if Japan were secure from attack in the Orient, her foreign policy would be carried on for an indefinite period in a liberal spirit; the promoters of the Kellogg Pact believed in it too much when they hoped that a promise not to resort to war would prevent war; many, many Americans believed in it too much when they advocated the demobilization of our great armies in 1945 and 1946 and trusted in the essentially benevolent intentions of the masters of the Kremlin. Here is a point of view that has undeniably had its drawbacks in practice.

And yet, in this special case, where we are obliged to agree that American doctrine has sometimes sacrificed national interest, or at any rate not clearly perceived the realities of international intercourse, we can at least say that this emphasis on good faith and good will has been no more disastrous to the United States than undiluted cynicism and blind reliance on force have been to other nations. Where now are Hitler and Mussolini? What have been our sufferings from excessive trust as compared with those of the Germans and the Italians for confiding their affairs into the hands of cynical believers in power? And is it not in the nature of democracy, in the nature of popular government at its best, that opinion forms slowly and hesitantly in favor of the assertion of force? Can it be otherwise in a nation practiced in the maintenance of social harmony through compromise and in the solution of public questions by the processes of give-and-take?

On the whole, it does not appear that the American people have suffered more than other peoples through their attachment to general principles and the frequent enunciation of these principles. They have usually managed to combine high-sounding precepts with practical action. But let us turn to the second question: have the interests of the United States been damaged by the extraordinary publicity given to foreign affairs in this country and by the practice of open diplomacy?

The dangers of the American system in this regard are certainly worth examining. What would be said by its critics? First of all, it might reasonably be contended that heated discussion of international problems in the public forum tends to expose the divisions in national opinion and to encourage aggressive action on the part of our enemies. In the second place, it may be said that the public conduct of negotiations may make it difficult to attain a reasonable compromise; it may stiffen both sides, exacerbate the national pride, and create a situation in which a challenge of arms is inevitable. In the third place, excessive publicity may damage the relations of allies. In the fourth place, it is difficult in a democratic state to keep the diplomatic antagonist in ignorance of one's purpose: the objectives of the administration in power become clearly defined through discussion, and the hostile state knows precisely how far it can go and when it must abstain from pressing further. Or still worse, a public statement of intention and of limited purpose may actually encourage aggression. Finally, as in the field of diplomacy so in the field of military action which is the complement of diplomacy, secrets may be revealed that ought to have been kept; plans may become known, and counterplanning thus made easier; weaknesses may be stressed in public debate and encourage aggressive action where otherwise it might not be undertaken; the ends of military action may be defined in such a way as to encourage ambitious projects on the part of another state beyond those limits.

Such are some of the arguments that can readily be brought against the American diplomatic method and against the weaknesses inherent in the conduct of foreign affairs under a democratic government. To what degree are these arguments valid?

Before answering this question, it is just as well to establish a correct perspective by reminding ourselves that nondemocratic governments conducting foreign policy in secret make mistakes of their own. The Austrian Foreign Minister, Count Berchtold, when he concocted his ultimatum to Serbia in 1914, was acting in the spirit of the old diplomacy; the result was the dissolution of the empire of which he was the servant. Hitler and Mussolini were masters of secret intrigue; they failed miserably. The Japanese militarists had no intention of taking the Japanese people into their confidence; yet they contrived ill. It is too much to say that had the issues with which these men dealt been submitted to a democratic public opinion the result would have been different; this would be history by hypothesis. But the result could scarcely have been worse. Human error is about as easy under one technique as under another, and behind all techniques there lie fallible human beings.

To expand the point a bit further, open diplomacy has never plunged the United States into a disastrous war or since 1812 into one on which the country was deeply divided; on the contrary, as I showed in an article in *The Yale Review* (Winter, 1949),* public discussion may well serve to postpone a decision

* See pp. 16–36 above.

in favor of taking up arms and compel even the most bellicose of statesmen to count the cost of a conflict for which the nation is not prepared from the point of view of national unity.

Nonetheless, there are weaknesses in open diplomacy; the points against it as stated above are in part sound; the real question is to assess accurately their importance.

As to whether divided opinion encourages aggression, there is something to be said on both sides. There are certainly instances in the history of Europe where totalitarian states have taken advantage of internal division in democratic countries. This, indeed, was an essential technique of Hitler. But it does not appear to be so easy to find examples of this kind of thing in American foreign relations. In 1916 the large vote for Wilson on a peace platform may have encouraged the German Imperial Government to resume the submarine warfare and thus to bring about war; but the pressure for such action was strong before the Presidential election, and gross miscalculation of the military potential of the United States also entered into the final decision. When the Japanese militarists decided upon the attack on Pearl Harbor, they obviously counted upon the element of surprise for the winning of the war, more than on the state of American opinion. The German and Italian declarations of war on the United States were, in a sense, long delayed (they might well have come after the passage of lend-lease) and followed logically on the Japanese action. The North Korean aggression was due, it is true, to a misreading of American opinion, but, as we shall see, this misreading was based on something more concrete than a general feeling that the United States was not united in its opposition to a possible aggression. All in all, it would be dangerous to put too much emphasis, then, on the thesis that the natural differences of opinion that exist in a democratic state are the major factor in encouraging violence by others.

What of the argument that when two nations join in a public debate the chances of a peaceful settlement of the dispute that has arisen between them are reduced almost to a nullity? In its extreme form, this statement is almost certainly false. In the campaign of 1844, when the Oregon controversy was at its height, the air resounded with cries of "fifty-four forty or fight"; yet the very administration that came in on this slogan made an accommodation with Great Britain. When an American vessel seized the confederate commissioners on board the British vessel, the *Trent*, in 1861, the act was greeted with tremendous applause in the United States, yet it was found possible to surrender the Southerners, despite the popular clamor. In 1895 Grover Cleveland demanded the arbitration of a boundary between Venezuela and British Guiana, and for a little the war spirit flamed; but the matter was settled, and the terms of arbitration to which the United States assented represented a considerable concession to Great Britain. Nor are the examples of this kind of thing all in the past. "Unconditional surrender" was the slogan of the Roosevelt administration in the Second World War; but in the case of Japan, a concession was made in the permission to the Japanese to keep their Emperor, and, though the matter is less clear, there was certainly some negotiation with the Italians in connection with the armistice agreement of 1943. When the United States entered Korea in 1950, the proclaimed objective was the unification of Korea; yet in the armistice negotiations not yet concluded there is certainly an intimation that we might settle for something considerably less. It is certainly not an absolute rule, then, that a democratic government cannot retreat from a position once publicly assumed.

In one sense, too, the problem of public debate and public challenge wears a new guise when the diplomatic antagonist of a democracy is a totalitarian state. It may make little difference, for example, whether an American demand made on the Kremlin is open or secret. For, if the Politburo wishes to yield, it may either never tell its public what has been asked or may invent its own reasons for yielding, or perhaps it may not even confess that it has yielded at all. To put the matter another way, the embarrassments of open diplomacy are minimized when only one of the two parties to a dispute is a practitioner of this type of policy.

Yet the case does not run all one way. There are plenty of instances in the history of foreign policy when conflict between two powerful nations has been avoided, or at any rate postponed, by diplomatic deals, often by diplomatic deals at the expense of third powers. The "sphere of influence" diplomacy is too familiar in its broad outlines for us to need to embroider the point. Such deals are repugnant to the spirit of popular government. Whatever we may think of President Roosevelt's decisions at Yalta, there is little doubt that they have been widely condemned, by no means only by the partisan opponents of the administration or by those who would denigrate Roosevelt's immense role in history. It is safe to assume that it would be very difficult for the American government in dealing with Russia to purchase concessions in one part of the globe by making concessions in another. The mood of the American people is clearly shown by the declarations of both the Republican and Democratic platforms with regard to the enslaved peoples of Eastern Europe and by the widespread reluctance on the part of many persons to recognize the finality of the great acquisitions to the Russian Communist empire that have been made since the war. It is possible, of course, that some rough balance may in the future be struck between the two great antagonists of today; but it would be very difficult indeed to put this in the form of a diplomatic agreement. Such agreements, to be sure, have in the past rarely proved lasting; but they have often operated to ease the tension for a period of years and permitted a temporary improvement in relations. They are, very possibly, impracticable for a democratic diplomacy.

It is doubtful, to my mind, whether open diplomacy much weakens an alliance. It is, of course, true that unscrupulous politicians often play on nationalistic feeling and arouse irritation by so doing; and it is also true that the unquenchable energy of American journalists is sometimes occupied in discovering and exploiting differences of opinion between those who are co-operating in their common interest. We have, undoubtedly, something to learn as to restraint in this regard. But alliances that rest upon a true community of interest can stand a good deal of this kind of thing, as the Second World War demonstrated. It would be premature to make a dogmatic judgment; but it is fair to say that there is no reason, as yet, to believe that the record of the self-governing peoples is a bad one. The powerful pressure toward unity exerted by the ambition of the Soviet Union may well prove an antidote to national selfishness and misunderstandings.

It must be conceded that public debate of national purposes does something to remove the element of bluff from international negotiation. In the Korean matter, for example, we have made it fairly clear to our enemies that we do not intend to attack Communist China unless we are further provoked, and this was certainly good news for the Kremlin. More doubtfully, the Kremlin may well understand (if it is not completely saturated by suspicion) that there is little danger of a preventive war on the part of the United States. Ultimata can hardly be a part of a democratic diplomacy unless the nation is completely united, and they are a dangerous weapon for popular governments.

There is always the risk, too, of misunderstanding when a statesman attempts, for the public instruction, to define the national purpose. When Mr. Acheson, in his famous speech of January, 1950, attempted to define the defense perimeter of the United States (qualified though his words were), his omission of Korea almost certainly did something to encourage the aggression of the following June, and the indiscretions of Senator Connolly may well have contributed to the same result. The fact that there are, under our system, several different persons who, in the eyes of foreigners, may be thought to speak authoritatively on questions of diplomacy increases the danger of misunderstanding. Presidential press conferences, Senatorial laxities, and sometimes the interviews of relatively minor officials may all be dangerous.

With regard to the revelation of military secrets, it is more difficult to come to a conclusion. Certainly, a great deal is published in a democratic state that would be carefully concealed in a totalitarian one. But what most of us do not know is how far the major facts of military position and purpose can be effectively concealed. Americans are still a bit naïve with regard to the problem of espionage; there has been, is, and will be on both sides far more of it than meets the eye. None but those closest to the facts can possibly decide just how far it is possible really to keep from the assumed enemy a reasonably wide knowledge of the total situation.

What is the general conclusion to which we must come? Certainly not an unqualifiedly cheerful one. The problems of open discussion should be faced; we should appreciate and learn to counteract the dangers. But, on the other hand, we should not exaggerate them. And this, too, we must say. We cannot expect a great self-governing nation not to wish to know what so vitally concerns it; and, if we have faith in democracy, we may hope that an enlightened people will learn how to reduce the dangers of discussion while it derives a peculiar strength from the collective wisdom characteristic of popular government.

4

The Department of State and American Public Opinion [*]

THE study of social history, highly desirable and fruitful, has led in some instances to a distorted concentration on trends and movements, and to an undue minimization of the part played by highly individual decisions. In American foreign policy, as elsewhere, the importance of resolutions taken *in camera* by a few persons is not to be disregarded. Yet in a fundamental sense, the diplomatic history of the United States does not resemble the diplomatic history of Europe. Essentially, the professional diplomat has always played a subordinate role. There are few Légers, few Vansittarts, few Holsteins in the record of American action. Occasionally, we have a House, or a Hopkins, or a Harriman— a non-professional—who plays a significant role; and, in the 1930's, a career diplomat, Sumner Welles, had great influence. But, for the most part (and the longer the perspective the truer is the generalization), men of this type are rare. The elements in the formation of policy are at once more subtle and more complex

* Reprinted by permission from *The Diplomats, 1919–1939*, ed. by Gordon A. Craig and Felix Gilbert (Princeton, N.J.: Princeton University Press, 1953).

than they are in many other states. We may, therefore, before describing the diplomacy of the 1920's, properly examine the various factors that enter into it.

In a sense that is true in no such degree in other nations, American diplomatic action has been determined by the people. There were ardent debates on foreign policy in the first days of our national history. There have been such debates ever since. Uninstructed though the average citizen may be in the facts of international life, he still has an opinion with regard to them. If he does not know, he thinks he knows. And this conviction on his part is one that cannot be disregarded. Nor do those who conduct our affairs in the main desire to disregard it. The democratic tradition is deeply rooted in our history. The men who stand at the levers of control are almost always men with substantial political experience. Their habits, their prepossessions, their convictions all lead them to pay heed to the voice of the great body of citizens, to shape their decisions with that voice in mind.

This does not mean that the minutiae of diplomatic action can be determined by the masses. Nor does it mean, if we are careful in our use of terms, that "public opinion," in the sense of a carefully thought-out view of a specific problem, is the fundamental factor. It means, rather, that the general sentiment of the people lies at the root of every great issue. There have been times when the mood of the American people was essentially militant. The government has responded to this militancy. There have been times when the mood was essentially one of withdrawal, of *reculement* as the French would put it. The government has responded to this mood likewise. Presidents have been powerless to withstand these deep-seated feelings. President McKinley was a man of peace, yet he was swept into war. President Franklin D. Roosevelt was certainly by conviction no isolationist, yet his first administration was essentially isolationist in spirit. This overmastering popular emotion rationalized, perhaps, into convenient slogans, often influences policy. To say this is not to praise or condemn. It is simply to state a fact. One may believe, if one is a convinced democrat, that in the main the popular instincts are sound. Or one may be cynical enough to distrust them. The important thing is to recognize that they exist.

But once this essential generalization has been made, there are others that need to be added to it. So far as individuals make policy, the balance of influence in the United States is always tipping, now this way or that, now to the executive, now to the legislature, and rarely to the professional diplomat. For example, there have been many Presidents of the United States who have exercised a remarkable personal influence on diplomatic action. This was true of Polk, of Theodore Roosevelt, of Woodrow Wilson, of Franklin D. Roosevelt, to mention only a few. But there have also been Presidents who delegated a large part of their power to their Secretaries of State. Except perhaps at the beginning of his administration, Lincoln did so. Grant did so. Harding and Coolidge did so. The role of the Chief Executive in foreign policy is a shifting thing, now great, now small, depending upon the type of individual happening to hold the office.

It is the same way with Secretaries of State. Some have been strong personalities, the true makers of policy. Others have recorded the views of Presidents, or depended upon their professional staffs. The one thing that is certain is that no definite and fixed role can be assigned to the Secretary under our constitutional system.

But we cannot end here. The conduct of American diplomacy is substantially affected by our constitution forms. It is not, of course, merely that the legislative body, through the treaty-making power, participates in the formation of policy. In other states some control of foreign affairs can be exerted by the law-making power. What is more important is that, under our type of government, there is no certainty of harmony between the executive and the legislature. Under the parliamentary system with cabinet responsibility there naturally exists between the government of the day and its majority in parliament an intimate and cooperative relationship. But in the United States the Congress does not feel bound to pay any very extraordinary deference to the views of the executive, and its attitude is all the more likely to be critical if the Congressional majority is, as it may be under our system, of a different political complexion from that of the executive. Furthermore, the chairmen of the great committees, especially the chairman of the Senate Committee on Foreign Relations, may be veterans in political life, and men of strong convictions who feel no obligation to take their views from the other end of Pennsylvania Avenue. They may insist not only on being consulted but on being heeded.

Let us look for a moment at the manner in which these generalizations apply to the period under examination in this essay. It is the period of the Harding, Coolidge, and Hoover administrations, from 1921 to 1933. First, as to the mood of the American people. When the Harding administration entered power, the country had just emerged from a great war. There had been much disillusionment and a severe letdown from the mood of exaltation induced by the leadership of Woodrow Wilson. The question of the role of the United States in world affairs had been under constant and vigorous debate. On the whole, I think it fair to say, the country had reacted against a policy of extensive commitments in the world at large. In the struggle over the League, there was so much pettiness and partisanship that it is difficult to discover its essential meaning. Yet it seems reasonable to say that between the President and his opponents there was a real issue involved and that this issue centered upon that part of the Covenant which projected the United States most deeply into the international scene. Article 10, with its pledge of territorial sovereignty and political independence, may or may not have been, as Wilson claimed, the heart of the whole matter. But, if one reads the Senate reservation to that article,[1] one becomes convinced that there was a real and fundamental question at stake, the question whether the United States should participate in the fullest sense in the development of a system of collective security for the maintenance of peace. And the answer that the American people gave, with the election of Harding to the Presidency, was that they did not care much about the matter. This renunciation must not be understood as implying that the withdrawal of the United States from world affairs was to be anything like total, or that there was not much devotion to the peace ideal as an abstraction. It merely means that the American mood was not one in which a sense of world responsibility played a dominant part.

Moreover, the mood of 1920 was the mood of virtually all of the period we shall consider. The immense prosperity of the United States, and the profound reaction from that prosperity, both concentrated American attention upon domestic rather than foreign matters. Those who conducted the foreign affairs of the nation, while often far ahead of public opinion in the breadth of their vision and in their sense of the large role which the country ought to play, had to take account of that essential fact.

As to the role of the Executive, neither President Harding

---

[1] The Senate reservation reads as follows: "The United States assumes no obligation to preserve the territorial integrity or political independence of any other country by the employment of its military or naval forces, its resources, or any form of economic discrimination, or to interfere in any way in controversies between nations, including all controversies relating to territorial integrity or political independence, whether members of the League or not, under the provisions of Article 10, or to employ the military or naval forces of the United States, under any article of the treaty for any purpose, unless in any particular case the Congress, which, under the Constitution, has the sole power to declare war or authorize the employment of the military or naval forces of the United States, shall, in the exercise of full liberty of action, by act or joint resolution so provide." D. F. Fleming, *The United States and the League of Nations* (New York, 1932), p. 433.

nor President Coolidge was fitted to assume the function of leadership in the field of foreign affairs. Harding was an easy-going man of very mediocre intellectual gifts, if the word gifts may be used at all, and when he thought at all he thought in stereotypes. Coolidge was congenitally cautious, incapable of powerful or effective leadership, essentially the exponent of the laissez-faire philosophy. Neither exercised any really powerful influence on the diplomacy of the period. The same thing cannot be said of Herbert Hoover. Few Presidents were more conscious of their responsibilities than he, and, as we shall see, in some essential matters the opinion of the Chief Executive was of great significance during his administration.

The Secretaries of the period we are examining present an interesting picture, and interesting contrasts. Charles Evans Hughes, Secretary from 1921 to 1925, was undoubtedly one of the ablest men who ever held that office. His personal role in the formation of policy was a most important one. Secretary Kellogg, on the other hand, was much less disposed to initiate action of any kind, much more conscious of the limits imposed upon him by public opinion and by the Congress. Henry L. Stimson, Hoover's Secretary of State, was a man of powerful and strongly-held convictions, but was compelled in some matters, as we shall see, to defer to his chief.

All three Secretaries had to consider the legislative branch. The great concentration of powers inevitable to the waging of the first world war had inevitably led to a reaction, and the Congresses of the 1920's were in many respects jealous of their own position, and none too disposed to defer to the Executive. Despite the obstacles thrown in his way, Hughes often succeeded in by-passing the legislators, and in shaping policy by his own personal force. Kellogg was exceedingly deferential to Senators, and he had to deal with a man of great force, and of capacity superior to his own, in William E. Borah, chairman of the Senate Committee on Foreign Relations. Stimson was, on the whole, on good terms with the Senate, and was more confined by the views of his chief than by the opposition of the legislature. Yet on some questions, as we shall see, he could make little headway over Congressional resistance. The pattern, in other words, changed with each Secretary of State.

As for the permanent personnel of the Department, it is not easy to estimate its role. But it seems fair to say that Hughes dominated his department, Kellogg was often much influenced by his professional advisers, and Stimson, like Hughes, had strong views of his own. From all of which it can be understood how difficult it would be to write the diplomatic history of this period in terms of any single personality.[2]

Since the personal interpretation of American foreign policy is denied to us by the facts of the American scene, it seems wise to center our examination of the 1920's about certain key ideas. The emphasis, as in all these essays, is on Europe, and much, therefore, will be omitted that is not relevant to the European picture. Such emphasis is wholly justified. For whatever may have been the case before 1914, the relations of the United States with the great communities of the West are, in the period with which we are dealing, of great significance to the world as a whole.

II

Let us choose, as the first theme for our examination, the attitude of the United States towards the idea of collective security, as it was reflected in the three administrations from 1921 to 1933. First of all, it is necessary to reiterate that the opposition to the famous Article 10 of the Covenant was nothing more or less than opposition to the collective security idea. That arti-

---

[2] It is relevant to remark that in the brief period between 1921 and 1933 there were no less than six Under-Secretaries of State. No single fact indicates more strikingly the contrast between the American and the European diplomatic scene.

cle was designed by its framers to prevent physical aggression on the part of one state against another. The members of the League agree, it read, "to respect and preserve as against external aggression the territorial integrity and existing political independence of all members of the League." This was not, as has sometimes been said, a freezing of the *status quo*. It was a prohibition on the alteration of the *status quo* by force. But it involved, and involved very deeply, the notion of common action against an aggressor, and it became the focus of the most fundamental attacks upon the Covenant itself. While the materials for a judgment are not so satisfactory as we might desire, it seems clear that a majority of the Senate were not ready to accept such an obligation, and when President Wilson attempted to make an issue of the matter in the election of 1920, he utterly failed. The great vote for Harding in that year showed, so it seems to me, that the mass of the people, to put it mildly, attached no very great positive importance to this central idea—if, indeed, they apprehended it at all clearly.

It seems clear, too, that Mr. Hughes, soon to become Secretary of State, was not enamored of the collective security idea, either. He was not a foe of the League idea in general but, as his correspondence shows, he thought of it in quite a different way from Wilson. "There is plain need for a league of nations," he wrote, "in order to provide for the development of international law for creating and maintaining organs of international justice and machinery of conciliation and conference, and for giving effect to measures of international cooperation which may from time to time be agreed upon." [3] There is not a word in this interesting statement with regard to the machinery of coercion. It is, moreover, abundantly clear that he was opposed to Article 10. Indeed, he expressed such opposition as early as March of 1919, and this position he consistently maintained. Whether or

[3] C. E. Hughes to Senator Hale, July 24, 1919, quoted in M. J. Pusey, *Charles Evans Hughes* (2 vols., New York, 1951), I, 397.

not the treaty was to be ratified by the new administration, there seems no reason to believe that Hughes was ready to fight for the principle of common action against aggression. In point of fact, however, the question was never discussed in the early days of the Harding regime. For so bitter was the opposition of the irreconcilable Republicans to the whole Wilsonian edifice that Hughes, despite his own desire to see the Versailles pact ratified with reservations, was obliged to abandon this idea, and to abandon it even in the face of the assurances that he had offered to the American people in the campaign of 1920 that a vote for Harding was a vote for entry into the League under reasonable conditions.[4]

Despite the rebuff administered by the new administration to the idea of collective security, the idea itself showed a remarkable vitality. This is not to say that it was ever close to general acceptance in the 1920's; such a proposition, I think, cannot be maintained. But there were important discussions of the problem, and we should understand these discussions before we can examine the American attitude with regard to them.

First of the attempts to strengthen the machinery of the Covenant was the Draft Treaty of Mutual Assistance of 1923. This treaty gave to the Council considerably greater power than that conceded in the League constitution itself. It permitted that body, for example, in case of the outbreak of hostilities to designate the aggressor nation, and bound the contracting parties to furnish each other mutual assistance against the nation so designated, on a basis determined by the Council itself. It assumed that both military and financial aid would be accorded the aggressed state, and implied that an international force would be created to give effect to the obligations of the treaty. It sought at the same time to limit the operation of sanctions by declaring that in principle no state in a continent other than that in which

[4] For a discussion of this point see Pusey, *Charles Evans Hughes*, II, 431–434.

the operations would take place would be required to co-operate in military, naval, or air operations.[5] The Draft Treaty was transmitted to the various governments by the Fourth Assembly, and comment invited.

There is little reason to believe that there was ever much chance of the adoption of this ambitious scheme, even by the members of the League. Indeed, the opposition to more extensive commitments than those of the Covenant had been expressed by not a few states in the deliberations which preceded the drafting of this instrument, and in the Fourth Assembly itself. In the debates at Geneva, indeed, it is possible to discern a distinct reaction against the idea of collective security, a reaction by no means wholly due—perhaps not even chiefly due—to the attitude of the United States. Nevertheless, it is interesting to observe the extremely cold tone in which Mr. Hughes replied to the note of January 9, 1924, in which the Draft Treaty was presented to the American government. Delaying his answer until June 16, and expressing a "keen and sympathetic interest" in "every endeavor" for the reduction of armaments, an end towards which the treaty was directed, he pointed out that wide powers were given to the Council of the League of Nations. "In view of the constitutional organization of this government," he declared, "and in view of the fact that the United States is not a member of the League of Nations, this Government would find it impossible to give its adherence."[6]

The reference in this note to the constitutional obligations of the United States deserves a word of comment. What Hughes is talking about is perfectly clear. Obviously effective action under any agreement looking to the application of collective meas-

[5] For a scholarly discussion of the mutual assistance treaty, see B. S. Williams, *State Security and the League of Nations* (Baltimore, 1927), pp. 151–182. See also Gordon A. Craig and Felix Gilbert, eds., *The Diplomats, 1919–1939* (Princeton, N.J., 1953), chs. i sec. 3, iv sec. 3, and x sec. 1.

[6] *Foreign Relations,* 1924, I, 79.

ures for the maintenance of peace can, under our form of government, only be taken by the Congress of the United States. But this is not to say that the Executive cannot enter into an engagement which would bind Congress to act. Many another treaty, and not merely a treaty of the type we have been discussing, can be made effective only by affirmative action of the legislative branch. The question is not constitutional but moral. When an obligation is incurred, it is morally imperative that the Congress should carry it out. It should not be incurred, of course, unless there is good reason to believe that it would be honored. But it is quite unnecessary to speak, as did Mr. Hughes, as if our governmental forms prevented the signature by the United States of agreements for the maintenance of peace.

Practically speaking, we repeat, the Hughes note was not of very great importance. The Draft Treaty was probably doomed from its inception. The point to be made is that in this instance the Secretary showed no enthusiasm for—indeed no interest in— the idea of collective security.

The Secretary was to take a still more drastic stand with regard to the Geneva Protocol.[7] In 1924 the European diplomats tried their hand once again at the problem which the Treaty of Mutual Assistance had failed to solve. The result was the Geneva Protocol for the Pacific Settlement of International Disputes. This Protocol erected an elaborate system for the solution of international difficulties, first by extending the compulsory jurisdiction of the Court of International Justice, and, second, by providing for the settlement, either by the Council of the League or by compulsory arbitration, of all disputes which did not fall within the jurisdiction of the Court. At the same time it made

[7] For a discussion of the protocol, see Williams, *State Security and the League*, pp. 182–205, also D. H. Miller, *The Geneva Protocol* (New York, 1925), and P. J. Noel Baker, *The Geneva Protocol for the Pacific Settlement of International Disputes* (London, 1925); and Craig and Gilbert, eds., *The Diplomats, 1919–1939*, chs. i sec. 3, iv sec. 3, and x sec. 1.

it possible to define an aggressor with more precision than was possible in the Covenant, and bound the signatories to participate loyally and effectively in the application of sanctions, but with the proviso that aid should be given by each state "in the degree which its geographical position and particular situation as regards armament allows." It is important to note that the Geneva Protocol was unanimously approved by the Fifth Assembly of the League on October 2, 1924.

The Geneva Protocol has a far greater significance than the Draft Treaty. The leaders of the greatest states of Europe were at the meetings of that famous Assembly of 1924, Ramsay Mac-Donald for Great Britain, Eduard Herriot for France. The Protocol was launched at a favorable moment and under favorable auspices, with the end of a period of tension in the relations of France and Germany, and in an atmosphere favorable to constructive achievement. It is true that the position was somewhat altered by the fall of the Labor government in November of 1924. Still, without overstressing the matter, it is possible to say that, on the mere basis of the significance of the instrument, the attitude of the United States towards the Protocol was bound to be of considerable importance.

The Foreign Relations of the United States for 1925 contain a very remarkable account of conversations on the subject between the Secretary and the British ambassador in Washington. The first occurred on January 5, 1925. It is important to quote this document, recorded in a memorandum by Mr. Hughes himself. It was Sir Esmé Howard who opened the conversation. Declaring that "it was a cardinal point in British policy to maintain friendly relations with the United States, and to cooperate with this Government wherever possible," he added that "there might be interference with this policy if contingencies should arise in which through the operation of the Protocol the British Government was brought into opposition to the interests of the United States." "On the other hand," he continued, "it seemed to the British Government that it would not be well to throw out the Protocol entirely. . . ." "The only alternative to such a competition in armament with all its possible consequences would seem to be the adoption in some form of such an arrangement as the Geneva Protocol proposed." [8]

In reply to these observations the Secretary took what can only be described as a rather high tone. "There were," he remarked, "two aspects, at least, of the Geneva Protocol which might give concern to this Government." "If the Protocol were taken as having practical value and actually of portending what it set forth," said Hughes, "there would appear to be a proposal of a concert against the United States, when the Powers joining in the Protocol considered that the United States had committed some act of aggression, although the United States might believe itself to be entirely justified in its action, and in fact be acting in accordance with its traditional policies. The Secretary said that he did not believe that such a concert would actually become effective but he supposed that the Protocol must be taken as it is written and in this view the United States would be compelled to view it with disfavor. The Secretary said there was another class of cases where the action of the United States itself might not be involved but that of some other country with which the United States had trade relations, and the action of the Powers who had joined in the Protocol might turn out to be inimical to the interests of the United States in such relations with the country in question." Alluding still further to the possibility of collective action against some other nation, Mr. Hughes went on to remark that "there was one thing he believed could be depended upon, and that was that this Government from its very beginning had been insistent upon the rights of neutrals and would continue to maintain them." He "did not believe that any Administration, short of a treaty concluded and ratified, could commit the country against assertion of its neutral

[8] *Foreign Relations,* 1925, I, 16–17.

rights in case there should be occasion to demand their recognition." [9]

All this could hardly be described as encouraging. But Mr. Hughes went further. He declined at one and the same time to approve or to disapprove the Protocol. He intimated that the British sounding was a mere maneuver and excuse for inaction, and expressed the hope that if other governments did not approve of the Protocol, they should deal with the matter from the point of view of their own interests and not put the responsibility on the United States. To the suggestion that the matter might be handled by a reservation on the part of the British, he declared that he would not wish anything to be said that might imply that this way of dealing with the problem might be satisfactory to the United States.

It is difficult to describe this commentary of Mr. Hughes as other than a dash of cold water thrown in the face of Sir Esmé. Indeed, it is hard to see how the tone could have been much more intransigent and unconciliatory. Nor was the effect of this interview diminished three days later when the British ambassador returned to the State Department and was told that the Secretary had consulted with the President and that the Chief Executive approved the point of view previously expressed.[10] And it is worth noting that the position then assumed was in no sense due to any particular political pressure. The date, it will be noted, was January 1925. The presidential elections were over, and the Republican party had been brilliantly victorious. It may be that Mr. Hughes believed that he was expressing the mood and temper of the American people. It is certain that he was not acting on the basis of any particular exigency of the moment.

On the other hand, it is by no means clear that the action taken by the Secretary was a determining factor in the final collapse of the effort to strengthen the League through the Protocol. The British elections of November 1924 brought the Conservatives

[9] *Foreign Relations,* 1925, I, 17.   [10] *Foreign Relations,* 1925, I, 19.

into power with an overwhelming majority, and the new Secretary of State for Foreign Affairs was not an enthusiast for the arrangements that had been worked out at Geneva. The Dominions, when consulted, also were disposed to avoid the rather sweeping commitments contained in the League proposals.[11] True, the position of the United States afforded an excellent argument against these new commitments, and the British government made a good deal of this argument in its memorandum of March 1925.[12] But the most that can probably be said is that the position assumed by Mr. Hughes reinforced a point of view that the London government might have assumed in any event. It is useless to speculate, of course, on what would have been the course of events in the 1920's if the United States had wholeheartedly accepted the engagements of the Covenant itself.

The dislike of the League idea, it must be stressed, did not, in the secretariat of Mr. Hughes, prevent the taking of steps which expressed American interest in the idea of peace. There was, for example, in 1923, a proposal put forward by the administration for American adhesion to the protocol creating the Court of International Justice.[13] Such a proposal was consonant with American traditional thinking, which connected peace, not with power, but with orderly process. But this proposal got nowhere. When the United States Senate in 1926 voted to adhere to the protocol, it did so with reservations that created new problems and that carried the whole controversy with regard to the Court over into the Roosevelt administration.[14]

But let us return to the movement for collective security. The failure of the Protocol was followed by the very significant ne-

---

[11] See some of their comments in Williams, *State Security and the League*, pp. 310–320. See also Craig and Gilbert, eds., *The Diplomats, 1919–1939*, ch. i, note 91.

[12] Williams, *State Security and the League*, p. 306.

[13] On the World Court question, see D. F. Fleming, *The United States and the World Court* (Garden City, 1945).

[14] *Ibid.*

gotiations, lasting through a great part of 1925, that finally resulted in the treaties of Locarno. By these treaties specific agreements strengthening the principles of collective security were approved in place of generalized understanding. Thus the French, British, Italian, Belgian, and German governments entered into engagements by which the territorial *status quo* with regard to the frontiers between France and Germany and Belgium and Germany were guaranteed, and by which the countries concerned mutually undertook in no case to attack each other or resort to war against each other. They also agreed to settle all disputes arising between them by resort to arbitration, and to extend mutual assistance to one another against any one of their number which resorted to war in violation of the pact. The Eastern frontier settlements of Versailles, that is, the frontier between Germany and Poland and Germany and Czechoslovakia, were not similarly guaranteed. But treaties of arbitration were drawn up between Germany and Poland and Germany and Czechoslovakia, and these treaties were buttressed by antecedent agreements between France and Poland and France and Czechoslovakia to give each other immediate aid and assistance in case of an unprovoked recourse to arms. The Locarno agreements, signed at the end of 1925, represent the high-water mark of the movement for collective guarantees in the period between the wars.[15]

By the time the Locarno treaties were under discussion, Secretary Hughes had laid down his charge at the State Department and had been succeeded by Secretary Kellogg. The new director of American foreign policy was a man of far less force than his predecessor, far less likely to adopt any initiative in the field of foreign policy. Yet the very fact that the Locarno agreements were regional in their character was calculated to relieve the

[15] For a convenient summary see Williams, *State Security and the League*, pp. 206–226. See also G. Glasgow, *From Dawes to Locarno* (New York, 1926).

United States of any embarrassment with regard to them. To such partial understandings the American government could have no such objections as pertained to the strengthening of the Covenant. Mr. Kellogg, of course, when informed of what was going on, firmly declined to have anything to do with any guarantee.[16] But President Coolidge speaking in July of 1925 gave the negotiations his blessing,[17] and in his message of December 1925, the cautious Chief Executive declared that the recent agreements "represent the success of the policy on which this country has been insisting . . . of having European countries settle their own political problems without involving this country," and went on to suggest that the way was now clear for the reduction of land armaments, while underlining the fact that this was primarily a European problem.[18]

III

The question of American participation in the movement for the reduction of land armaments was, in due course, to take another turn. In no little time the American government began to participate in discussions at Geneva looking to such reduction. But, since the climactic moves in this discussion came in the early 1930's, it will be convenient to postpone discussion of this subject for a moment, and to examine first that remarkable movement which culminated in the famous Kellogg Pact, or the Pact of Paris, for the maintenance of peace.[19] This pact,

[16] *Foreign Relations*, 1925, I, 21.

[17] See the *New York Times*, July 4, 1925.

[18] The *New York Times*, December 9, 1925.

[19] On the Kellogg Pact, see the full discussion in *Foreign Relations*, 1928, I, 1–234. See also J. T. Shotwell, *War as an Instrument of National Policy and Its Renunciation in the Pact of Paris* (New York, 1928), D. H. Miller, *The Peace Pact of Paris: A Study of the Briand-Kellogg Treaty* (New York, 1928), and D. P. Myers, *Origins and Conclusion of the Paris Pact. The Renunciation of War as an Instrument of National Policy* (Boston, 1929).

finally signed on August 28, 1928, was a simple pledge on the part of the contracting parties "not to have recourse to war as an instrument of national policy, and to settle all disputes arising between them by peaceful means." At first blush this compact looks like a denial of the very principle of collective security, a substitution of peace by promises for peace by common action. But whoever studies the background of the Kellogg Pact in detail will, I think, come to a somewhat different conclusion. For the friends of the Pact were by no means always clear on the matter of sanctions. Mr. S. O. Levinson of Chicago, who very early espoused the idea of the outlawry of war and who was one of those who pressed it most tenaciously throughout the 1920's, though certainly not depending on force as the essential element in his own view of the problem, at one time seems to have believed that in flagrant violations of a no-war pledge force might be used.[20] Senator Borah, who had a great deal to do with the promotion of the Kellogg Pact, on one occasion declared that it was "quite inconceivable that this country would stand idly by in case of a grave breach of a multilateral treaty to which it was a party." [21] Statements such as these ought not, it is true, to be given an exaggerated importance. They certainly do not represent the prevailing mood or conviction of the two men just mentioned, both of whom seem to have had a naïve faith in the power of public opinion. But neither can they be entirely disregarded. To this fact must be added another. Some of the friends of the Pact were quite clear as to what they hoped would flow from it. Believing in the principle of collective action against aggression, they took the view that once the treaty was ratified there would arise, almost inevitably, a demand that it be "implemented." And this demand, they hoped, would in due course lead the United States into closer relations with the

[20] See J. E. Sloner, *S. O. Levinson and the Pact of Paris: A Study in the Techniques of Influence* (Chicago, 1943), esp. pp. 27 and 185.

[21] See Shotwell, *War as an Instrument of National Policy*, p. 224.

League of Nations. If once the principle that war was inherently illegal, as well as immoral, were accepted, a way would be found by which the American people would take action in support of the principle they had affirmed. This point of view appears most clearly in Professor Shotwell's interesting book on *War as an Instrument of National Policy*.[22] But one can find it in many other pronouncements of the period as well.[23]

Perhaps the most interesting thing about the Pact of Paris, however, is the illustration it affords of the way in which American foreign policy on occasion comes up from the grass roots rather than down from the State Department or its Secretary. It is a well-known fact that the initial step in the negotiations that led to the Pact came from a proposal of the French Foreign Minister Aristide Briand, made on April 6, 1927, to enter into a bilateral treaty for the renunciation of war. This proposal, incited by Professor Shotwell on a visit to Paris, passed almost unnoticed at the time, and was indeed completely ignored by Secretary Kellogg. The situation was in some degree changed when Nicholas Murray Butler, then president of Columbia University, in a letter to the *New York Times*, called attention to the significance of the Briand offer, and when Professor Shotwell and Professor Chamberlain put the idea in the form of a draft treaty. In June of 1927, the French government presented a formal proposal to the United States.[24] Still the administration hesitated, indeed the State Department declared that no such compact was necessary, and that it would not even be desirable.[25] But the outlawry of war proposal aroused an increasing interest, and the crucial factor in securing official consideration for it was doubtless the attitude of Senator Borah, the powerful chairman of the Senate Committee on Foreign Relations. On December 27,

[22] *Ibid.*, pp. 254ff.
[23] See, for example, Miller, *The Peace Pact of Paris*, and J. B. Whitton, *What Follows the Pact of Paris* (New York, 1932).
[24] Shotwell, *War as an Instrument of National Policy*, p. 72.
[25] *Ibid.*

1927, Borah introduced a resolution calling for the outlawry of war, the establishment of an international code, and of an international court by the decisions of which the nations of the world should be bound to abide.[26] On the very next day, Secretary Kellogg, in a note to the French government, proposed that "the two governments, instead of contenting themselves with a bilateral declaration of the nature suggested by M. Briand, might make a more signal contribution to world peace by joining in an effort to obtain the adherence of all of the principal powers of the world to a declaration renouncing war as an instrument of national policy." [27] Thus were initiated the negotiations that finally led to the Pact of Paris.

I do not think it desirable to trace these negotiations in detail. There were substantial obstacles to be overcome. The French were by no means enthusiastic about the alteration of their original proposal, and they feared that the proposed agreement might weaken the structure of the League of Nations, and the machinery of sanctions embodied in the Covenant. Other difficulties soon arose. The British, in particular, seemed to fear that their freedom of action in certain parts of the world might be limited by the proposed engagement. Matters ended happily, however. By making it clear, as he did in a speech of April 28, 1928, that the Pact did not affect the right of self-defense, Mr. Kellogg calmed the apprehensions of the critics, and at the same time (having regard to the flexibility of the term self-defense itself) whittled away some of the significance of the Pact itself.[28] By the spring of 1928, with a Presidential election coming on, there was only one course of action to be followed, and that was to press matters to a conclusion. And so the Pact was signed.

[26] The resolution is found most easily in Shotwell, *War as an Instrument of National Policy*, pp. 108–109.

[27] *Foreign Relations*, 1927, II, 626–627.

[28] The speech is in the *New York Times*, April 29, 1928.

What effect did the Pact have on American diplomacy in the years that followed? The first attempt to invoke it concerned a dispute between China and Russia in 1929 and need not concern us here save to remark that the appeal made by the American government exposed the United States to a severe rebuff from the Soviet Union.[29]

The fiasco which resulted in this particular case led Mr. Stimson to meditate on possible means by which the Kellogg Pact might be made more effective. Thus arose the idea of consultation, or of a consultative pact.[30] This idea was discussed with the French ambassador in the fall of 1929.[31] It also came up at the London naval conference of 1930. At that conference the French again brought it forward and threw out the hint that the reduction of their own naval armament might be facilitated by some understanding on the matter. The Secretary was at first cold to the suggestion since it smacked of a diplomatic bargain, and President Hoover was still more opposed. But, as the conference proceeded, it appeared possible that the French and the British might agree on some strengthening of their association under the Covenant of the League, and Stimson played with the idea of encouraging such a strengthening by some agreement for consultation. On March 25 he issued a somewhat cryptic statement to the press on the matter, intimating that some positive step might be taken. He seems at this moment to have had the support of the American delegation of which he was the head. There was, however, less enthusiasm in Washington; the President was distinctly nervous with regard to the matter and feared the reaction in the Senate. He was, indeed, strongly opposed to any generalized engagement to consult. Though he gave his

[29] The voluminous correspondence is in *Foreign Relations*, 1929, II, 186–435.

[30] For this whole matter of consultation, see R. M. Cooper, *American Consultation in World Affairs for the Preservation of Peace* (New York, 1934).

[31] See *Foreign Relations*, 1929, I, 59–64.

approval to a watered-down version of a consultative clause in the naval treaty, the project was, in the last analysis, abandoned.[32]

But Stimson was tenacious of the general objective. When the Manchurian crisis broke in the fall of 1931, he maintained close contact with the League, even to the extent of permitting the American representative at Geneva to sit in on meetings of the Council, and of sending General Dawes to Paris to participate at arm's length in the League deliberations. There was an American member on the commission which the League appointed to investigate the situation and make recommendations, and the League and the United States co-operated in the winter of 1932 in proclaiming the so-called Stimson doctrine by which it was declared that there could be no recognition of an illegal situation arising out of the violation of the Kellogg Pact. In the course of the year 1932, moreover, both party nominating conventions declared in favor of the principle of consultation,[33] and Stimson underlined the desirability of accepting this principle in a speech of August 8.[34] Nonetheless, no formal engagements were entered into during any part of the period which we are reviewing.

Taken all in all, however, it cannot be said that the American government, between 1921 and the advent of the Roosevelt administration, had gone very far towards the acceptance of the idea of collective security. There was very distinctly a difference between the attitude of Hughes and the attitude of Stimson,[35] but the difference was by no means so wide as practically to affect the policies of the European nations. On the whole, the dogma of freedom of action dominated American policy during the period, and none was more deeply attached to it, it should

[32] See *Foreign Relations*, 1930, II, *passim*, esp. pp. 36–92.
[33] Cooper, *American Consultation in World Affairs*, p. 58.
[34] *Ibid.*, p. 59.
[35] Stimson was disposed to acquiesce in sanctions against Japan in 1931.

be said, than was President Hoover.[36] It seems likely that in this respect he expressed the dominant opinion of the nation.

Interesting as it is to speculate on "what might have been," in summarizing the attitude of the United States in the years under review, all that can really be said is that the general line of policy was unfavorable towards common action against an aggressor, but that the Kellogg-Briand Pact, by branding war as immoral, reflected something of the sentiment of the American people, and may have provided a basis for the more active diplomacy of the United States at a later period.

IV

The dislike of the administrations of this period for the League idea is well illustrated in the manner in which they dealt with the problem of reduction of armaments. There was, at the end of the war, an immense sentiment for such reduction, and Mr. Hughes, in the very first year of his administration of the State Department, boldly capitalized on such sentiment. The Washington Arms Conference of 1921–1922 was, in many ways, a great diplomatic achievement. Though the British would have liked the credit for calling it, Mr. Hughes insisted on garnering that credit for himself. He electrified all observers when, at the very outset, he laid down a plan for the scrapping of a substantial part of existing building programs and for the establishment of fixed ratios in capital ships and aircraft carriers. He secured that parity with the British which American opinion (for no very clear reason, it must be conceded) demanded, and he persuaded the Japanese to accept a subordinate position. He brought about these striking results without what the enemies of the League would have described as "entanglement." The nearest approach to such an entanglement, indeed, was a Four Power pact, consultative in nature, with regard to "the regions of the Pacific."

[36] See President Hoover's recent article in *Collier's, The National Weekly*, for April 19, 1952, p. 57.

(Somehow or other, such a pact could, even in 1922, be regarded as innocent if it applied to the Orient.) In the course of the negotiations, moreover, assisted by the pressure exercised by the Dominions, and especially by Canada, he broke up the Anglo-Japanese alliance which had existed since 1902. But this story is not for us to tell here in detail.[37] The point is that the American theory with regard to arms reduction was essentially different from the thesis upheld by many influential Europeans, and especially by the French. To the latter, the building of a system of external security was a condition precedent to the reduction of armaments, and it was only under very heavy pressure that the Quai d'Orsay yielded even on the partial limitation of naval armaments at Washington. But American statesmanship stoutly insisted that there was no necessary connection between the curtailment of armed forces and a network of treaties to punish aggression. It succeeded, in this particular instance, in making its point of view prevail by giving up, in the face of Japanese pressure, the right to fortify Guam and the Philippines. In other words, it abdicated so far as the use of force in the Far East was concerned. No doubt, as was frequently maintained at the time, because of the state of American public opinion, it would have been impossible to secure funds for such fortifications in any case. But however this may be, the significant thing is that the American outlook on the whole question of armaments was so very different from that involved in acceptance of the League.

The success of the Washington Conference in the field of naval armament was to be repeated and extended in the administration of President Hoover. For a time after 1922 it seemed as if the rivalry of the United States and Great Britain, partially exorcised so far as capital ships were concerned, was to break out in new construction of vessels of inferior tonnage. An at-

---

[37] The best brief account of the Conference is in A. W. Griswold, *The Far Eastern Policy of the United States* (New York, 1937), pp. 269–332.

tempt to come to an agreement in 1927 in a conference at Geneva aborted, largely because the preparations for the conference were inadequate and because the admirals were allowed a very important, if not a central, role in the negotiations. But at London in 1930, the three Great Powers, the United States, Great Britain, and Japan, came to an agreement which limited ships of every kind and which was, indeed, a remarkable achievement.[38] It ought, perhaps, to be said parenthetically, that one of the reasons for the success of both the Washington and London conferences was the appointment of influential Senators as members of the American delegations. This specific is not infallible, but it has frequently proved efficacious in smoothing the way to successful negotiation.

The naval agreements of the period seemed at the time to be remarkable achievements. In the short run they were rightly so regarded. But they did not survive the tensions of the 1930's, and their long-time effects were certainly not entirely happy. The United States was for a time lulled into a false security and neglected its naval establishment, failing to build up to the agreed quotas. The British were compelled at London, or in the negotiations preceding London, to reduce their cruiser strength in order to propitiate the American government, and this was to be a serious handicap in the 1940's. Naval disarmament was an expression of the temper of the 1920's and of a distinctively American point of view. But it was very far from affording a long-time guarantee of peace, and it contributed little to the stabilization of Europe. It is for this reason that I have dealt with it so summarily.

Let us turn to examine the American role in the effort carried on from 1925 to 1933 to reduce land armaments. As early as 1925, eschewing the very cautious view of the matter expressed by Secretary Hughes, and responding, no doubt, to the pres-

[38] The London negotiations are given in much detail in *Foreign Relations*, 1930, I, 1–186.

sure of powerful elements in American opinion, Secretary
Kellogg permitted the United States to take part in the deliberations of the Preparatory Commission on Disarmament that
assembled at Geneva. For years a long discussion went on in this
Commission which finally culminated in the Geneva Conference
of 1932. In this conference bold proposals were put forward
for the curtailment of land armaments as well as sea armaments,
and in June of 1932 President Hoover presented a sweeping
program which laid the emphasis on the abolition of "offensive
weapons." [39]

But firmly, at all times, the United States adhered to its idea
of no entanglement, of making no engagements that might tie
its hands. And, equally firmly, the French insisted that such engagements were essential to any understanding. Thus the arms
conference was to end in a fiasco; the way was blocked to any
concrete accomplishment, and though the attitude was slightly
changed when the Roosevelt administration came into power,
the advent of Hitler in Germany dimmed the prospects of any
accord. The world, instead, was to march down the long road
to war.

Let us summarize at this point the policies of the United States
with regard to peace and security as they relate to Europe. We
shall have to begin by saying once again that these policies were
narrowly circumscribed by public opinion. There are those who
believe that if the American government had been able to take
part wholeheartedly in a program of military guarantees the
catastrophes of the 1930's might have been avoided. Certainly,
in this year of grace 1953, the assumptions of American diplomacy are based on the idea of such guarantees. But different
times, different manners. Neither Secretary Hughes nor Secretary Kellogg ever believed in the principle of collective action,
and Stimson, believing in it more, had to contend with a President who was deeply set against any such conception. It is easy,

[39] See *Foreign Relations*, 1932, I, 180–182.

if one will, to bewail the situation. But it is perhaps more judicious merely to recognize the fact that in democratic countries it is not possible to proceed in defiance of, or in opposition to, a powerful body of opinion.

V

Let us turn from the questions of politics to the principal economic problems that vexed the administrations of the 1920's. And here the two principal matters to be considered are the war debts [40] and reparations. On the former a position had been taken at Paris by President Wilson from which it was impossible at any time in the next fifteen years to depart. This position was that the cancellation of the debts could not be considered. It is obvious that, in assuming this position, Wilson was interpreting American opinion. It would have been impossible to take any other course. In the wave of postwar nationalism most Americans saw only that they had come to the rescue of the Western democracies in a great war, that they had played a decisive part in the winning of that war, and that the United States had little to show, in the way of material gain, for the immense sums of money that had been expended and for the loss of American lives. The suggestion that they should now forgive borrowings which had been understood to be such at the time they were made was hardly to be tolerated.

Accordingly, the Harding and Coolidge administrations were bound to base their own policy on the position assumed by the previous administration, and to turn a deaf ear to European appeals for a scaling down of both the war loans and reparations. The American attitude was first defined in an explicit manner, that is, by legislation, in the winter of 1922. The act of February 9 of that year created a special War Debt Commission to preside over the liquidation of these debts into long-term obligations.

[40] On the war debts, see especially H. G. Moulton and L. Pasvolsky, *War Debts and World Prosperity* (Washington, D.C., 1932).

The Secretary of State, the Secretary of the Treasury, and members of both Houses of Congress were to constitute this commission. The original act narrowly confined the Commission as to the terms on which refunding could take place. No new bonds were to be issued the date of maturity of which was later than June 15, 1947, and the rate of interest was not to be fixed at less than 4¼ per cent.

The legislation of 1922 produced no great enthusiasm in the breasts of our European debtors for refunding, and it was indeed fundamentally vulnerable. For as the rate of interest fell in the United States so that the American government could borrow at a rate substantially lower than that of the war years, it seemed unreasonable to exact a high rate from other governments. It was also apparent, as time went on, that if interest payments were to be added to principal, there was little chance of arriving at agreements which stipulated for the complete discharge of the debt by 1947. The Congress was therefore obliged to enact a much more flexible statute in the winter of 1923, which gave far more latitude to the Commission. It was undoubtedly influenced to that end by the negotiations with Great Britain which took place in January of the same year. Secretary Mellon was chairman of the Debt Commission, and it does not appear that the American Secretary of State took the leading part in the discussions. The first of these discussions, carried on for the British by Stanley Baldwin, who came to America for that purpose, ended in a deadlock. The problem was complicated, moreover, by the wholly unauthorized assurances of George Harvey, our ambassador in London, as to the rate of interest that the United States would demand, and as to the possibility of floating a tax-free loan in the United States.[41] Hughes had good reason to lament the good old American custom which confided the charge of the most important embassies to political supporters of the administration. But, in due course, an arrangement was

[41] Pusey, *Charles Evans Hughes*, II, 585.

arrived at, the rate of interest reduced, and the period of payments extended to 62 years, and this agreement was approved by the Congress. The method adopted, that is, legislative approval instead of the negotiation of a treaty, undoubtedly made easier the arrival at an accord, and is an interesting example of a method, which was to be more and more employed in the future, of circumventing the Senate.

Other debt agreements followed. It was the French who were the most obdurate in negotiation, and who were particularly insistent that the war debt problem be linked up to the question of reparations. Against any such proposition the War Debt Commission and the State Department alike took a very strong and unyielding stand. No connection between the two subjects was admitted, though it was obvious, of course, that if Germany defaulted on reparations, the burden of repayment of the debts would fall squarely upon the taxpayers of the debtor nations, and would, to some extent, at least, create a new situation. The first flurry with the French took place in 1925. When the French went home without an agreement, and in a good deal of a huff, the Italian government, nicely calculating the moment for a deal, took up the thread of its own negotiations, and, for reasons that are somewhat obscure, emerged with a settlement that reduced the average rate of interest on the Italian obligations to something like .4 of one per cent. A new effort at dealing with the French was undertaken in 1927, and in a much more favorable climate of opinion. Though the French continued to press for a recognition of the relationship between debts and reparations, an agreement was signed and payments began to be made.

In these negotiations for debt refunding, the principal burden was borne by the Treasury. But it was not so with reparations. Here the State Department played an important role, and this was particularly true under Secretary Hughes.

At Paris in 1919, it was impossible to arrive at any settlement with regard to Germany's payments to the victors. The problem was, at best, a very complicated one, and it was rendered more complex by the strong public feeling in both France and Great Britain. The exaggerated hopes of the mass of people had been encouraged by the politicians, and economic realism flew out the window. Accordingly, what was done was virtually to adjourn the settlement of the matter, to entrust the determination of Germany's indebtedness to a Reparations Commission set up by the treaty, which should by May 1, 1921, following certain principles laid down in treaty, determine the facts of the situation. In the meantime Germany was compelled to make certain types of payment, which we do not need to examine in detail.

Originally, it was expected that the United States would be one of the five nations represented on the Commission, and that the American member would be chairman. But the treaty of Versailles failed in the Senate, and when a separate treaty was negotiated with Germany, the Senate tacked on a reservation by which the representation on any of the numerous bodies functioning under the pact was forbidden, unless the explicit consent of Congress had been given. Mr. Hughes thus found himself in a most embarrassing situation. He could, of course, and did, appoint "unofficial" representatives to the Commission. But these individuals could wield very little authority; they could not vote on any issue. As a consequence, the control of the Commission gravitated into the hands of the French, and the attitude assumed became more and more rigorous. On a problem where the relatively objective attitude of the United States might have been of very great value, it became of almost no value at all.

The hamstringing of the State Department did not prevent Mr. Hughes from taking an active interest in the reparations question. At the outset of his term of office he was approached by the German government and asked to mediate the reparations question, and to fix the sum to be paid by Germany to the Allies.[42] This hot potato the Secretary naturally laid down hastily

[42] *Foreign Relations,* 1921, II, 41.

enough, but he urged that the German government itself formulate proposals that would form a proper basis for discussion. This suggestion was promptly accepted, and an offer made to pay a sum of 50,000,000,000 gold marks, present value, which would have amounted to something like four times this sum in annuities. The very afternoon it was received, the German proposition was submitted to the British and French ambassadors, and in the conversation that ensued Mr. Hughes raised the question whether a point had not been reached where it was better to take the proposal as a basis for further negotiations.[43] But the various European governments concerned remained obdurate. And on May 2 the word went forth to Berlin that the United States "finds itself unable to reach the conclusion that the proposals afford a basis for discussion acceptable to the Allied Governments." [44] The first American effort at a solution of the reparations question had met with failure.

As is well known, the reparations question became more and more aggravated in 1922, and the French government in particular manifested a more and more rigid point of view. The situation was shaping up towards sanctions and military pressure on Germany in the fall of the year. Very obviously, this development the Secretary profoundly deplored. Indeed, in December of 1922, he held a long conversation with Jusserand in which, in none too gentle a tone, he pointed out the difficulties to which further coercive measures by France would surely lead.[45] Moreover, there was germinating in his mind as early as September a proposal that the reparations question be taken out of the field of emotional debate, and submitted to the examination of financial experts, and this idea, too, he presented to Jusserand. On the other hand, he rejected as impracticable a proposal that came from Ambassador Houghton in Berlin, and which looked towards easing the general international tension by canceling the

[43] *Foreign Relations*, 1921, II, 48.   [44] *Foreign Relations*, 1921, II, 54.
[45] *Foreign Relations*, 1922, II, 187ff.

war debts in exchange for measures of disarmament, and a pledge on the part of the great nations of Europe not to go to war without a public referendum.[46] At the end of December, in a step only less remarkable than the dramatic proposal for arms reduction at the Washington Conference in November 1921, he laid bare to the public his views on the reparations question, in a speech before the American Historical Association at New Haven. The speech, it is true, indicated no concessions on the part of the United States. But it contained a key idea, which the Secretary stated as follows, "Why should they (the Allies) not invite men of the highest authority in finance in their respective countries—men of such prestige, honor and experience that their agreement upon the amount to be paid (by Germany), and upon a financial plan for working out the payments, would be accepted throughout the world as the most authoritative expression obtainable. I have no doubt that distinguished Americans would be willing to serve on such a commission." [47]

At the time that it was pronounced, the New Haven speech produced no effect whatever. On January 2, Britain dissenting, the Reparations Commission declared Germany to be in default, and authorized sanctions against her. Not many days later the French moved into the Ruhr, and there began one of the most disastrous political moves of the postwar decade.

During the summer and early fall of 1923 the situation in the Reich deteriorated in sensational fashion. There was, in Hughes' opinion, nothing that the United States could do that would not make the situation worse; any suggestion in favor of Germany would, he felt, irritate the French and weaken the force of the suggestion that he had made at New Haven. Only experience could alter the situation and provide a means of settlement. And experience did precisely that. Slowly the French, in the face of British and American criticism and German passive resistance,

[46] *Foreign Relations*, 1922, II, 181.
[47] *Foreign Relations*, 1922, II, 199–202.

yielded ground. They haggled over terms of reference to be laid down for the committees of experts and sought to limit the conclusions of the inquiry in time. But Hughes stood his ground, and at last he had his way. On November 23, 1923, the Reparations Commission approved of an inquiry of the type the Secretary had suggested, and two committees of experts were appointed to consider means of balancing the budget and stabilizing the currency and to investigate the amount of German capital that had been exported abroad. Since the Commission itself appointed the members of the committees, the limitation that the Senate had appended to the treaty of peace with Germany with regard to official representation on international bodies was of no effect, and that body was neatly outflanked.

The deliberations of these committees, appointed in November 1923, resulted, of course, in the Dawes plan. It is not possible to analyze that plan here. But it is important to note the part which Hughes played in seeing that its recommendations were carried into effect. Ostensibly going to Europe as President of the American Bar Association (a camouflage that seems a bit ineffective), he visited the various capitals of Europe and lent his influence to persuading the governments concerned to accept the program that General Dawes and his associates had laid down. He appears to have had his greatest difficulties in France, where Premier Herriot, himself not unfavorable to the plan, was mortally afraid of the hostile influence of Raymond Poincaré. But he saw both Herriot and Poincaré and made it clear that rejection of the scheme would have a very unfortunate effect.[48] Whether his role was decisive it is not possible to say. But, at any rate, the Dawes plan was put into effect.

Of course the new arrangements did not last long. They had to be revised in 1929 when the same technique of committees of experts was again employed. And then came the depression of 1929, forcing still further readjustments.

[48] Pusey, *Charles Evans Hughes*, II, 591–592.

These readjustments we must for a moment examine if only for the light they throw on the character of American foreign policy in general. As the depression deepened, it became increasingly clear that the whole structure of international indebtedness erected in the postwar years rested on a flimsy foundation. The crisis came in 1931, with the collapse of the Austrian bank, the Credit-Anstalt, and a serious deterioration in the economic situation of Germany. Though Congress was not in session, and though his only recourse was to telegraph Congressional leaders in both Houses, the President came forward with a proposal for a year's moratorium on reparations and war debts alike. In his recent memoirs Mr. Hoover declares that this proposal was his own.[49] Certainly there have been few examples of more forthright action on the part of the Chief Executive, and no one will deny that the decision took political courage. Even so, it was necessary to attenuate its effects by declaring that no question of cancellation was involved, and by stating (somewhat illogically, it must be confessed) that the question of German reparations was a "strictly European problem."

The President's bold initiative did not alter the fundamentals of the situation. It was accepted by the French only after some diplomatic haggling, and it did not prevent an increasing agitation for the reduction of German reparations. The European conference which met at Lausanne in the summer of 1932 reduced the obligations of the Reich to a minimum, while at the same time drawing up a "gentleman's agreement" which stipulated that these reductions would not go into effect if the United States persisted in maintaining its attitude with regard to the war debts. What followed is no part of our story, except to say that both reparations and war debt payments had broken down entirely by 1934. The essence of the matter is that here was a problem that the diplomats simply could not settle, one in which the prejudices and resistances of the masses were more powerful

[49] *Collier's*, May 10, 1952, p. 72.

than any appeal to intelligence could be. And outside the gesture of the Hoover moratorium, it is to be stated that American statesmanship in the last years of the debt question was never ready to face up to explaining to the American people the cold realities of the situation.

There is a peripheral aspect of this question of war debts and reparations that deserves a word of attention. The tariff attitude of the United States in the 1920's and early 1930's was in glaring contrast with its position on the refunding of the war obligations. It is an extraordinary commentary on the architects of American policy that they seem to have been so oblivious of the fact that if Europe were to pay up, it would be necessary to tear down, or at least to lower, customs barriers. Yet Secretary Hughes appears to have been little interested in the tariff act of 1922, and Secretary Stimson, though apparently more clearly aware of the problem, offered no effective resistance to the still higher tariff bill of 1930. The co-ordination of economic and political factors in the evolution of American diplomacy would, in any case, have been difficult; but in this one phase, at any rate, it does not seem even to have been attempted.

It is further to be noted that the edifice erected in the 1920's, the edifice of the naval treaties, of the Kellogg Pact, of the Dawes plan and the Young plan, was virtually completely to collapse in the 1930's, and here again the principal reasons were economic. When economic collapse came, an economic collapse for which the uncontrolled inflation in the United States must be regarded as a heavy contributing cause, the diplomats found their work in large degree undone. In the face of popular pressures based on economic discontent, they were powerless to prevent the deterioration of the general international situation in the 1930's.

The central question raised by this essay is, then, the question as to where, in the last analysis so far as America is concerned, foreign policy is made. And the conclusion is one suggested by the first pages of this text. It is made by the people, to no inconsiderable degree. It functions only within a frame of reference which they prescribe. Today, we seem to have embarked upon courses of action entirely antithetic to those of the 1920's. Then the thought was all of keeping American freedom of action, of avoiding Leagues and treaties which implied commitments. Today we think in terms of massing collective strength against a new menace, of alliances, of common action, and warning to aggressors that aggression will meet with punishment. Such policies are today dictated by the public mood, or are at least consistent with it. But the statesmen of the 1920's labored in a different climate of opinion, and were circumscribed by the prejudices which were typical of that climate. In the long run, they failed to erect a structure of peace. Will the formulas of the 1950's make success possible where it was not possible three decades ago? That is a question, not for the historian but for the prophets.

II ~

REVISIONISM

5 ~

American Wars
and Critical Historians *

ONE of the most curious and interesting paradoxes in the intellectual outlook of Americans lies in the attitude which they have frequently assumed towards war. Nowhere, perhaps, is the word "peace" more sure of a favorable emotional reaction than in the United States. A Presidential candidate may well profit from its use, as Woodrow Wilson did in 1916, when the politicians of his party invented the slogan "He kept us out of war," and as Roosevelt and Willkie did in 1940 when, though both favored assistance to Great Britain, both again and again emphasized their commitment to peace. Americans have fought, and fought on the whole not conspicuously less often than other great peoples in the nineteenth and twentieth centuries; the bloodiest war anywhere between 1815 and 1914 was their own civil conflict; and in the great wars of the twentieth century they have been swept into the whirlpool. But never have they as a people glorified war in principle; hardly any but a few professional militarists have taken this attitude, and those who have done so have commanded no widespread support. On the con-

* Reprinted by permission from *The Yale Review,* Summer, 1951.

trary, it is characteristic of Americans to think of past wars in rather objective terms, and even to display a somewhat guilty conscience in regard to them. This tendency deserves to be studied, and its effects observed.

Nowhere has this sense of guilt about American wars manifested itself more explicitly or more tangibly than in the national historiography. Repeatedly, historians have reviewed the record of one after another of America's wars, and have been so prone to assign war-responsibility to their own government that the term "revisionists" has become a standard designation for the writers who devote themselves to refuting the patriotic explanation of our part in wars, recent or remote.

In saying that this applies to all our wars, we should perhaps make an exception of the American Revolution. To suggest that the Revolution was a mistake, that the breach in the unity of the English-speaking peoples ought to have been avoided, that the cause of the dispute was too trivial to justify a resort to arms, has not been characteristic of the writers of history, though now and again an ardent Anglophile may have put forward such views.

But with the War of 1812 we reach a part of our history on which the revisionists have been at work. It is, for example, the thesis of Professor J. W. Pratt that the real purpose of the war was imperialistic, that a coalition of the South and West, with their eyes on Florida and Canada respectively, sought to bring the country into the conflict. It has been pointed out by other writers that the war was simply foolish: a war for neutral rights, it can be argued, is in its essence rather futile. You cannot vindicate such rights by fighting. You can only increase the dangers and perils to which your own commerce is exposed. Further, in this second conflict with Great Britain, the struggle ended without the faintest recognition of any of the principles for which the United States contended.

The argument that the War of 1812 was useless can also be

supported on the ground that the Madison Administration, which was entirely unprepared for the waging of the struggle, endangered national unity by leading the nation into war, since there was bitter opposition in New England—opposition so extreme that it even led to some talk of secession. The whole business, it has been argued, was a mistake, and it would have been better if the nation had never taken up arms.

Such, at least, is one thesis with regard to 1812. This is not to say, be it understood, that this thesis is a correct one; it is merely to say that these are samples of the highly critical views of a past war that seem to crop up in the United States.

Let us look next at the war with Mexico. Here the critical view has again and again been put forward, and is, of course, contemporary with the conflict itself. The action of President Polk, we have more than once been told, was highly provocative; he instructed General Taylor in the winter of 1846 to occupy territory which was in dispute between Mexico and the United States; Taylor himself behaved badly by blockading the Mexicans across the Rio Grande at Matamoras; and the Mexicans were thus goaded into armed action. Polk's real objective was conquest, and the war ended in our acquisition of California and the Southwest. It was a true war of aggression, and should be so regarded.

A similar interpretation has grown up with regard to the Spanish-American War of 1898—an interpretation perpetuated in that brilliant book by Walter Millis, "The Martial Spirit." According to this view, the Spanish government had virtually conceded the essential American demands in April of 1898; it had agreed to suspend the policy of concentration camps in Cuba, which had shocked American opinion; and it had indicated its willingness to grant an armistice to the Cuban insurgents. But President McKinley, who had in Theodore Roosevelt's picturesque phrase, "no more backbone than a chocolate éclair," gave slight emphasis to these concessions in his message to Congress, and in the prevailing temper of American public opinion, that body lost little time in declaring war. Thus, through the weakness of an American President (so runs the argument or the implication) the country was launched into an unnecessary conflict.

The same tendency of historians to regard a resort to arms as futile was manifest on a still larger scale after World War I. At the distance of about a decade from the end of the struggle, American revisionists made themselves heard with a new theory of the events of 1914–17. Matter-of-fact citizens had for the most part assumed that Germany's challenge to the United States on the high seas had been the cause of America's taking up arms. But the case was restated in a wholly different way. The policy of the United States was shaped (so it was contended) by considerations of a very different kind. British propaganda directed American opinion; President Wilson never honestly carried out a policy of neutrality. Moreover, the Administration was influenced by a desire to extend American trade. The munitions traffic produced profits that gave the United States a stake in the cause of the Allies; so, too, did Allied loans. Thus, economic forces afford the true explanation for the policy pursued—a policy confused and tortuous, and never candidly set forth.

World War II is only a few years behind us, but already the revisionist thesis has again been put forward, and from the pen of one of the most eminent, most respected, and most respectable of American scholars. The late Charles A. Beard has told us, in his book published a few years ago, precisely how it happened. President Roosevelt, it appears, committed himself to a policy of peace in the electoral campaign of 1940, but in 1941 he so shaped events that war, both with Germany and with Japan, became virtually inevitable. In regard to the war in Europe, he secured from Congress the so-called Lend-Lease Enactment, under the pretense that this measure of assistance to Great Britain would prevent our entry into war; he then extended aid to include first patrols and then convoys at sea; he instructed the American Navy to take action which would almost inevitably provoke the Germans to war; he misrepresented as an act of defense the famous episode of the destroyer *Greer*, which at the time it was attacked by a German submarine was following that submarine and reporting its position to British vessels and air patrols; he sought a showdown at the very time that he was professing to avoid it, and the showdown came.

In his relations with Japan, the Beard argument continues, President Roosevelt was no less ingenious; he extended aid to the Chinese government with which the Tokyo regime was at war; he applied economic pressure against that regime; he put aside the offer of a personal conference with Prince Konoye, the Japanese Minister in the summer and early autumn of 1941; he declined to accept proposals for a *modus vivendi* in November of 1941; by his action he encouraged the Japanese to make the "sneak attack" on Pearl Harbor, which indeed was more or less foreseen. Moreover, the war into which he led the United States is now revealed as a futility; for while it destroyed the power of Hitler and of militarist Japan, it left a new and more dangerous totalitarian state in a position of supreme power. It brought, not peace, but a situation more dangerous and troubled than ever. And, in attempting to challenge the Soviet Union, the United States is embarking upon a policy so sweeping and so perilous as to offer a new illustration of the dangers of ambitious policies such as those we have recently pursued.

If we were to put together the generalizations that have been stated in the preceding paragraphs, we would come to the conclusion that the foreign policy of the United States has been almost uniformly inept; that every war in which this country has been engaged was really quite unnecessary or immoral or both; and that it behooves us in the future to pursue policies very different from those pursued in the past. What are we to think of these revisionist theories? To what degree do they rest upon a sound basis and furnish a foundation for action?

In the first place, it is to be said that no one of these explanations of America's wars can be wholly accepted by the scientific scholar. Take, for example, the War of 1812. It may be true that one of the motives of that conflict was American imperialism. Not all students of the period assign to this motive the important place that was given it by Professor Pratt, but let us grant for the moment its significance. It still remains true that other factors can be brought into the account; it seems unreasonable to suppose that British violation of American rights on the high seas is to be set completely aside as one of the elements in bringing about American action. The measurement of a nation's opinion, the exact determination of the why of great events, is in all cases a very difficult matter; but it is more rational and more scientific to assume that a variety of forces was operating than to lay exclusive emphasis on some single factor.

It is easy, too, to declare that the War of 1812 was a futility; but Albert Gallatin, one of the wisest statesmen of his time, did not so regard it. "The war," he wrote, "has been productive of evil and good, but I think the good preponderates. . . . The war has renewed and reinstated the national feelings and character which the Revolution had given, and which were daily lessened. The people have now more general objects of attachment. . . . They are more Americans; they feel and act more as a nation; and I hope that the permanency of the Union is thereby better secured." Look at the matter from another point of view. It is true that the United States did not secure from Great Britain any recognition of its point of view with regard to impressments or its neutral rights at sea; but it is not true that the nation did not profit from the war. The connection of the Indian tribes of the Old Northwest with Britain was definitely broken; and whether it be a direct effect of the war or not, it can be said with some confidence that the British Foreign Office treated the United States with far more consideration after the Peace of Ghent than before.

It is difficult to defend wholeheartedly the attitude of President Polk in connection with the Mexican war; but any judgment of that period that fails to emphasize the fact that Polk sought, apparently in good faith, a peaceful settlement with Mexico, and that this settlement was rejected by the Mexicans themselves, does not rest upon sound grounds. Polk was *ready* to come to terms without acquiring California or New Mexico; greater wisdom on the part of those in authority in Mexico City would probably have prevented war. And it might well be asked of those who have judged the diplomacy of the rigid Tennessean most harshly if they would wish to undo what he actually did.

The war with Spain illustrates another aspect of the problem of moral judgment on America's wars. It would have been more candid and more courageous of President McKinley if he had underlined the important nature of the concessions made by Spain when he reported to Congress; but to assume that if he had done so, war would have been prevented, is a purely gratuitous assumption. For how do we know that the Cuban insurgents would have accepted the armistice that Spain was ready to offer; what interests would they have had in so doing? After all, they wanted not autonomy but independence; and their best chance of independence lay precisely in American intervention. And how can we be sure that a Congress that had already lashed itself into a passion against Spain, and a nation that had been for more than a year open to the incitements of a yellow press, would have paid much heed to the President's pronouncement even if it had been more emphatically made?

It is, of course, possible to argue, as Professor S. F. Bemis does, that the imperialist courses into which the United States was launched as a result of the war with Spain were a mistake;

but here again one may well avoid too sharp a judgment. For it is possible to point out the consequences of the decisions taken in 1898, while it is not possible to set up anything more than a hypothesis as to what would have happened if the decisions then made had been different. One has a right, of course, to deplore the entry of the United States into the affairs of the Far East— then or now; but to argue that without the war with Spain that entry would never have occurred is to indulge in pure assumption.

The revisionist judgment of World War I seems to this writer particularly and grossly unscientific—save in one respect. It ought today to be candidly admitted that the Administration of Woodrow Wilson adopted a double standard in the enforcement of the traditional principles of neutrality—that it was rigorous in dealing with Germany and generously lax in dealing with Great Britain—but it ought also to be admitted by every student that this partiality was in large measure a reflection of the drift of American opinion itself. Beyond this, in my judgment, it is impossible to go. Who can prove that British propaganda produced this partiality? Who can measure the effect of that propaganda as compared with the effect of some other elements in the situation, of the influence, for example, of the fact that it was Germany and Austria that first declared war, of the influence of the German violation of Belgian neutrality, of the influence of the general assumption that Britain and France were democratic nations, and that the Central Powers were certainly far less so?

And, to go further, by what process of reasoning can it be established that the Administration of Woodrow Wilson, with its far from cordial attitude towards American business interests, was directly affected by the desire to promote those interests? How, for that matter, can it be demonstrated that the economic well-being of the United States was better promoted by entrance into the conflict than it would have been by the continuation of a policy of neutrality? How can it be shown that if the Germans had not afforded a provocation to war with their resumption of the submarine warfare in the winter of 1917, it would have been possible for the American government to abandon its neutrality, especially in view of the fact that as late as January 22, 1917, the President was still talking of a peace without victory?

There is something to be said for our participation in World War I not only from the viewpoint of causes, but also from the viewpoint of results. Discount the menace presented by Imperial Germany, if you will. Ignore the argument that without the intervention of the United States the German government would have been able to bring Britain to her knees, that German naval power would have been supreme, and that the page of German ambition, written so bold and large by Adolf Hitler, would have been inscribed in the decade of the 'twenties, instead of in the 'thirties. Even when all this is left out of the reckoning, there remain some favorable results of World War I. The world of 1919, the world of Allied victory, was a relatively secure world, and one which was still to enjoy a decade of great prosperity and material advance; the aspirations of many national groups were satisfied to a remarkable degree; and a temporary reconciliation of the two great secular enemies, France and Germany, was brought to pass in the Treaties of Locarno. As a matter of fact, the war of 1917–18 opened up the fairest opportunities for a Europe free from the menace of a predatory ambition, and it is certainly not wholly irrational to maintain, as did Mr. Lloyd George in his memoirs, that, had the statesmen of the postwar period been equal to their opportunities, the Treaty of Versailles might have ushered in a long period of peace. Of course, this, too, is assumption; but it is assumption sufficiently reasonable to make one think twice about the contrary hypothesis that our entry into World War I was simply a gigantic mistake.

Again we come to World War II. We must examine it in some detail. Is it true that President Roosevelt "lied us into war"? Let us look at the record. The public opinion polls, imperfect as they are as a guide, suggest no such conclusion. They show that the American people, indifferent at first to the struggle in Europe, or perhaps foolishly optimistic as to the prospects of victory for the democratic nations, became genuinely aroused after the Fall of France, and that a great body of public sentiment was increasingly in favor of aid to the democracies, even at the risk of war. For example, as early as June, 1940, when people were polled on the question as to whether the President was right in making it possible for Great Britain and France to buy airplanes of models that were being used by our army and navy, the affirmative view was taken by 80 per cent of those questioned. This percentage was only slightly affected by partisan affiliation, 85 per cent of the Democrats being so recorded, and 76 per cent of the Republicans. When the destroyer-bases transaction was under discussion in August, it was approved by 60 per cent of those polled, and disapproved by only 37 per cent, and this vote, it should be emphasized, was taken before the deal was consummated, and at a time, therefore, when there was no incentive to support it as a national commitment irrevocably taken. By November of 1940, after the national election, the question was put, "If it appears that England will be defeated by Germany and Italy unless the United States supplies her with more food and materials, would you be in favor of giving more help to England?" and 90 per cent of those polled responded in the affirmative.

The Lend-Lease Bill came before Congress in the winter of 1941. In four successive samplings of public opinion, the percentage in favor of the measure was always twice as great as those opposed, with still more giving a qualified approval. Further, the implementation of the bill by authorizing convoys (a measure not taken until July) was already approved by 55 per cent in June, with only 38 per cent in the negative. When, indeed, the issue was defined in terms of a possible British defeat, the percentage in favor of the action increased to 71 per cent with only 21 per cent opposed. Similarly, in the fall, the arming of American merchant ships was approved by 72 per cent against 21 per cent, and the shooting of German warships on sight by 62 per cent to 28 per cent.

Many of the most important steps in the Roosevelt policy towards Germany were made the basis of legislative action. The adoption of national conscription in time of peace (surely some index of the concern of the American people with the menace of National Socialism) was adopted in the House of Representatives by a vote of 232 to 124, and in the Senate by a vote of 47 to 25 (almost two to one). Lend-Lease, after a prolonged debate that gave ample time for the expression of the public judgment, was passed by a vote of 317 to 71 in the House, and 60 to 31 in the Upper Chamber. The arming of American merchant ships in the fall was approved by a vote of 259 to 138 in the House, and, with an amendment ending the exclusion of American ships from the war zones, in the Senate by 50 to 37. Though the amended measure had a close call in the House, 212 to 194, it was nonetheless enacted. Such figures make it absurd to assume that the President was acting contrary to American public opinion, or that his own sounding of the alarm (a fact to be conceded) struck no responsive chord in the breasts of his compatriots. An additional point to be noted is that, on almost every vote, the defections in the ranks of the Democrats were fewer than those in the ranks of the Republicans; in other words, that where party allegiance did not operate, the drift was towards and not away from the Chief Executive.

There are other facts that deserve to be considered in any assessment of public opinion. The Republican nominating convention was one of those rare conventions in which the practiced players of the political game were persuaded to nominate

a candidate whose strength amongst the professionals was by
no means great. The foremost contenders in the months preceding the convention were Senator Taft, who took the isolationist
viewpoint with his usual courage, and Thomas E. Dewey, who
was at that time busily carrying water on both shoulders. Yet
the nominee was Wendell Willkie. Willkie stood for a policy
not very different from that of the President himself, and had as
early as April declared for aid to the Allies. The formation of
the Committee to Defend America by Aiding the Allies took
place in May of 1940, and the roster of its membership discloses
a strong non-partisan support for a policy of intervention. It
is certainly not very scientific to ignore these facts in an assessment of the policy of the Administration; honest students of the
period, especially those who believe that the foreign policy of a
democracy must take its shape from the opinion of the people,
cannot fail to accord them a very vital significance.

It is not possible to speak so categorically with regard to our
relations with Japan. There were, for example, no important
votes in Congress to serve as the basis for a judgment. Yet here,
too, there can easily be established a connection between the
broad lines of the Roosevelt policy and the sentiments of the
people. From as early as June, 1939, for example, 72 per cent
of those questioned as to their sympathies in the war between
Japan and China declared their sympathies were with China.
When the Vandenberg Resolution was brought forward in the
summer of 1939, calling for the denunciation of our trade treaty
with Japan, 82 per cent of those polled believed that we should
refuse to sell her any more war materials. When President
Roosevelt forbade the shipment of scrap iron to Japan, 96 per
cent of those questioned approved his action. By February of
1941, 60 per cent thought the interests of the United States
would be threatened by the seizure of Singapore and the Dutch
East Indies, though only 39 per cent were as yet ready to risk
war. And by November of 1941, 64 per cent thought the United

States should take steps to prevent Japan from becoming more powerful, even if this meant risking war with Japan.

These facts may not be decisive, but they certainly indicate that a powerful body of opinion was behind Roosevelt's actions. Furthermore, unless one is disposed to maintain that we had no interests worthy of protection in the Orient, the Philippines included, there was ample reason to look askance on Japanese policy, and on the multiplied aggressions of the Tokyo government. Consider the record: the Amau statement of 1934, and the doctrine of a Greater East Asia, the denunciation of the naval treaties, the fortification of the Pacific Islands, the war with China, the acquisition of Jehol, the occupation of northern Indo-China, the tri-partite alliance with the Axis, and the occupation of southern Indo-China.

In the revisionist gospel, these acts are of no significance. Attention is fixed on the American riposte to them, on loans to China, on the denunciation of the commercial treaty of 1911, on the severance of trade relations. By a curiously inverted logic, these acts are made provocative, and the acts of Japan appear as the expression of a legitimate national interest. Just how reasonable is such an approach? Just how reasonable is it to suppose that, under any administration, the country would have observed complacently the advance of Japan, and its alliance with German imperialism?

The revisionists also turn to the results of the war, and declare that we are now confronted by a danger greater than that which we attempted to destroy. They blandly assume that in Europe the two totalitarian giants would have bled each other white, and that in Asia we would have been able to live with an imperialist Japan. But how can they prove any such hypothesis? How do they know that Hitler would have been defeated? How do they know that Japan, inflamed by victory, would have kept her hands off the Philippines? To assert such things is to assume a degree of omniscience that is denied to mortal man. It is to brush aside as of no importance the assumptions (and they were assumptions, it is to be frankly admitted) which actually governed conduct, and received wide currency, in 1941. In international affairs, it can be argued, one meets one danger at a time, and the fact that a new peril presents itself is not proof, or anything like proof, of the unreality of the peril that preceded.

What, then, are we to think of revisionism? In the first place, it may be stated categorically that we will always have it with us. The evidence is conclusive that it lies deep in the temperament of the American people, with their innate dislike of violence, their instinct for re-examination of their own motives, the partisan impulses that prompt to criticism, the disillusionments that come with victory. The revisionists, moreover, will always have a great advantage with the unsophisticated and the naïve. For every war leaves many discontents behind, and it is always comfortable to trace these discontents to the war itself. It is easy to accept an hypothesis, if one wants to accept it; and revisionism is, in essence, merely the presentation of hypotheses, hypotheses that are bound to appear attractive to at least some segment of public opinion.

It is also fairly clear that, within narrow limits, revisionism may make for better history. Its challenge to the conventional view is not wholly without utility; it protects us against the nationalistic, or the chauvinistic, approach; it stimulates reflection as to the bases of our own policy; it tends to raise the question, the useful question, as to whether our own diplomatic action is unduly rigid and more concerned with theories than with the national interests, clearly understood and soundly and thoughtfully interpreted.

On the other hand, it must always have its dangers. It is sheer intellectual levity to imagine that, in matters so complex as international relations, we can accurately trace the consequences of an alternative course of action which never happened. It may, moreover, be actually harmful. The revisionist theory of the war of 1917–18 had only one obvious result: it encouraged the great militarist states to imagine that they could count on the indifference of the United States to the realization of their nefarious ambitions. A revisionist theory of World War II might well have the same result. It suggests that we can be secure if we abdicate our role as a world power; it suggests that we can and ought to watch the growth of a new totalitarianism without apprehension, without ever reacting emotionally against it, and that such an attitude can be indefinitely prolonged without any snapping of the nerves, without one of those indefinable changes of national mood which lead to the final acceptance of a challenge.

Revisionism rests, too, upon a very doubtful interpretation of human nature. Revisionists are often motivated by a dislike, perhaps even a noble dislike, of a resort to force. But, in fact, no institution is so deeply ingrained in human nature as war, and the attempt to flee from this fact is no solution of an age-old problem. No generation ought to be clearer on this point than our own; for when did great states ever submit to more humiliation, or watch with greater complacency the building up of aggression than did the states of Western Europe in the 'thirties? If this painful period shows anything, it shows that in the face of ruthless ambition, the pacific spirit will in time be undermined, in the very nature of the case; and that a nation which begins with appeasement is likely to end with war. This is, no doubt, an unpleasant truth; but it seems to have a good many facts to support it; and to treat all war as a gigantic mistake is not to advance materially the preservation of peace.

The matter, indeed, can be put in a nutshell. Behind revisionism often lies the spectre of appeasement, the assumption that the will to avoid war is sufficient to prevent war. The problem is more complex. When it is recognized to be such, the chances of avoiding conflict will be enhanced.

Revisionism is very largely wishful thinking after the event, history by unprovable hypothesis. It may sometimes open up new vistas, but it can establish no finalities. And it often fails to reckon with the deep passions that in practice stir men to action.

6 ～

Was Roosevelt Wrong?*

REVISIONISM may be defined as an after-the-event interpretation of American participation in war, with the accent on the
errors and blunders that provoked the struggle and on the folly
of the whole enterprise. If we accept this definition, we shall
certainly agree that there has been plenty of revisionism in the
course of our history. The war of 1812 has sometimes been
judged to have been futile and sometimes described as a war
of intended conquest. The Mexican War has come in for harsh
treatment as a war of unnecessary aggression. James G. Randall,
one of the foremost students of the Civil War period, suggests
that a less passionate view of the sectional problem might have
made that conflict avoidable. Again and again it has been stated
by reputable historians that William McKinley might have
prevented the war of 1898 had he stressed in his message to Congress the very large concessions that had been made by Spain.
The First World War was brilliantly represented by Walter
Millis as the product of a blundering diplomacy and of economic
pressures not entirely creditable. And since 1945 we have had

* Reprinted by permission from *The Virginia Quarterly Review*,
Summer, 1954.

a crop of historians, headed by so eminent a member of his historical generation as Charles A. Beard, attempting to show that the maddest folly of all was our entry into the conflict that ended less than a decade ago. Clearly, revisionism is an American habit; though, in saying this, I do not mean to imply that it is unknown in other lands.

The roots of the revisionist tendency are worth speculating about. Such a point of view, I take it, is particularly apt to find expression in a country where peace is highly treasured and where the glorification of war is relatively uncommon. Just as many Americans easily put away the hates and resentment of war at the end of the struggle and display a tendency towards reconciliation with the vanquished, so they tend to forget the passions that animated them and drove them into the conflict, and to view what at the time seemed reasonable and natural as something that with a little more forbearance or wisdom could have been avoided. And there are other factors that reinforce this point of view. Wars are apt to end in disillusionment. After the glorious hopes of the years 1917 and 1918 came the clash of national selfishnesses at Versailles, and a distraught and threatened world. In 1945 the defeat of Hitler and Japan was soon seen to have left grave problems ahead. In the East, the American defense of China and the hopes of a strong democratic nation in the Orient ended in the victory of the Chinese Reds. And in Europe, though the peril from the ambitions of Hitler was exorcised, the United States found itself face to face with a new totalitarianism, far-ranging in its ambitions like the old. In such a situation it was natural to forget the menace that had been defeated, and to ask whether there might not have been a better solution to the problems that ended with the capitulation ceremonies at Rheims and on the deck of the *Missouri*.

After every large-scale war, moreover, there is a reaction against that strong executive leadership which is almost inevitably associated with periods of crisis in the life of the nation.

This was true in 1920; and it was true after 1945. During the conflict the personality of Mr. Roosevelt loomed large, and almost immune from attack. But under the surface there was hostility, and this was to take the form of criticism of his war policies. Sometimes this criticism came, as in the case of Frederic R. Sanborn in his "Design for War," from one who had a strong animus against the New Deal, and who approached the record of the administration in the field of foreign policy with this animus. Sometimes, on the other hand, as in the case of Charles A. Beard, it came from one who regarded the Roosevelt diplomacy as jeopardizing and perhaps wrecking far-reaching programs of internal reform. In these two cases, and in virtually every other, strong emotions entered into the account. It has been a satisfaction to the revisionists to tear down the President; and there has always been—and it was inevitable that there should be—a reading public to fall in with this point of view, either from personal dislike of Roosevelt or from partisan feeling.

Revisionism, then, has roots in the very nature of the case. But, if we analyze it coolly, what shall we think of it? This is the question I propose to examine in this essay.

It seems to me fair to say at the outset that it is impossible to avoid the conclusion that revisionism is essentially history by hypothesis. It suggests—indeed in some instances it almost claims—that the world would have been a better place, or that at any rate the present position of the United States would have been happier, if this country had not intervened in the Second World War. Such a proposition can be put forward, but it cannot be established like a theorem in geometry. We cannot go back to 1939 or 1941 and re-enact the events of those stirring and tumultuous years. In a sense, we are bound by the past.

None the less, it seems worth while, even though we are in the realm of speculation rather than scientific history, to state the revisionist point of view. First, with regard to Germany, the point of view is advanced that the United States was in no essential danger from Adolf Hitler, that he demonstrated no very great interest in the American continents, that he desired until almost the day of Pearl Harbor to keep out of trouble with the United States, that there is no reliable evidence that he meditated an assault upon the New World. It is possible for the revisionist to go further. The ambitions of Hitler, it would be maintained, would have been checked and contained within limits by the presence of the great totalitarian state to the East. The two colossi would act each as a restraint on the other. It needed not the intervention of the American government to preserve the safety of the New World. As to Asia, the argument runs somewhat differently. Less emphasis is placed on the question of national security and more on a certain interpretation of national interest. The United States, we are told, had only a meager interest in China; its trade and investments there were insignificant, and were likely to remain so. They were distinctly inferior to our trade and investments in Japan. The shift in the balance of the Far East that might come about through a Japanese victory over Great Britain was no real concern of the United States. As to the Philippines, they might have been left alone had we stayed out of the war, or conversely, they were not worth the sacrifice involved in maintaining our connection with them. Such are the assumptions, implied, if not always expressed, in the revisionist view of the problem of the Orient.

Now some of the assertions in this rationale are unchallengeable. It is true that Hitler desired to avoid a clash with the United States until just before Pearl Harbor. It is true that the economic interests of the United States in China were inferior to our interests in Japan. These are facts, and must be accepted as facts. But there still remain a good many questions about the revisionist assumptions. For example, was there in 1940 and 1941 no danger of the destruction of British naval power, and would that destruction have had no unhappy consequences for the United States? Granted that the documents show great reluctance on the part of the Fuehrer to challenge the United States, would this reluctance have outlasted the fall of Great Britain? Granted that the Kremlin might have exercised a restraining influence on the Germans, is it certain that the two powers might not have come to an understanding as they did in 1939, and had at other periods in the past? Just how comfortable a world would it have been if the psychopathic leader of Germany had emerged from the Second World War astride a large part of the Continent, with the resources of German science at his command? There are questions, too, that can be asked about the Orient. Did the United States have no responsibility for the Philippines, and would the islands have been safe for long if the Japanese had dominated the Far East? Could the United States divest itself of all concern for China, abandoning a policy of nearly forty years duration and a deep-seated American tradition? Was the destruction of British power in this part of the world a matter of no concern to this country? Could the defeat of Britain in the East be separated from the fate of Britain in the world at large? These are extremely large questions, and it is a bold man who will brush them aside as inconsequential or trivial, or who will reply to them with complete dogmatism. Indeed, it is because they raise so many problems cutting to the root of our feelings, as well as our opinions, that they arouse so much controversy. Nor is there any likelihood that we can ever arrive at a complete consensus with regard to them.

We must, I think, seek a somewhat narrower frame of reference if we are to answer the revisionists with facts, and not with speculations. One of the ways to answer them, and one particularly worth pursuing with regard to the war in Europe, is to analyze the policy of the Roosevelt administration in its relation to public sentiment.

Foreign policy, in the last analysis, depends, not upon some logical formula, but upon the opinion of the nation. No account of American diplomacy in 1940 and 1941 can pretend to authority which does not take into account the tides of sentiment which must always influence, and perhaps control, the course of government. It is not to be maintained that a President has no freedom of action whatsoever; he can, I think, accelerate or retard a popular trend. But he does not act independently of it; the whole history of American diplomacy attests the close relationship between the point of view of the masses and executive action. A peacefully-minded President like Mc-Kinley was driven to war with Spain; a President who set great store by increasing the physical power of the nation, like Theodore Roosevelt, was limited and confined in his action; and Franklin Roosevelt himself, when, in the quarantine speech of October, 1937, he sought to rouse the American people against aggression, was compelled to admit failure, and to trim his sails to the popular breeze. These things are of the essence; to fail to observe them is to fail to interpret the past in the true historical spirit.

Let us apply these conceptions to the period 1939 to 1941. It will hardly be denied that from the very beginning of the war public sentiment was definitely against Germany. Indeed, even before the invasion of Poland, the public opinion polls show a strong partiality for the democratic nations. As early as January, 1939, when asked the question whether we should do everything possible to help England and France in case of war, 69 per cent of the persons polled answered in the affirmative, and the same question in October produced a percentage of 62 per cent on the same side. No doubt this sentiment did not extend to the point of actual participation in the war, but it furnished a firm foundation for the action of the President in calling Congress in special session, and in asking of it the repeal of the arms embargo on shipments of war in the interest of the Allies. The measure to this effect was introduced in the Congress towards the end of September; and it was thoroughly debated. There are several things to be said in connection with its passage. The first is that after its introduction there was a consistent majority of around 60 per cent in the polls in favor of passage. The second is that, though there was a strong partisan flavor to the debate, the defections when they came were more numerous on the Republican than on the Democratic side. It is true that, without the leadership of the President, the repeal could not have been enacted. But also it did not fly in the face of public sentiment (so far as that can be measured), but on the contrary reflected it.

With the fall of France there took place a deep and significant development in public opinion. This change the revisionists usually do not mention. They prefer to treat of American policy as if it were formed in a vacuum without regard to the moving forces that have so much to do with the final decisions. Yet the evidences are ample that in June of 1940 the American people were deeply moved. Take, for example, the action of the Republican nominating convention. There were several outstanding professional politicians in the running in 1940, Senator Taft, Senator Vandenberg, Thomas E. Dewey. Each one of these men represented a policy of caution so far as Europe was concerned. Yet what did the convention do? It turned to a relatively unknown figure, to a novice in politics who had, however, more than once declared himself as advocating extensive assistance to the democracies. The choice of Wendell Willkie as the Republican candidate for the Presidency is a fact the importance of which cannot be denied. It is worth while calling attention to other like phenomena. One of these is the overwhelming majorities by which the Congress appropriated largely increased sums for the armed forces, not only for the navy but for the army and the air force as well. Perhaps the American people, or the representatives of the American people, ought not to have been perturbed at what was happening in Europe. But the fact is that they were perturbed. They were perturbed in a big way. And the votes in the legislative halls demonstrate that fact.

Or take another example. The movement for a conscription law in time of peace developed rapidly after June of 1940. It developed with very little assistance from the White House. It cut across party lines. And it resulted in a legislative enactment which reflected the excitement of the public mind. How can we interpret the measure otherwise? Was there not a substantial body of opinion in the United States that feared a German victory?

Another important factor to be noted is the formation in June of 1940 of the Committee to Defend America by Aiding the Allies. It is highly significant that this movement arose at all. It is doubly significant that it found a leader in a Kansan Republican such as William Allen White. It is trebly significant that, once initiated, it spread like wild-fire, and that by September there were more than 650 chapters in the United States. And it is also to be noted that in New York there soon came into being a more advanced group, the so-called Century Group, which advocated war if necessary to check the aggressions of Germany.

And it is further to be observed that out of the Committee to Defend America came an agitation for what was eventually to be the bases-destroyer deal of September 2, 1940. This deal, by the way, was approved by 62 per cent of the persons polled on August 17, 1940, two weeks before it was actually consummated.

Let us go further. The next important step forward in American policy was the lend-lease enactment of the winter of 1941. This measure, it would appear from the polls, was based on a very distinct evolution of public sentiment. In July of 1940 59 per cent of the persons polled preferred to keep out rather than to help England at the risk of war, and 36 per cent took the contrary view. In October the percentages were exactly reversed: they were 36 to 59. By January of 1941 68 per cent of those interviewed thought it more important to assist Great Britain than to keep out of war. And the lend-lease enactment, when presented to the Congress, passed the Lower House by the impressive vote of 317 to 71 and the Senate by 60 to 31. As in the legislation of 1939, though the vote again had a partisan flavor, there were more defections from the Republicans in favor of the measure than of Democrats against it. And there is something more to be added to the account in this instance. By the winter of 1941 the America Firsters had appeared upon the scene. A counter-propaganda was now being organized against the administration. Yet this new group, despite its vigorous efforts, failed signally to rally majority opinion. And Senator Taft, who represented the most thoughtful opposition to the administration, himself proposed a measure of assistance to Great Britain.

I shall treat a little later of the various measures requiring no legislative sanction which the President took in the course of the year 1941. But it is important to observe that throughout the period there was a strong public sentiment that believed that it was more important to defeat Germany than to keep out of war. This view was held, according to the polls, by 62 per cent of those interrogated in May of 1941 and by 68 per cent in December of 1941. As early as April, 1941, 68 per cent of the pollees believed it important to enter the war if British defeat was certain.

We should next examine the legislation of the fall of 1941. By this time the Congress was ready to authorize the arming of American merchant ships, and this by a heavy vote. The measure was passed by 259 to 138 in the House and the Senate amended it and passed it by 50 to 37. Congress was ready, more reluctantly, to repeal those provisions of the neutrality acts which excluded American vessels from the so-called war zones. It was moving in the direction of fuller and fuller engagement against Hitler. We shall never know, of course, what the next step would have been had not that step been taken by Germany. It was the dictator of the Reich who declared war on the United States, not the American national legislature that declared war on the Fuehrer and his minions. But in the period between 1939 and 1941 it seems safe to say that the foreign policy of the Roosevelt administration was in accord with the majority public opinion of the nation. It seems incontestable that the President was acting on assumptions which majority opinion accepted, and pursuing a course of action which majority opinion approved.

This circumstance is naturally either ignored or obscured in the revisionist literature. And what makes it easier to forget is the undeniable fact that Franklin Roosevelt was unhappily sometimes given to equivocation and shifty conversation. Very early, it is true, as early as the quarantine speech of October, 1937, he sounded the alarm against the totalitarians. Very often he stated his conviction that their continued progress presented a threat to the United States. On occasion he took his courage in his hands as, when at Charlottesville in June of 1940, in an election year, he came out frankly in favor of aid to the democracies, or in the declaration of unlimited emergency in the address of May 27, 1941. There is little doubt that he deemed the defeat of Hitler more important than the avoidance of war (as did many other Americans, as we have seen). Yet he was often less than frank in his approach, and the emphasis he laid on his devotion to peace was often excessive. He shocked even his ardent admirer, Robert Sherwood, in the election of 1940. His presentation of the case for lend-lease does not at all times suggest candor; indeed, the very phrase seems a bit of cajolery. With regard to the question of convoy, in the spring of 1941, he was clever and, though verbally correct, hardly wholly open in his approach to the problem. In the famous episode of the *Greer* (an attack by a German submarine on a vessel which was reporting its position to a British destroyer), he misrepresented the facts, or spoke without full knowledge of them. All this it is only right to admit. Yet we must not exaggerate the importance of these considerations. The country knew where it was going with regard to Germany. It accepted lend-lease as desirable. Of the patrolling of the ocean lanes which followed, the President spoke candidly in the speech of May 27, 1941. There was nothing clandestine about the occupation of Greenland or Iceland. The pattern in the fall of 1941 would most probably not have been much altered if Roosevelt had been more scrupulous with regard to the *Greer*. In the last analysis we come back to the essential fact that Roosevelt represented and expressed in action the mood of the country with regard to Germany.

The question is, I believe, more difficult when we come to examine American policy towards Japan. We can say with some assurance that the denunciation of the treaty of commerce of 1911, undertaken by the administration in July of 1939 as an indication of American displeasure with Japanese policy, was distinctly well received. Indeed, if the State Department had not acted, the legislature might have. We can also say that in August of 1939 there was an overwhelming feeling against sending war materials to Nippon. When in September of 1940, an embargo on the export of scrap iron was imposed, 59 per cent of the persons polled on this issue approved the step that had been taken. And in 1941 the number of persons who believed that some check should be put on Japan even at the risk of war rose from 51 per cent to 70 per cent between July and September, and stood at 69 per cent at the time of Pearl Harbor.

But we have fewer indications of the direction of public sentiment in the action of Congress, and no actual votes on which to base our estimate of how the representatives of the American people felt with regard to the important problem of our course of action in the Orient. We must, I think, speak less confidently on this question of public opinion than in the case of Germany. We must turn rather to an analysis of the policy of the administration, and to revisionist criticism of that policy.

First of all, let us look at some of the uncontroverted facts. We know that there were militarist elements in Japan. We know that as early as 1934 Japan proclaimed its doctrine of a Greater East Asia in the famous Amau statement. We know that in the same year it upset the naval arrangements made at Washington and London. We know that it set up a special régime in North China in 1935. We know that it became involved in a war with China in 1937. This, of course, was only prelude. The outbreak of the European conflict in Europe, and the collapse of France, offered to the sponsors of further aggressive action a great opportunity. The occupation of Northern Indo-China followed. In the summer of 1940, the impetuous and aggressive Matsuoka came to the Foreign Office. On September 27, 1940, there was signed a tripartite pact with Japan, which bound Nippon to come to the assistance of the Axis powers if they were attacked by a power then at peace with them. In other words, the Tokyo government sought to confine and limit American policy. In April of 1941 came a neutrality pact with Russia which freed the hands of the Japanese militarists for a policy of advance towards the South. In July came the occupation of the rest of Indo-China. The occupation of *northern* Indo-China made some sense from the point of view of blocking the supply route to the Chinese Nationalists. The occupation of *southern* Indo-China made no sense, except as the prelude to further acts of aggression. And in due course the aggression came.

Admittedly, this is only one side of the story. The question to be examined is, did these acts take place partly as a result of American provocation? Was it possible for a wiser and more prudent diplomacy to have avoided the rift that occurred in December, 1941? Revisionist criticism of our Oriental policy has been expressed in a variety of ways. In its most extreme form, it suggests that the President and his advisers actually plotted war with Japan. In its less extreme form, it directs its shafts at a variety of actions, of which I shall examine the most important. They are the conversations with the British as to the defense of the Far East, the commitments made to China, the severance of commercial relations, the failure to accept the proposals of Prince Konoye for direct conversations with the President, and the breakdown of the *modus vivendi* proposal of November, 1941. I shall examine each of these briefly, but let us first turn to the accusation that American policy was directed towards producing and not avoiding an armed conflict in the Orient.

It seems quite impossible to accept this view on the basis of the documentation. During the greater part of 1940 and 1941, it was certainly not the objective of the Roosevelt administration to bring about a clash in the Far East. On the contrary such a clash was regarded as likely to produce the greatest embarrassment in connection with the program of aid to Britain. The military and naval advisers of the President were opposed to it, and said so again and again. Even on the eve of Pearl Harbor this was the case. In addition, Secretary Hull was opposed to it. Ever the apostle of caution, he made his point of view quite clear almost up to the end. And as for the President, it is worth pointing out that on the occasion of the Japanese occupation of southern Indo-China he came forward with a proposal for the neutralization of that territory in the interests of peace, and that in August he frankly stated it to be his purpose to "baby the Japanese along." That he feared Japanese aggression is likely, almost certain; that he desired it is something that cannot be proved.

But let us look at the various specific actions which have awakened criticism on the part of the revisionists. In the first place I cannot see that staff conversations with the British were open to any objections whatsoever. If the object of the Roosevelt administration was to limit Japanese aggression in the Far.

East, then it seems wholly rational to take precautions against such aggression, and surely it could reasonably be expected that such precautions would serve as a deterrent rather than as an incitement to action. It is, in my judgment, rather distorted thinking that regards such action as provocation. This is precisely the point of view of the Kremlin today with regard to the North Atlantic treaty and the European defense pact, or, to take anoher example, very like the contention of the Germans when they invaded Belgium in 1914. Because the British had engaged in military conversations with the Belgians looking to the possible violation of the neutrality treaty of 1839, it was claimed by apologists for Germany that the violation of neutrality was defensible. Where is the possible justification for such reasoning?

There is more to be said with regard to the breaking off, by the United States, of commercial and financial relations with Japan on the heels of the Japanese occupation of southern Indo-China in the summer of 1941. Undoubtedly this created an extraordinarily difficult situation for the government in Tokyo. Undoubtedly the cutting off of the oil supply from the United States gave great additional force to the arguments of the militarists. Undoubtedly, in the absence of a far-reaching diplomatic arrangement, it presented a strong reason for "bursting out" of the circle, and going to war. If the administration put faith in this measure of economic coercion as a substitute for physical resistance, its faith was to turn out to be groundless. For myself, I have for a long time believed that economic coercion against a strong and determined power is more likely to produce war than to prevent it. But there are circumstances that ought to be mentioned in favor of the action of the administration. It is to be emphasized that the severance of commercial and financial relations resulted not in a breach of the negotiations with Japan but in a resumption of those negotiations. It is to be remembered that Prince Konoye's proposal for a personal conference with the President came after and not before the President's action. American policy by no means put an end to the efforts of those substantial elements in Japan who feared a clash with this country and who were laboring to prevent it. It must be pointed out, also, that the alternative was by no means a pleasant one. At a time when we were deeply engaged in the Atlantic, when we were being more and more deeply committed with regard to the war in Europe, when our domestic supply of oil might have to be substantially curtailed, the continuation of our exports to the Far East to assist Japan in possible projects of aggression was a very difficult policy to follow. It may even be that it would have proven to be totally impracticable from a political point of view.

We come in the third place to the efforts of Premier Konoye to establish direct contact with President Roosevelt. It is well known that Ambassador Grew believed at that time, and that he has more than once stated since, that a good deal was to be hoped from such a meeting. And it is by no means clear why, if the objective were the postponement of a crisis, the experiment should not have been tried. Secretary Hull brought to this problem, as it seems to me, a rigidity of mind which may properly be criticized. In insisting on a previous definition of the issues before the meeting was held, he was instrumental in preventing it. While we cannot know what the result of such a meeting would have been, we are entitled, I think, to wish that it had been held. All the more is this true since it would appear likely that Prince Konoye was sincere in the effort which he made to avoid war.

But there is another side to the matter. We cannot be absolutely sure of Konoye's good faith. We can be still less sure of the willingness of the Tokyo militarists to support him in the far-reaching concessions that would have been necessary. And in the final analysis we cannot be sure of the ability of the American government to make concessions on its own part.

And here we come, as it seems to me, to the crux of the matter. It was the American policy in China that created an impassable barrier in our negotiations with Japan. It is necessary to examine that policy. From one angle of vision the patience of the American government in dealing with the China incident seems quite remarkable. There was a good deal to complain of from 1935 onward, certainly from 1937 onward, if one were to think in terms of sympathy for an aggressed people and in terms of the traditional policy of the United States with regard to this populous nation. The Roosevelt administration moved very slowly in its opposition to Japan. It made its first loan to Chiang Kai-shek in the fall of 1938. It denounced the commercial treaty of 1911 with Nippon only in the summer of 1939. And it embarked upon a policy of really substantial aid to China only contemporaneously with the signing of the tripartite pact in the fall of 1940. Its increasing assistance to Chiang is intelligible on the ground that to keep the Japanese bogged down in China was one means of checking or preventing their aggressive action elsewhere.

The fact remains, however, that it was the Chinese question which was the great and central stumbling block in the long negotiations that took place in 1941. Though the Japanese had entered into an alliance with the Axis powers, it seems not unlikely that, in 1941, as the issue of peace or war defined itself more clearly, they would have been willing to construe away their obligations under that alliance had they been able to come to terms with the United States on the Chinese problem. But by 1941 the American government was so far committed to the cause of Chiang that it really had very little freedom of maneuver. The various Japanese proposals for a settlement of the China incident would have involved a betrayal of the Chinese Nationalist leader. The proposal for a coalition government, a government of the Nationalists and the puppet régime of Wang Ching-wei, could hardly have been accepted. The proposal that

America put pressure on Chiang to negotiate, and cut off aid to him if he refused, was by this time equally impracticable. And the question of the withdrawal of the Japanese troops in China presented insuperable difficulties. True it is that in October of 1941 the idea of a total withdrawal seems to have been presented to Mr. Welles by Mr. Wakatsuki, Admiral Nomura's associate in the negotiations. But the idea was emphatically rejected by the militarists in Tokyo, and perhaps there was never a time when they would have agreed to any proposal that at the same time would have been acceptable to Chungking. The American government had been brought, by its policy of association with the Chinese Nationalists, to the point where understanding with Japan was practically impossible.

This fact is dramatically illustrated by the negotiations over the *modus vivendi* in November, 1941. At this time, as is well known, proposals were brought forward for the maintenance of the *status quo*, and a gradual restoration of more normal relations through the lifting of the commercial restrictions, and through the withdrawal of the Japanese from southern Indo-China. At first it seemed as if there were a possibility of working out some such proposal. But the Chinese objected most violently, and Secretary Hull dropped the idea. In the face of Chinese pressure, and of the possible popular indignation which such a policy of concession might produce, and acting either under the orders or at least with the assent of the President, he backed down. We must not exaggerate the importance of this. There is no certainty that the *modus vivendi* would have been acceptable to Tokyo, and, judging by the Japanese proposals of November 20, there is indeed some reason to think otherwise. But the fact remains that our close association with Chiang was a fundamental factor in making the breach with Japan irreparable. And it seems fair to say in addition that our hopes with regard to Nationalist China were at all times, in 1941 as later, very far removed from political reality.

Let us not, however, jump to absolute conclusions with regard to questions that, in the nature of the case, ought not to be a matter of dogmatic judgment. If there was a party in Japan, and a substantial one, which feared war with the United States and earnestly sought for accommodation, there was also a party which regarded the course of events in Europe as a heaven-sent opportunity for national self-aggrandizement. That this party might in any case have prevailed, whatever the character of American policy, does not seem by any means unlikely. It is significant that in July of 1941 the fall of Matsuoka brought no change in policy in the Far East, and that the so-called moderate, Admiral Toyoda, gave the orders for the crucial and revealing occupation of southern Indo-China in the summer of 1941.

Let us not forget, either, that after all it was the Japanese who struck. The ruthless act of aggression at Pearl Harbor was no necessary consequence of the breakdown of negotiations with the United States. If new oil supplies were needed, they were, of course, to be secured by an attack on the Dutch East Indies, not by an attack on Hawaii. Though there were strategic arguments for including America in any war-like move, there were strong political reasons for not doing so. No greater miscalculation has perhaps ever been made than that made by the militarists at Tokyo in December, 1941. By their own act, they unified American opinion and made their own defeat inevitable. It will always remain doubtful when the decisive involvement would have come for the United States had the bombs not dropped on Pearl Harbor on the 7th of December of 1941.

What, in conclusion, shall we say of revisionist history? There is a sense in which it is stimulating to the historian, and useful to historical science, to have the presuppositions, the conventional presuppositions, of the so-called orthodox interpreters of our foreign policy, subjected to criticism. There is surely some reason to believe that the candid examination of the views of these critics will, in the long run, result in a more accurate and a more objective view of the great events of the prewar years and in a better balanced judgment of President Roosevelt himself.

But there is another side of the question which, of course, must be recognized. It is fair to say that virtually all revisionist history (like some orthodox history) is written with a *parti pris*. It is hardly possible to speak of it as dictated by a pure and disinterested search for truth. It is, on the contrary, shot through with passion and prejudice, with passion and prejudice that may spring from comprehensible or even good motives, but which are passion and prejudice none the less. It also rests upon hypotheses which, in the nature of the case, cannot be demonstrated, and assumptions that will, it is fair to say, never be generally, or perhaps even widely, accepted. As to its practical effects, there are no signs that the isolationism of the present era has important political effects, so far as foreign policy is concerned. Conceivably, it provides some reinforcement for partisan Republicanism. But even here it seems considerably less effective than the unscrupulous campaign of Senator McCarthy and his colleagues to represent the previous administration as one saturated with Communists. The urgency of present issues may make revisionism less of a force in our time than it was two decades ago. As to this, we shall have to see what the future unfolds.

7 ～

The State Department Speaks[*]

FOR a long generation historians will concern themselves with the entry of the United States into the present war. Each will have his own interpretation of these momentous events; each will seek, in his own way, to collect the "truth" with regard to what actually happened. The documents recently published by the state department will be a primary source in the search for this "truth"; and the question with which we must concern ourselves here is the question: "Precisely how valuable are they likely to be?" [1]

It is obvious, of course, that the history of the diplomatic interchanges of the last ten years that culminated in Pearl Harbor cannot yet be written with any pretense at finality or complete-

---

* Reprinted by permission from *The Journal of Modern History*, June, 1944.

[1] *Peace and war: United States foreign policy, 1931–1941*. Department of state. Washington: U.S. Government Printing Office, 1943.

Paper relating to the foreign relations of the United States. Japan: 1931–1941. Department of state. Washington: U.S. Government Printing Office, 1943. 2 vols.

The United States and its place in world affairs 1918–1943. Edited by Allan Nevins and Louis M. Hacker. Boston: D. C. Heath & Co., 1943.

ness. No one knows better than the diplomatic historian that any study which even pretends to "definitiveness" must be based on a variety of archives and upon a vast amount of work in each. No mere selection of documents by one of a number of foreign offices can possibly suffice. There is a large number of questions that the state department publications leave unanswered; the omissions, as we shall see, are fully as striking as the inclusions; and so it must inevitably be in the existing circumstances. For, after all, in general, no government is free to publish its diplomatic exchanges with other governments without that other government's consent; and, while the rule can be broken with regard to countries with which we are at war, it may still be true, even in this case, that reasons of high policy will dictate many omissions and the slurring-over of many essential facts. It does not imply the faintest criticism of the state department's effort to say that in time of war governments naturally tell us what they want us to know; they are fully justified in acting on this basis from the standpoint of practical statesmanship; they would get themselves into difficulty if they did otherwise. They need not practice deception, but they must practice discretion; they need not be dishonest, but they can hardly be expected to tell all that will ever be told. It would be a most ridiculous pretense to imagine that we have here in these three red-bound volumes the whole story of American diplomacy since 1931; we have, I think I should be inclined to say, a less complete record than Seward gave to the country with regard to the Civil War in the diplomatic correspondence of the years 1861–65. But we have —and the point should be stressed—a more complete record than any other government in the world today is likely to give its people; and there can be little question that from documents just published we are able to understand the underlying philosophy and the basic assumptions which those responsible for the conduct of American policy believed during the fateful decade that ended with the day of infamy at Pearl Harbor.

This last statement of mine I think the reader should ponder on. For, as time goes on, something is lost, as well as gained, in the appreciation of the truth of history; and there is melancholy evidence that the diplomatic historians of a postwar period—with far greater stocks of information, with far more painstaking research, with many-sided knowledge—often miss completely the essence of the very period that they describe and do great harm by that very fact. Take, for example, the story, now frequently met with, that McKinley might have prevented the Spanish-American War if he had been more courageous, and especially if he had stressed the point, in his message of April 11, 1898, that the Spanish government had virtually yielded to the American demands. This statement has been repeated again and again by reputable historians. Yet it is nothing more nor less than history by hypothesis. How can anyone be sure what *would* have happened if McKinley had acted otherwise? How can one be sure that, because Spain, at the request of the United States, had offered an armistice, the Cuban insurgents would have accepted it? How can one be sure that congress would not have overridden the president no matter how pacific his tone? There is only one set of facts that we really know as to 1898, and those are the facts that really happened. And to set up a different set of facts, or rather of imaginings, is to fail to understand fully the actual climate of opinion of the time, the then-accepted assumptions or emotional states on which action depended. This kind of historical writing has a very limited value, and it may perform a genuine disservice. I am not at all sure that it has been a good thing for teachers of history to make it appear, as they often have made it appear, that this or that war in the past has been, after all, a good deal of a mistake, or one that should have been avoided; it might be wiser, as well as more "scientific," if they sought rather to enter into the spirit of the time and to interpret with accuracy and good conscience what it was, precisely, that did occur.

Or, take again the diplomacy of the war of 1914–18. That very able editorial writer, Walter Millis, in one of the best-written and, therefore, one of the most insidious, of the books of the middle thirties, so described the diplomacy of Woodrow Wilson as to make it appear little more than a series of stupid blunders. As has been well said, he reproduced everything but the spirit of the war years. In so doing, he missed the whole point of the period. It may have been true that Wilson assayed British and German violations of American neutral rights in different scales; but, if he did so, there was a reason in his own temper and in the temper of the time. It does not seem utterly ridiculous today to most of us to find him declaring, at the very beginning of the war, that the victory of Germany might lead to the militarization of the United States; we can understand—or at least many of us can—why he thought that the security of the American people was connected with the victory of the Allies. But, even if we could not, why should we seek, as Millis in some fashion sought, to persuade the American people that the war of 1917 was a mistake; why should we believe, as such a judgment implies, that we can measure exactly and with precision what the balance of forces would have been if the Germans had issued victorious from the struggle of a quarter of a century ago? Our business, as historians, is to understand what happened and not to build a dream picture of a world that never was. The thing which we call "perspective" may be merely an excuse for our failure to enter into the thoughts, the feelings, the aspirations, of those about whom we write. And so these state department documents, incomplete as they may be, from one angle, as an historical record, have at least the merit of reproducing the climate of opinion in which American diplomacy operated, of reflecting the point of view of those responsible for its conduct, and of providing the essential background for the study of the period. From this point of view, in particular, they deserve careful study.

In emphasizing this consideration, however, I do not wish to be understood as saying that there is nothing novel in these voluminous collections of state papers. They do not alter the broad lines of the story of American diplomacy; but they do, of course, illuminate some significant episodes and provide an opportunity for a fuller consideration of American foreign policy in the fateful years 1931–41.

With this general understanding of the nature of the documents we are studying, let us look first at those which deal with European affairs in the period covered and which extend from Hugh Gibson's address to the General Disarmament Conference at Geneva on February 9, 1932, to the Declaration of the United Nations on January 1, 1942.

As the problem of rearmament became more and more acute in Europe, the policy of the United States was directed toward its solution. But that policy was at all times limited by a basic reluctance to assume any effective responsibility for the maintenance of peace. Positive participation in coercive measures of any kind was not to be thought of. The furthest that the American government would go in implementing any agreement with regard to armaments or any understanding for the preservation of world order was stated in the speech of Norman H. Davis, chairman of the American delegation to the World Disarmament Conference, on May 22, 1933. According to the terms of this address, the American government would participate in a system of adequate supervision "to insure the effective and faithful carrying out of any measure of disarmament." [2] It would agree to consult in case of a threat to peace. In case other states took common measure against a violator of the peace, it would agree to refrain from any action tending to defeat such collective effort. Beyond these measures it would not go.

Such was the American position only a few months after

[2] *Peace and war,* Doc. No. 17, p. 189.

Adolf Hitler came into power. The story of the years from 1933 to 1941 is the story of the advance from this position to full participation in a general war and the punishment of an aggressor nation by the collective force of mankind.

It is clear from the documents in *Peace and war* that the administration received early warning of the sinister character of the new German regime. As early as June 26, 1933 our very able consul-general in Berlin, G. S. Messersmith, wrote frankly that "those who hold the highest positions [i.e., in the German government] are capable of actions which really outlaw them from ordinary intercourse" and that they wish to "make Germany the most capable instrument of war that has ever existed." [3] This warning was repeated in November [4] and in the most definite and concrete terms in a memorandum prepared by Douglas Miller in April of 1934.[5] The idea of a German entente with Japan, or, at any rate, of "unusually close and friendly relations . . . even to the extent of a possible secret alliance," was suggested as early as May 17, 1934.[6]

In the face of these warnings, it is clear that the administration was uneasy. As early as May 5, 1934 Secretary Hull warned that it would be both a blunder and a crime for civilized peoples to fail to take notice of present dangerous tendencies,[7] and this warning was repeated in June.[8] Indeed, the secretary's tone mounted with time; and the warnings attained a new solemnity with the year 1935. But, it should perhaps be said, the warnings were in general terms; and they certainly made no deep impres-

[3] Messersmith to the under secretary of state (Phillips), June 26, 1933, *ibid.*, pp. 191–92.

[4] Messersmith to Phillips, Nov. 23, 1933, *ibid.*, pp. 194–95.

[5] *Ibid.*, pp. 211–14.

[6] Memorandum by the United States military attaché, *ibid.*, p. 222.

[7] Address delivered by the secretary of state at Washington, May 5, 1934, *ibid.*, pp. 217–19.

[8] Address delivered by the secretary of state at Williamsburg, Virginia, June 11, 1934, *ibid.*, pp. 231–33.

sion upon the American people. In the years of the first Roosevelt administration the set of public opinion was very far from
favorable to any kind of positive or preventive action. The administration could not even persuade the congress of the United
States to give it discretionary power to impose an arms embargo,
which it might apply against an aggressor nation; and the proposed adherence to the World Court protocol failed dismally
in the senate.

There is something distinctly pathetic about the position in
which the president and Secretary Hull found themselves at
the time of the Ethiopian war and the attempt of the League to
apply sanctions against Italy. The administration was well informed of the imminence of Italian action. It is clear that it desired to be helpful. But it could do very little. It could, and did,
put an embargo on the sale of arms and ammunition to both
parties; but with regard to all other trade it could only make a
painfully futile appeal to American citizens not to sell to the
belligerents (which meant Italy, of course) materials useful in
war. It was thought necessary definitely to instruct the United
States delegation at Geneva to discourage any invitation "to
join in any committee organized to consider sanctions." [9] And
the secretary of state, in a conversation with the Italian ambassador, was obliged twice in a single interview to state that the
American people were almost "wildly against war"; that "if
those participating in the war were double cousins and twin
brothers of the American people, the people of this country
would be just as violently and eternally against the war and in
favor of peace, and, above all considerations, in favor of keeping
away from and out of the war as would be possible." He even
went so far as partly to justify this attitude, declaring that "with
the extremely disastrous and unsatisfactory experience of the
American people in going to Europe and aiding Italy and other

[9] The secretary of state to the United States delegation at Geneva, *ibid.*,
p. 284.

countries to the extent they did, they are almost wild in their demand that we not only avoid being drawn into the war but that we stay entirely away from the same," and pointed out that, far from complaining of the American attitude, the Italian government should recognize how much less hostile than the attitude of the League was the attitude of the United States.[10] In this remarkable interview, one feels, is reached the point of most profound discouragement in the effort of the administration to arouse American public sentiment with regard to the danger of the European situation. The evidence of this discouragement is found not only in Mr. Hull's interview with Count Rosso but in the absence from the documents of even a single dispatch or instruction (to say nothing of a public speech) dealing with the occupation of the Rhineland in the winter of 1936, and in the secretary's frank declaration in September of the same year that the United States "would not depart from our traditional policy and [would not] join with other governments in collective arrangements carrying the obligation of employing force, if necessary, in case disputes between other countries brought them into war." [11] Was not this public announcement an unnecessary encouragement to the forces of aggression in Europe; or is it to be judged merely as an expression by the executive of what was already clear through the passage of the neutrality legislation of 1936, with its obvious limitations on the freedom of American action?

It was only slowly that the pendulum of foreign policy, swinging toward isolation in 1935 and 1936, reversed its action. With regard to Europe, 1937 was a quiet year; and the famous Quarantine Address of October 5, as well as the president's demand for the stepping-up of American armament, may well be

[10] Memorandum by the secretary of state regarding a conversation with the Italian ambassador (Rosso), Nov. 22, 1935, *ibid.*, pp. 293–301.

[11] Address delivered by the secretary of state at New York, Sept. 15, 1936, *ibid.*, p. 335.

connected with the situation in the Far East. But it is interesting to observe that as early as January 14, 1938, Secretary Hull, confronted with an unofficial German representation as to the utterances of Ambassador Dodd, responded to Ambassador Dieckhoff with some very pertinent observations on the importance of law and order in international affairs,[12] and that in March, shortly after the German occupation of Austria, Hull made a public speech in which he attacked in blistering language the "doctrine of force" which would "bring in its wake, inexorably, international anarchy and a relapse into barbarism." [13] There was no specific mention of Germany; but it is obvious that in this critical year the administration set out, more vigorously than ever before, to educate the American people to the moral implications of what was happening in Europe and in Asia.

I want to emphasize that phrase "moral implications." Cynics, and sometimes diplomatic historians, seem to assume that self-interest is the sole propulsive force in foreign affairs; and, in so assuming, they misread and distort the history to which they appeal. I believe that any student of American diplomacy in the years 1914–17, or in the years 1938–41, who studies the documents objectively and sincerely will not fail to recognize the place which moral conceptions play in the development of foreign policy. I make this remark neither in praise nor in blame of anyone. It merely seems to me important to insist that the American people, perhaps, more than other peoples, are profoundly moved by ideas and ideals in the field of foreign affairs and that any interpretation of the crucial years we are discussing which does not take account of this fact will be only a partial and incomplete record of what actually occurred.

[12] Memorandum by the secretary of state regarding a conversation with the German ambassador (Dieckhoff), Jan. 14, 1938, *ibid.*, pp. 402–3.
[13] Address delivered by the secretary of state at Washington, Mar. 17, 1938, *ibid.*, p. 417.

Nor can there be any question that the administration in the fall of 1938 was seeking, on its side, to sharpen the moral cleavage between the United States and National Socialist Germany. The president's personal intervention in behalf of peace at the time of the Czechoslovak crisis [14] could hardly have had any other purpose; the speech of Secretary Hull on November 1; the recall of the German ambassador from Berlin in the same month as a protest against the disgusting persecution of the Jews —these things clearly pointed in that direction. The Lima conference at the end of the year, with its declaration of American ideals and its machinery for consultation in the event of war, was directed, of course, to the same end. The extraordinary proposal of April 14, 1939, in which the president appealed to Hitler and Mussolini to give their personal assurances that they would not attack or invade any of the independent nations of Europe and the Near East, was also, one suspects, in part an educational measure, a clarification of the issue, though it may have had a deeper significance. One would like to know, and one will not, for some time to come, if there is any truth in the assertion made by Alsop and Kintner that the presidential maneuver was directed against an imminent danger of war and was effective in forestalling that danger for a few months at least.[15]

However this may be, the emphasis in the administration's public pronouncements changes with the president's speech of January 4, 1939. For the first time—and this eight months before the outbreak of war in Europe—Mr. Roosevelt strikes the note of actual danger, the note of security. "The world has grown so small," he declares, "and weapons of attack so swift that no nation can be safe in its will to peace so long as any other

[14] *Ibid.*, pp. 423–30.
[15] J. Alsop and R. Kintner, *American white paper* (New York, 1940), pp. 35–38.

single powerful nation refuses to settle its grievances at the council table." [16] The president goes on to embroider this declaration in language that has a new significance now that we are in the midst of war. It is a new man speaking here—a man gravely aware of present danger and of danger yet to come. There were those, of course, who thought that he exaggerated the danger; but whether this was the case or not, of one thing we may be certain: from this time forward, the president and his closest advisers were convinced that Nazi Germany constituted a positive menace to the United States. In the speeches of the next two and a half years this emphasis on security becomes more and more pronounced, until it reaches a culmination in the radio speech of May 27, 1941.[17]

Before leaving this matter, it is worth while to call attention at this point to the pronounced difference between the viewpoint of Woodrow Wilson and that of Franklin D. Roosevelt. That Wilson feared the consequences of German victory is clear from any study of his private utterances.[18] After the actual involvement of the United States in the war he painted in many of his speeches a striking picture of the perils of German militarism. But in the period of neutrality he carefully abstained from any such public castigation of the Central Powers. The issue of 1917 was an issue of neutral rights. The issue, as it developed under the president's guiding hand in 1939–41, was an issue of actual security.

For some time, of course, the president was by no means reflecting, but rather seeking to guide, public opinion. In the first nine months of the European war he succeeded in securing the

[16] Address delivered by President Roosevelt to congress, Jan. 4, 1939, *Peace and war*, pp. 447–51.

[17] Radio addresses delivered by President Roosevelt from Washington, May 27, 1941, *ibid.*, pp. 662–72.

[18] See, e.g., the conversation with Cecil Spring Rice in the fall of 1914 in Stephen Gwynn, *Letters and friendships of Sir Cecil Spring Rice* (Boston, 1929), II, 223.

lifting of the arms embargo, which hampered shipments to the Allies; but he had to buy even this small concession with the tightening, rather than the relaxation, of the rest of the neutrality law. His diplomatic action was apparently confined within narrow limits until the disasters of the spring of 1940. But in the days when Italy was trembling on the verge of war, the documents reveal a very heavy diplomatic pressure on the part of the United States.[19] Here, indeed, are some of the most interesting documents in the entire series. As early as April 29, Mr. Roosevelt uttered a veiled threat in pointing out to Mussolini that no one could tell what the ultimate result of a further extension of the struggle might be.[20] The threat was made more specific in the communication of May 30, in which it was stated that Italy's decision for war "might well bring with it the involvement of countries at present remote from the scene of the hostilities" and "would at once result in an increase in the rearmament program of the United States itself and in a redoubling of the efforts of the Government of the United States to facilitate in every practical way the securing within the United States by the Allied Powers of all the supplies and matériel which they might require." [21] It was accompanied by an offer to undertake to act as go-between in negotiations with France for the satisfaction of Italian legitimate aspirations and for the obtaining of assurances from Great Britain and France that such agreements would be faithfully executed at the end of the war.[22] But the Fascist dictator was, of course, untouched either by warning or by offers of propitiation. He had made up his mind, even as early as the first of May, that Germany could

[19] *Peace and war*, pp. 519–22, 536–40.

[20] President Roosevelt to the premier of Italy (Mussolini), Apr. 29, 1940, *ibid.*, pp. 519–20.

[21] The secretary of state to the ambassador in Italy (Phillips), May 30, 1940, *ibid.*, p. 539.

[22] President Roosevelt to the premier of Italy (Mussolini), May 26, 1940, *ibid.*, p. 537.

not be beaten.[23] He made his choice; he would not even see Mr. Phillips, the American ambassador, to discuss the matter when Phillips called upon him under express direction of the president in the last days of May. The "stab in the back" followed shortly.

One cannot help admiring the promptitude and the range of American diplomacy in the days that followed the fall of France. On June 10 came the Charlottesville speech in which, in an election year (the cynical should be reminded), the president pledged to the forces of democracy "the material resources of this nation." [24] On June 13 and on June 17 came encouragement to France at least to keep the French fleet out of the hands of the Germans.[25] On June 19 came a sharp reminder to the Axis nations that the United States could not recognize any transfer of territory in the New World.[26] On July 5, when a tart and insolent reply came from the Wilhelmstrasse, it was answered not only with a reasseveration of the Monroe Doctrine but with the statement that the United States would co-operate "in its own best interests" for ". . . the purpose of advancing the cause of international law and order of which the world stands so tragically in need today." [27]

From July, 1940 to the actual outbreak of war there is hardly a document in *Peace and war* bearing on the European situation that was not published at the time that it was drawn up. The

[23] The ambassador in Italy (Phillips) to the secretary of state, May 1, 1940, *ibid.*, pp. 520–22.

[24] Address delivered by President Roosevelt at Charlottesville, Virginia, June 10, 1940, *ibid.*, p. 548.

[25] President Roosevelt to the president of the French council of ministers (Reynaud), June 13, 1940, *Peace and war*, pp. 550–51; and the secretary of state to the ambassador near the French government at Bordeaux (Biddle), June 17, 1940, *ibid.*, pp. 553–54.

[26] Press release issued by the department of state on June 19, 1940, *ibid.*, pp. 555–56.

[27] Statement by the secretary of state, July 5, 1940, *ibid.*, p. 562.

reader will look in vain, therefore, for any new illumination on American foreign policy. What he will gain from the further perusal of this volume is what comes from reflection on facts already known, not on the discovery of new facts. He will be interested to note the extraordinary definiteness of the president's language on the great issue of security, to observe the mounting tone in which he described the menace of naziism in its relation to the New World; he will see the same temper in the speeches of Secretary Hull; he will, not for the first time, marvel at the boldness of conception that lay behind the meeting of Churchill and Roosevelt in August, 1941 and that resulted in the far-reaching declarations of the Atlantic Charter— this at a time when America was ostensibly at peace; he will realize, if he has not already done so, that informal war on the sea began with the president's speech of September 11, 1941, after the episode of the "Greer," and will once more be amazed at the lengths to which the executive then carried us; he will recognize in the revision of the Neutrality Act in November the support which public opinion, as expressed in the congress, gave to presidential policy. But he will know no more than he might have known had he followed the newspapers and the bulletins of the department of state; and there will be all sorts of things that he would like to know. He can find out some of these in Davis and Lindley's *How war came*,[28] which seems to have had official sponsorship; he will still be very curious as to others. In particular, he would like to know a lot more about Anglo-American relationships in this fascinating period; and he would be almost equally interested in the detailed historical record of our association with Vichy France. But these things must wait for a long time, and we need be under no illusion that the complete story is or can be in our hands at present.

[28] New York, 1942; reviewed in *The Journal of Modern History*, XIV (1942), 551–56.

The observation with which I have just closed my analysis of American diplomacy and the European crisis must apply also to the problems of the Far East. Here, it is true, the documents are indeed voluminous. The two volumes on Japan contain nearly 1,800 pages, and the documents run from the autumn of 1931 down to the actual outbreak of the war. But there are many things that they do *not* contain. On the Manchurian question, for example, there is material in Secretary Stimson's own book on the subject which is not to be found in *Foreign relations;* and for the years 1939–41 the interrelation of American and Japanese policy to the problems of the Indies and of Malaya is hardly touched on (with a few exceptions to be noted later). The American policy of aid to China hardly takes the place that it deserves in the broad perspective of the story, nor are its details much emphasized. In short, we must not expect to find in these volumes a satisfactory basis for the full story of American policy in the Orient.

Nonetheless, the reading of these documents is suggestive and illuminating. Take, for example, the Manchurian question. We have known for a long time that the Japanese army ran amuck in Manchuria in the fall of 1931. But the impressions become clearer and more definite as we read the dispatches. The moderate elements in Japan and the Japanese foreign minister, Shidehara, as late as October 14, were still talking of a solution of the problem that was essentially moderate in its terms.[29] The tone of Ambassador Debuchi was very often almost apologetic, and on one occasion he very definitely declared that "he believed in his people and that sooner or later the moderate elements would not disappoint us." [30] At the other end of the line, in Tokyo, the same language was heard. A prominent peer said to a member of

[29] Memorandum by the under secretary of state (Castle) of a conversation with the Japanese ambassador (Debuchi), Oct. 14, 1931, *Foreign relations,* I, 24.

[30] Memorandum by the secretary of state, Feb. 27, 1933, *ibid.*, p. 117.

Mr. Grew's staff, in the summer of 1932: "I hope they will change their minds before they wreck the country." [31] But the plain fact was that these moderate elements could not stand up against the clique of the militarists. Secretary Stimson was right in declaring in the winter of 1933 that "the Japanese government was in the control of a group of younger officers, none of them of a higher rank than a Lieutenant Colonel, and . . . that he must recognize that as long as that situation lasted I could not regard Japan as a normal Government. . . ." [32] From the very outset—indeed, from September 1931—not only were the militarists in control, but they had created the very situation which they proceeded to exploit. As early as July 1932, General McCoy, the American member of the Lytton investigating commission, revealed to Ambassador Grew that the commission was unanimous in the conviction that "the blowing up of the railway and every subsequent incident in Manchuria since September 18, 1931, were carefully planned and carried out by the Japanese themselves." [33]

There have been those students of American foreign policy who have raised the question whether all this was the business of the United States. Our material interests in Japan and in Japanese trade were far greater than those in China. In theory, at any rate, we could have stood aside and let Japan absorb Manchuria, as we let her establish a protectorate over Korea in the administrations of Theodore Roosevelt and William Howard Taft. But it is very clear why we did not do so. We had erected a treaty system in the Far East by the Nine-Power Treaty. We had, by national policy and by the promotion of the Kellogg Pact, taken a position against aggression from which it would have been difficult to withdraw. To have done nothing would

[31] The ambassador in Japan (Grew) to the secretary of state, July 16, 1932, *ibid.*, p. 95.

[32] Memorandum by the secretary of state, Jan. 5, 1933, *ibid.*, p. 107.

[33] The ambassador in Japan (Grew) to the secretary of state, July 16, 1932, *ibid.*, p. 94.

have been a diplomatic retreat of the first order. It would have involved the abandonment of the Nine-Power Treaty and of the policy of encouragement to renascent China which had, on the whole, been consistently pursued during the decade of the twenties. It would have been an act of self-stultification from the point of view of the Kellogg Pact, by which the United States had sought to outlaw war as "an instrument of national policy." It would have put the American government in the position of merely standing by, while the League of Nations wrestled with this difficult question. Such things mattered in 1931, and mattered much.

There are reasons to believe that the Roosevelt administration, in its initial months, was less militant in its position with regard to the Far East than was its predecessor; at any rate, its tone toward Japan was somewhat more cordial. But no one can read the record of the subsequent years without perceiving that appeasement would have involved the attenuation of American rights to the vanishing-point. The state department began to complain with regard to a Japanese oil monopoly in Manchuria as early as October 1933.[34] It was met with the ridiculous assertion that Manchukuo was now an independent state and that Tokyo could not interfere. Its continued representations were disregarded. In the spring of 1934 the famous Amau statement with regard to the Japanese position in the Far East made it clear that Japan was virtually aspiring to hegemony over China. Coincidentally, Mr. Saito transmitted to Under Secretary of State Phillips the actual instructions of the Japanese foreign minister to the Japanese minister in China.[35] These instructions contain such ominous sentences as the following: "As to the maintenance of peace and order in Eastern Asia the recent development of affairs has brought about a situation in which Japan will

[34] The secretary of state to the ambassador in Japan (Grew), Oct. 14, 1933, *ibid.*, p. 126.

[35] The Japanese ambassador (Saito) to the under secretary of state (Phillips), Apr. 25, 1934, *ibid.*, pp. 228–30.

have to undertake it upon her own responsibility and even single-handedly. Japan is determined to fulfill this mission." And they make it clear that Japan, still theoretically at peace with China, intended to "oppose" the granting of supplies, the naming of foreign military advisers, or the furnishing of "political loans" to the Chinese. It is not strange that Washington was disturbed and that Secretary Hull frankly expressed his displeasure to Saito in a long and interesting interview.[36]

The flurry of the spring of 1934 was followed by the denunciation of the Washington arms treaties by Japan and by Japan's insistence in the naval conference of 1935 upon quantitative equality with Great Britain and the United States. And while this conference was sitting, it is interesting to note, Saburo Kurusu, then chief of the Bureau of Commercial Affairs, had an interesting and revealing talk with the first secretary of the American embassy in Tokyo. He declared frankly, if flamboyantly, that "Japan was destined to be the leader of the Oriental civilization and would in course of time be the 'boss' of a group comprising China, India (*sic*), the Netherlands East Indies, etc." Great Britain, it appeared, was decadent, and Russia a nation of dreamers. The United States would lead the Occidental civilization, and Japan the Oriental. This interesting document goes on: "I asked Mr. Kurusu how he reconciled this theory with the treaties for collective security which Japan had signed. Mr. Kurusu said that he had always been opposed to Japan's hypocritical attitude toward such things. He said that he had just recently made a speech . . . criticizing his own country for signing agreements which could not be carried out if Japan wished to progress in this world." [37] Is it strange that such language created a certain amount of nervousness in Washington and suggested that, unless the United States intended to abdi-

[36] Memorandum by the secretary of state, May 19, 1934, *ibid.*, pp. 233–36.

[37] Memorandum by the first secretary of the United States embassy in Japan (Dickover), Dec. 23, 1935, *Peace and war*, pp. 302–3.

cate completely in the Far East, it would have to look to its fences there?

In 1937 came the undeclared war on China. We need no new collection of documents to understand that this new aggression on the part of Tokyo produced a change in the policy of forbearance which had, up to this time, characterized the course of the administration, and that it was followed by the Roosevelt Quarantine Speech of October 5, 1937. But what stands out from the 239 pages of correspondence in *Foreign relations* which deal with the bombing of civilians and other acts endangering the life and welfare of American citizens in China is the arrogance of the Japanese and their frequent indifference to American representations. By the end of 1938 there had been 298 cases of injury to American persons and property and 135 bombings in which American interests suffered. In a small number of these cases the Japanese foreign office made some kind of payment or solatium; but in many others—the great majority—the representations of Ambassador Grew passed unanswered. In the meantime discrimination against American commercial interests became more and more flagrant in areas controlled by the Japanese, and Grew had handed in a strong protest as early as October 6, 1938. At about the time that this protest was framed, it is interesting to observe, Secretary Hull told the Hungarian minister in Washington that he was proceeding (and had proceeded since last August) on the theory that "Japan definitely contemplates securing domination over as many hundreds of millions of people as possible in eastern Asia and gradually extending her control through the Pacific islands to the Dutch East Indies and elsewhere, thereby dominating, in practical effect, that one-half of the world; and that she is seeking this objective by any and every kind of means; that at the same time I have gone on the theory that Germany is equally bent on becoming the dominating colossus of continental Europe." [38]

[38] Memorandum by the secretary of state of a conversation with the Hungarian minister (Pélenyi), Sept. 21, 1938, *Foreign relations*, I, 475–76.

In the Orient, as in the Occident, the fall of 1938 was marked by the increased diplomatic activity of the United States. The first loan to China came at this time, although of this there is almost no mention in the diplomatic correspondence; and it is further to be remembered that the notice of the abrogation of the commercial treaty of 1911 with Japan came in the summer of 1939, before the outbreak of the European war. The tone of the American government in announcing this latter step was extremely mild; but by September, Secretary Hull's conversations with the Japanese ambassador had become distinctly acrimonious,[39] and there was certainly no lack of frankness in Ambassador Grew's speech before the American-Japan Society in October.[40] The United States was definitely taking its stand against Japanese imperialism. As for the Japanese, the widening scope of their ambitions and the trend of their diplomacy soon became clear. As early as February 1939 Grew had notified his government that Japan was negotiating with Germany and Italy for an alliance.[41] The Japanese had set up monopolies for the development of the trade of northern China;[42] they took advantage of the outbreak of the war to request the withdrawal of foreign warships from the rivers of China and to suggest a change in the status of the International Settlement at Shanghai.[43] In February of 1940 Mr. Arita, the Japanese foreign minister, referred to Japan's war in China as a "Holy War";[44] in April, Japan was beginning to refer to her special interest in the Dutch East Indies; a very heated conversation with Secretary

[39] *Ibid.*, II, 15–19.

[40] Address delivered by the ambassador in Japan (Grew) before the America-Japan Society at Tokyo, Oct. 19, 1939, *ibid.*, pp. 19–29.

[41] The ambassador in Japan (Grew) to the secretary of state, Feb. 8, 1939, *ibid.*, p. 162.

[42] The secretary of state to the ambassador in Japan (Grew), Dec. 8, 1939, *ibid.*, p. 48.

[43] The chargé in Japan (Dooman) to the secretary of state, Sept. 5, 1939, *ibid.*, pp. 9–10.

[44] The ambassador in Japan (Grew) to the secretary of state, Feb. 29, 1940, *ibid.*, p. 55.

Hull on this question took place in May; [45] and the collapse of France freed the hands of Tokyo for an advance into Indo-China. At the same time the foreign minister conveyed a broad hint to Grew that aid to China should cease. [46] By October the Japanese government was talking of its interest in "greater East Asia, that is, East Asia including the South Seas," and of Japan's claim to "equality with every other country" to "carry on enterprises, trade and emigration in and to each and every land in greater East Asia and thereby be enabled to solve its population problem." [47] By this time, of course, there had been signed the tripartite pact of September 27, 1940, by which the government at Tokyo not only became the ally of Germany and Italy but by which it virtually bound itself to come to the aid of these powers if the United States entered the war against the Reich.

It is safe to say that no government, certainly no government representing one hundred and thirty millions of people, would have taken lying down the attempt of another government to encircle it diplomatically. Secretary Hull certainly minced no words in talking to the Japanese ambassador at Washington. "I made it clear," says a memorandum of October 8, "that it is the view of this Government that two nations, one in Europe and one in Asia, are undertaking to subjugate both of their respective areas of the world, and to place them on an international order and on a social basis resembling that of 750 years ago." [48] Franker than this it was impossible to be.

In the meantime, of course, the United States was drawing nearer to Britain. The destroyer-bases deal had come in the summer of 1940; but to what extent and when Washington made clear to Japan its intention to support the British in the Orient

[45] Memorandum by the secretary of state, May 16, 1940, *ibid.*, pp. 285–88.

[46] Memorandum by the ambassador in Japan, July 11, 1940, *ibid.*, p. 95.

[47] The ambassador in Japan (Grew) to the secretary of state, Oct. 5, 1940, *ibid.*, p. 172.

[48] Memorandum by the secretary of state, Oct. 8, 1940, *ibid.*, p. 227.

the documents do not tell us in satisfactory detail. Here is a matter of great significance for the diplomatic historian. But it is certainly very important to note that, as early as February 1941 (and so before the passage of lend-lease), the counselor of the American embassy at Tokyo made it very clear to Mr. Ohashi, the vice-minister for foreign affairs, that if Japan were to attack Singapore there would be war with the United States.[49] This statement is worth quoting:

Mr. Ohashi could readily understand that the American people, being an eminently practical people, are quite aware that an adequate supply of airplanes and other munitions is not the only prerequisite to a British victory . . . it would be absurd to suppose that the American people, while pouring munitions into Britain, would look with complacency upon the cutting of communications between Britain and British dominions and colonies overseas. If, therefore, Japan or any other nation were to prejudice the safety of those communications, either by direct action or by placing herself in a position to menace those communications, she would have to expect to come into conflict with the United States.[50]

This warning was accompanied by a repetition of the views of the United States with regard to the Dutch East Indies. Certainly, the counselor would never have used such language except under instructions. We must, therefore, conclude that there existed a very close diplomatic entente between the United States and Great Britain in the Orient as early as February 1941, something like a month before the formal approval by congress of the lend-lease enactment of March 11, 1941.

On its side, Tokyo did not hesitate to threaten and bluster. In May, Mr. Matsuoka, having just returned from Moscow, where he had signed the Russo-Japanese neutrality pact, spoke

[49] The ambassador in Japan (Grew) to the secretary of state, Feb. 26, 1941, *ibid.*, p. 137.
[50] Memorandum by the counselor of the embassy in Japan (Dooman), Feb. 14, 1941, *ibid.*, p. 139.

in a very "bellicose" tone to Ambassador Grew. He spoke of the "patience and generosity" of Hitler "in not declaring war on the United States." He said that "if, in spite of previous forbearance, Hitler should not (*now?*) sink our ships in the Atlantic and if we Americans should then attack the German submarines he would regard it as an act of American aggression which would call for deliberation as to the applicability of article III of the Triple Alliance Treaty of September 27, 1940, and he thought there was no doubt that such deliberation would lead to war between Japan and the United States." [51] Could the language of menace go further?

In the meantime the famous Hull-Nomura conversations had begun in Washington. The evaluation of these talks is difficult, and delicate questions of motive (the most baffling of all questions for the historian) are involved. That they were undertaken, on the part of the United States, partly with the motive of "babying the Japanese along," was stated by the president in a press conference and is reiterated in the summary of these conversations in the correspondence.[52] It is highly likely that the delay was useful also to Japan, while she was completing her preparations for the day of attack on Pearl Harbor. But it would, I think, on the basis of the documents, be a mistake to imagine that there was in Tokyo no sentiment for understanding with the United States, no genuine desire to arrive at some kind of agreement. It may be that Admiral Nomura was speaking only diplomatically when he declared that he did not approve the Japanese advance into southern Indo-China, which came in the midst of, and which temporarily suspended, the Washington conversations.[53] But one feels something real about Grew's re-

[51] The ambassador in Japan (Grew) to the secretary of state, May 14, 1941, *ibid.*, pp. 145–46.

[52] *Ibid.*, p. 335.

[53] Memorandum by the acting secretary of state, July 24, 1941, *ibid.*, p. 528.

port from Admiral Toyoda, foreign minister in the summer of 1941. "[He] told me that he had hardly slept at all during recent nights and he appeared greatly discouraged at the turn of events and especially distressed that the present situation should have arisen at the very time of his assumption of the post of Minister of Foreign Affairs." [54] The proposal of Prince Konoye to seek a conference with President Roosevelt may very well have been sincerely meant. As Admiral Nomura pointed out, such a step was "unprecedented in history" and was all the more remarkable when Japan was allied with Germany and Italy.[55] The view that this overture was sincere and of good omen was certainly held by Ambassador Grew, who, in one of the most interesting documents in the whole series, made himself the partisan of such a meeting and warned against prolonged negotiations or against expecting from the Nomura conversations "clear-cut commitments which will satisfy the United States Government both as to principle and as to concrete detail." [56] When Konoye fell in October, the emperor himself intervened in favor of peace. He called a meeting of the leading members of the Privy Council and of the Japanese armed forces and "inquired if they were prepared to pursue a policy which would guarantee that there would be no war with the United States. The representatives of the Army and Navy who attended this conference did not reply to the Emperor's question, whereupon the latter . . . in an unprecedented action, ordered the armed forces to obey his wishes." [57] Even Admiral Togo, the foreign minister in the new cabinet of General Tojo, seems to

[54] Memorandum by the ambassador in Japan (Grew), July 26, 1941, *ibid.*, p. 534.

[55] Document handed by the Japanese ambassador (Nomura) to the secretary of state, Sept. 29, 1941, *ibid.*, p. 653.

[56] The ambassador in Japan (Grew) to the secretary of state, Sept. 29, 1941, *ibid.*, p. 648.

[57] Memorandum by the ambassador in Japan (Grew), Oct. 25, 1941, *ibid.*, p. 697.

have wished to find a way out of the situation. He "realizes that his own life is at stake," wrote Grew, quoting a Japanese informant, "but . . . nevertheless he has the courage to make this final attempt in full cognizance of the consequences of failure." [58] In the frequent urgings for haste made by Nomura and later by Kurusu, one gets again and again the feeling of men struggling to arrest the flood that threatened to overwhelm them.

Yet, as one goes over the documents, one discovers very little reason to believe that an understanding was really possible. The division between the two countries was too deep to be bridged. Especially was this true on the problem of China. Fundamentally, what the Japanese desired of the United States was that it abandon the Chungking government to the mercies of Tokyo. The United States, on the other hand, wished nothing less than the evacuation of China by Japan and the establishment of a regime of nondiscrimination in that vast country. Furthermore, the United States was by this time in such diplomatic relations with Chungking as would make the desertion of that government impossible. Its action was necessarily limited,[59] its commitments too far-reaching. When a government comes to the assistance of another, to a certain extent it ties its own hands and makes its course somewhat dependent upon the temper of its beneficiary. To settle the "China incident" on terms agreeable to Chiang Kai-shek, the Tokyo militarists, and Washington was a formidable job; and it is not strange that it could not be done. There is no hint that at any time the American government was ready to abandon, or even put pressure upon, China; to the Japanese, peace implied one of these two things.

It was also difficult to get around the tripartite pact. Secretary Hull's deep resentment at that agreement is intelligible enough. To him Hitler was "the most flagrant aggressor that has

[58] Memorandum by the ambassador in Japan (Grew), Nov. 12, 1941, *ibid.*, p. 720.

[59] *Ibid.*, p. 348.

appeared on this planet in the last two thousand years," as he told Nomura.[60] That Japan should strike hands with this aggressor was monstrous. The Japanese, on the other hand, found it difficult to extricate themselves from their obligations, though there are hints that they might have sold out if the price had been right. The furthest they went was in the Kurusu letter of November 20, which speaks of interpreting the obligation "freely and independently" and declares that Japan is "not obligated . . . to become a collaborator in or cooperator in any aggression whatever by any third Power or Powers," and will "accept warfare only as the ultimate inescapable necessity for the maintenance of its security and the preservation of national life against active injustice." [61] Such language was interesting; but it could hardly be convincing, particularly after all that had gone before.

The Hull-Nomura conversations, moreover, were poisoned by the events of the summer of 1941. The Japanese occupation of southern Indo-China could have no justification and only one meaning. Nomura himself was apologetic about it. On the other hand, the suspension of commercial relations by the United States acted only as an incitement to the militarists. There is nothing in the experience of those crucial months, as there is nothing in the experience of 1935 with regard to the application of sanctions against Italy, that suggests that economic pressure is a useful substitute for war. In such an atmosphere even the efforts at a *modus vivendi* could not get very far. We do not know, and certainly are not told in the diplomatic correspondence, the whole story. In particular, one would like to have fuller information on the conversations with the Chinese and with the governments of the South Pacific area. It was the thesis of some of the Japanese that, if the trend toward war could be reversed, the

[60] *Ibid.*, p. 361.
[61] Draft letter handed by Mr. Saburo Kurusu to the secretary of state, Nov. 21, 1941, *ibid.*, p. 757.

danger in time might pass. But the most that Tokyo would offer was withdrawal from southern Indo-China in exchange for the restoration of commercial relations and to agree not to extend its military operations southward. The state department was unwilling to accept this proposal, in view of the "contemporary manifestations of Japanese policy and action" such as the "augmentation and speeding up of Japanese military preparations at home, the continuing bombing by Japanese armed forces of Chinese civilian populations, the constant agitation in the inspired Japanese press in support of extremist policies, the unconciliatory and bellicose public utterances of Japanese leaders, and the tactics of covert or open threat which had become a constant feature of Japanese diplomatic procedure." It felt that there was needed "evidence of a positive intention to pursue policies in conformity with the liberal and constructive principles" of the United States.[62] There was no arresting the trend; and it is interesting to read that in mid-October Mr. Wakasugi, minister counselor of the Japanese embassy, warned that, if the settlement did not come quickly, there might be a military coup in Japan, and that war would inevitably follow.[63] The final exchanges marked not an improvement, but a deterioration, in the atmosphere; the American proposals of November 26 [64] were such that acceptance could hardly have been expected. But it was, of course, the Japanese who took the solemn responsibility of breaking off the negotiations—at the very moment when their planes were circling over Pearl Harbor in the surprise attack of December 7.

The story of Pearl Harbor belongs primarily to military and naval, rather than diplomatic, history. But there seems no doubt that the state department had done its part to make the situation clear to the armed services.[65] It seems astounding—all the more astounding on reflection—that the proper precautions had not

[62] *Ibid.*, p. 355.
[64] *Ibid.*, p. 769.
[63] *Ibid.*, p. 357.
[65] *Ibid.*, p. 359.

been taken and that the Japanese were able to wreak the damage which they did.

As a diplomatic matter Pearl Harbor may be the worst blunder that could have been made. As militarists will never understand, the division of opinion which is likely to exist in a democratic country disappears in just such circumstances and national unity takes its place. Perhaps by the attack of December 7 the Japanese contributed more than they could have in any other way to the will of the American people to victory.

III ~

POPULAR LECTURES

8 ~

The Constitution
and the American Spirit *

THE Constitution of the United States, whose one hundred and fiftieth anniversary we are celebrating, is now one of the oldest written constitutions, if not the oldest, in the world. In 1787, when it was drawn up, the United States consisted of thirteen colonies on the Atlantic sea-board, with a population of between three and four million. Today, this same instrument of government is the fundamental law of a great nation, stretching from ocean to ocean, and containing close to 130,000,000 people. It is an astounding thing that this should be true, all the more astounding because, though the Constitution has undergone amendment from time to time, it remains, so far as its text is concerned, to an extraordinary degree the same document that it was in 1787.

This is not to say, of course, that the men who framed it had any prevision of what lay ahead over the decades. They were men of extraordinary competence, all the more extraordinary when one considers the provincial, and limited, society from which they came; but in many respects their thoughts and their

* Address delivered before a community observance of Constitution Day, Rochester, New York, 1937.

point of view were far removed from those of our own day. The representatives, almost without exception, of the propertied classes of their own time, in an epoch where the propertied classes were usually the governing classes, they had, many of them, little sympathy with democracy, and a deep distrust of the wisdom of the people. They did not think of government as an instrument for the correction of social inequalities, or for the alleviation of the lot of the unfortunate. They were willing enough to condone, and even to sanction by implication, the institution of slavery. And yet they framed a document under which universal manhood suffrage, and then universal suffrage without distinction of sex, was to become possible; under which a federal government of limited powers was to widen its role immeasurably with the passage of time, and adapt itself to a totally different outlook from their own; under which the most extraordinary social changes have taken place without any great social upheaval save that which was caused by the destruction of the slave system in the middle of the nineteenth century. The achievement is a remarkable one, a tribute to the founding fathers themselves, but still more to the genius of the American people.

It was a knotty problem, the problem of drawing up the Constitution of the United States, of reconciling the strong sense of local autonomy with the need for national government, and the fathers solved it well and ingeniously; but it has been a still greater problem to make this Constitution work over a hundred and fifty years. What I am proposing, therefore, tonight, is no eulogy, well deserved though such a eulogy would be, of the men of 1787; what I am proposing is a eulogy of the American spirit in government, which has reconciled growth and change with the language of a document older than any other written constitution in existence, which has conserved old values while creating new ones, which, today, no less than in earlier times, is loyal to the ideal of ordered freedom and of progress under the law.

When we say that the world has greatly changed since the fathers wrought at Philadelphia in 1787, we do not mean that some of the ideals which were then prevalent have become outmoded. On the contrary, there is much in the American spirit today that was there when our existence began, sometimes expressed in the Constitutional convention itself, sometimes expressed in the views of its critics in the great campaign for the ratification of the Constitution which took place in 1788 and 1789. Not only the fathers, but the opponents of the fathers, had something vital to contribute to American theory and American practise one hundred and fifty years ago.

The point is a vital one, and one to which we may have occasion to return from time to time in the course of these remarks this evening. For America has thriven on the spirit of criticism, on free and open discussion of important public issues, on the fullest and widest discussion. This is itself one of the most important things about us, and about the success of our governmental system; and it is made clear by the experience of the constitution-making years themselves. For the critics of the document drawn up at Philadelphia from the very beginning criticised it as giving too much power to government; they feared that it would endanger liberty; and the Constitution could never have been ratified at all if assurance had not been given that there would be added to it amendments which protected the liberties of the citizens from the encroachments of state authority. That notion of liberty still has much to do with the American governmental system today.

Now liberty is a mouth-filling word. Behind it every selfish interest can entrench itself; and if it were regarded as an unqualified human good, there would be no need of government at all. Reasonable men recognize that some restraints on human nature and human selfishness are necessary in every society; and reasonable men, also, ought to be able to comprehend that in a complex industrial society, such as that which exists today, the restraints must inevitably be more numerous than they were in the simple farming communities of one hundred and fifty years ago. The word "liberty" must constantly undergo new definition, as indeed it does, in the practise of our courts. The 5 to 4 decision of the Supreme Court of the United States, for example, in the famous case of Lochner vs. New York, handed down in 1905, declaring that a law limiting the hours of work in bakeshops to ten hours a day was a deprivation of the liberty of the bakers, seems now only a bad joke. The 5 to 3 decision of the Supreme Court of the United States in the Adkins case, declaring a minimum wage law to be an interference with the liberty of the employer, has recently been pronounced by a majority of the present bench to be such a construction of the word as the present age cannot justify. We have seen for the last fifty years, and shall see, in all probability, in the years ahead, an extension of the area of governmental action, and in this sense a restriction of the liberty of the individual.

But it by no means follows that the idea of liberty itself is dead, or that the feeling for liberty does not still play a vital part in American affairs. In the realm of sentiment, for example, one fact stands out clearly throughout the whole course of American history, and that is the distaste of the American for personal government, for that exaltation of the role of the individual which leads straight on towards dictatorship. Every President of the United States, the greatest perhaps even more dramatically than the mediocre, has met this feeling and been compelled to yield to it. The heroic Washington found himself more and more bitterly opposed as his years in the Presidency lengthened, and was subjected to the most violent opposition before he laid down his office. The gentle Lincoln, trained politician as well as statesman, had aroused immense resentment before the end of his first term, and would have faced a tremendous revolt if the assassin's bullet had not cut his life short. Woodrow Wilson, elevated to such a pinnacle of power and moral influence as no American has ever equalled, found himself thwarted in his fondest dreams, and went out of office a broken and defeated man. The present President of the United States, exercising remarkable personal power as it seemed in 1933 and 1934, has shared the experience of his predecessors.

It may be that the distrust of personal leadership in the United States is sometimes excessive. Washington, Lincoln, and Wilson may have been wiser than their critics. And certainly our government has functioned most successfully when we have had strong executive leadership as compared with those periods when we have had Presidents who confined themselves to their administrative functions and essayed no further role. But the distrust of personal power is none the less fundamentally sound. It will not be easy for the American people to hand themselves over to a clever demagogue, a strong man, or a social revolutionary, who promises to solve their problems for them. They intend to solve those problems for themselves. They do not intend to abdicate those rights of self-government which they have exercised since the nation began.

There is another sense in which liberty is alive today, and will remain alive in the United States, alive in the hearts of the people, guaranteed by the venerable instrument whose one hundred and fiftieth anniversary we are celebrating. The guarantees of free speech and a free press, the right of assemblage, written into the first amendment of the Constitution, are as cherished today as they ever were. In America we always have an opposition and an outspoken opposition. It is not compelled to resort to subterranean and revolutionary agitation and sabotage, as in Russia. It is not terrorized and reduced to subservience, as in Germany or in Italy. It functions freely, in the halls of Congress, in the public press, over the radio. At a given place, and at a given time, one or another of these channels may be choked. But they are never really dammed up, completely, not even in time of war. They must never be. They lie at the very heart of democratic government. The public official who denies to a law-abiding minority the right to express its views, the newspaper which denies its news columns to all opinions but those which happen to express the views of its proprietor, the business man who seeks to terrorize his employees into silence, these men, fortunately a small minority of our whole people, are the enemies of the Constitution and a menace to our political integrity. It is fundamental to free government that there should be constant criticism. It is out of the composition of ideas freely expressed that wise public policies are formed. A regime in which criticism is treason, in which dissent must be timidly expressed or not expressed at all, in which blood purges or wholesale executions are the weapons of those in power, can never hope to profit by its mistakes, to modify its policies before they become disastrous, to raise the level of intelligence of its own people. It may, at a given moment, appear efficient or successful; it may even meet the needs or the mood of the people it serves; but, sustained by violence, it will in due time perish by violence. Only a government based upon consent, whose decisions are the result of free debate, where opposition loses its explosive force because it is not repressed, can hope to weather every storm of opinion, and, even amidst the violence of party spirit, maintain an even keel in the stormiest seas.

With political liberty goes religious freedom. We have been made aware, and that within the decade, that there are powerful forces of religious intolerance in this country. But they can never hope to restrict freedom of worship, or make laws which discriminate against one group or another. Religion is not, nor will it be in any future that we can foresee, the handmaid of the state or the object of its persecution. The deep human need that expresses itself through faith has, in this country of ours, never been outlawed, as in Russia, nor made to conform to the purposes of some arbitrary politician, as in Germany. We have put religious liberty, as we have put political liberty, under the special protection of this Constitution of ours, to be protected by the courts against the caprice or arbitrary power of those in authority. Intolerance in America must generally do its work by stealth; it cannot express itself in law. No church dares claim for itself a privileged position in government. No religious group dares call upon the state to restrict the liberty of another religious group. No government dares invade the temple of worship, or challenge the religious liberty of the citizen.

Moreover, these forms of freedom, religious freedom, and political freedom, freedom of worship, freedom of the press, freedom of speech, freedom of assemblage, are protected by the very language of the Constitution itself, or, more properly, of the first amendment imposed upon the makers of the Constitution by its critics. Laws which limit these fundamental liberties have, on more than one occasion, been overturned by the Courts. Whatever may be thought in broad terms of the power of the Supreme Court of the United States to declare statutes unconstitutional (a power which the fathers probably intended that it should exercise) it cannot be denied that in such questions as the above the record has been a reassuring one.

Just as Americans have, for a hundred and fifty years, cherished and respected the liberty of the individual in the matters that are fundamental, so, too, with rare exceptions, they have recognized the rights of minorities. There are some Americans, of course, who seem to believe that a majority, even a majority of one, has a right to override the minority completely. But such is not the spirit of our governmental system. The theory of the Constitution is that the action of the majority ought to be considered action, not the mere whim of the moment. Thus it is that we have a two-chambered legislature, one house of which acts as a check upon the other; thus it is that we have a Senate the composition of which changes by degrees, a third every two years; thus it is that we have a Presidential veto; thus it is that we have a Supreme Court which can declare statutes unconstitutional; thus it is that we require much more than a majority to amend the fundamental law itself. The mechanism of delay in our constitutional system expresses an age-old American conviction that it is the considered judgment of the people, and not its ephemeral mood, that is to be expressed through our constitutional forms.

I should not maintain, no informed student would maintain, that this system always works well. It is to be expected that selfish interests of every kind will entrench themselves behind this machinery, that at times not the passing sentiment, but the considered temper of the American people, may be defeated, or at least unduly delayed. Just for this reason (and I shall recur to the point hereafter) we need to be sure that our public servants, and especially our judges, are able to take a statesmanlike view of the problems submitted to them, and do not view all change through the spectacles of a bilious and immovable Toryism. But in general this emphasis on delay is not unsound. Persons of a reforming temper, of generous sympathies, are apt to think that the legislative process stands by itself, and that once they have secured a majority of one for this or that measure of social amelioration they have accomplished the largest part of their end. But in reality any enactment that rests upon a basis as narrow as this is a most insecure achievement. The slightest shift of temper may bring its repeal; and if it does not prove prudent to repeal it, its foes are likely very successfully indeed to emasculate it by hostile administration. The delay, then, which so infuriates some of our most impatient and some of our most humane apostles of change, is by no means an unqualified evil. It allows time for a genuine consensus to develop; and it ensures that when a measure is once enacted there will be behind it a weight of opinion that will not permit it to be reversed with a change of administration, or undermined in its actual operation by its foes.

There are things, moreover, which a majority ought not to try to do. Government is not a mere matter of counting heads. There are measures which, because of the widespread resentment they arouse, because of the type of resistance which they provoke, are unwise and disruptive in their effects. Our system of checks and balances has not always prevented them. When, for example, at the end of the Civil War, the North attempted to force upon the South certain standards of action with regard to the Negro, it found that the civil power and the military arm combined were powerless to accomplish its purpose. When, at a more recent date, the foes of alcohol attempted to impose complete abstinence on a large minority which did not believe that the use of alcoholic beverages was inherently evil, they found themselves frustrated, and their very action created more evils than it solved.

In the main, Americans have recognized in practise the unwisdom of stretching majority powers too far. It is difficult to point to many instances of important legislative measures in our history which have been enacted by the narrowest of margins. Governmental policies have not oscillated between extremes, and the work of one administration has rarely been undone by another. Changes have come slowly, with due regard for the forces of the opposition; when they have come they have usually been permanent.

This respect for minority interests reflected in our constitutional mechanism is in theory sometimes pushed to absurd lengths from the standpoint of majority rule. It seems ridiculous, in the abstract, for example, that some of the small states of the prairie region or of the Rockies should have the same representation in the Senate of the United States as does the great state of New York. But, if one examines the make-up of the Senate more carefully, as did Woodrow Wilson in his great work on

Constitutional Government some thirty years ago, one discovers that that body represents regional, rather than numerical interests, and that it provides for our widespread agrarian populations a counterpoise to the influence of the industrial East. In theory, one might object to the Presidential veto as an impairment of the majority principle. But in practise it is a much needed element in our governmental system. For Congressmen and Senators are likely to be affected by local, or at least by state-wide, interests; the President is the only one of our public officials who can be said by his very position to be free to think of the nation as a whole. His negative, therefore, is a wholesome check on the action of sectional majorities, or of group interests too powerful for Congress to resist, but by no means coincident with the welfare of the nation as a whole.

When it comes to the courts, and to their role in checking the action of the majority, the question is a more complicated one. No informed student of the history of the Supreme Court would seek to defend its every decision. The judges are but men, moved, as are other men, sometimes by profound prejudices to which, through their judicial position, they can give the force of law. Nor is it easy to alter their decision by constitutional amendment. While it is true that the Constitution of the United States has been amended twenty-one times,* it is to be remembered that ten of these amendments came at the very outset, that three more relate to minor problems of constitutional mechanism arousing no very considerable opposition, that three more were the product of a bloody Civil War, that two more were the result of a new war era, and that the processes of social and political change which would be deemed most fundamental are touched by none of them. A question which arouses powerful opposition is by no means easy to settle through the channel of a constitutional amendment. As an his-

---

* The twenty-second amendment, limiting the President to two terms of office, was adopted in 1951.

torical matter, the major changes in the operation of our governmental system have not come about in this way, and will not come about in this way in the future. The powers of delay which are lodged in the Supreme Court, therefore, are extremely significant. If our judges are men who, in the words of Mr. Justice Stone, proceed on the assumption that "the responsibility for the preservation of our institutions is the exclusive concern of any one of the three branches of government, or that it alone can save them from destruction," our constitutional system is bound to be subjected to severe strain. But as an historical matter, this has hardly been the case! Rarely, indeed, in our history has the Court resisted a sustained public mood. It has forced reconsideration, but it has not, over the one hundred and fifty years of American history, frustrated the public will. In the course of the last year, indeed, with its decision on the Wagner Act and the Social Security Act, it has given evidence that it is not unaware of the spirit of the times. It is an agency of government, and not a collection of demi-gods. It should be, as Chief Justice Taft so often insisted, no more exempt from criticism than any other part of our governmental machinery. Its composition is a proper subject of popular debate. But that it has formed a dangerous obstruction to the expression of the national purpose is a proposition which most close students of its activities would be inclined to deny. Nor have all of its decisions, by any means, been on the side of one economic group, —of one minority. It set aside an income tax law in one of the most criticized of its decisions. But it set aside a law for the compulsory adjudication of labor disputes, which barred the right to strike. It set aside a minimum wage law, but sustained employees' compensation acts at every turn of the game. It is well that the American people should, from time to time, re-scrutinize its role in their affairs. But it is clear that, despite frequent attacks upon it, it remains an accepted part of our constitutional system.

The moderation of the American mind, one of its most valuable qualities, so clearly evidenced in the practical treatment of minorities, and in its constitutional system, is evidenced in a third phase of our political order, which helps to account for the continued existence of the Constitution, as it does for its original drafting. The heart of the American way, politically, consists in *the habit of compromise,* and in the acceptance of the verdict of the people when that verdict has been pronounced. On this question of compromise, I cannot do better than to cite to you the language of Benjamin Franklin on that September afternoon of 1787 when the Constitutional Convention finished its momentous labors:

I confess that there are several parts of this constitution which I do not at present approve, but I am not sure I shall never approve them: For having lived long, I have experienced many instances of being obliged by better information or fuller consideration, to change opinions even on important subjects, which I once thought right, but found to be otherwise. It is therefore that the older I grow, the more apt I am to doubt my own judgment, and to pay more respect to the judgment of others. Most men indeed as well as most sects in Religion, think themselves in possession of all truth, and that wherever others differ from them it is so far error. Steele, a Protestant in a Dedication tells the Pope, that the only difference between our Churches in their opinions of the certainty of their doctrines is, the Church of Rome is infallible and the Church of England is never in the wrong. But though many private persons think almost as highly of their own infallibility as of that of their sect, few express it so naturally as a certain French lady, who in dispute with her sister, said "I don't know how it happens, Sister, but I meet with nobody but myself, that's always in the right—Il n'y a que moi qui a toujours raison."

I doubt too whether any other Convention we can obtain may be able to make a better Constitution. For when you assemble a number of men to have the advantage of their joint wisdom, you inevitably assemble with those men, all their prejudices, their passions, their errors of opinion, their local interests, and their selfish views.

This is the truly American temper. We have our political and economic fundamentalists, of course, who know, not only the past, but the future, who believe that they speak from inspiration, and are the sole repositories of truth and righteousness. But they are equally offensive to the average man, whether they speak the language of left-wing revolutionary thought, or the doctrines of standpattism which pervade a certain section of our business class. Fair play, the recognition of interests and opinions other than one's own, this is a part of the American creed. American political leaders, American leaders in the world of business or of labor, do not as a rule set out to rule or ruin. And when they do, the condemnation of American opinion is prompt and sweeping. Compromise is of the essence of our system and our thought.

The Constitution itself is full of this spirit. There was, for example, the rivalry of the small and the large states to be taken into account. It was settled on no dogmatic basis, but on the basis of mutual concession, with the House of Representatives elected on the basis of population, and the Senate chosen on the principle of the equality of the states. There were the economic interests of the North and South to be considered. The new government was given the power to regulate commerce and to levy tariffs, as a consequence, but it was forbidden to levy export taxes in the interest of the South. There was the question of the slave trade which the Lower South wished to maintain, and the North to abolish. It was permitted for twenty years. There was, most delightful of all, the question of counting slaves in fixing the population ratios for the House. They were counted as 3/5 of their number, a procedure utterly illogical and yet satisfactory at the time. It was by such means as these that a document was drawn up that has lasted one hundred and fifty years.

And what followed? The Constitution, despite the romantic notion of some Americans, was ratified after a bitter battle. If universal suffrage had then existed, the probability is that it would not have been ratified at all. If the state legislatures had not been gerrymandered against the frontier, it would probably not have been ratified. But once the battle was over, the result was accepted. There were few irreconcilables, none who turned from the battle of ballots to other weapons. And from that day to this we have, with one exception, never had to face the possibility of an appeal to force. Even when in 1876, in the most closely contested Presidential election in our history, the body selected to make the final decision decided by a strictly partisan vote, and in a fashion which was widely believed to be in contradiction of justice, the American people maintained its political *sang-froid*, and accepted the result.

Once indeed in our political history, the instinct for compromise failed to assert itself successfully. On the question of slavery, involving a change in the social system of a considerable part of the country, the American method failed. Yet it failed only after every effort at adjustment had been tried. Once in 1820, and once again in 1850, American statesmen successfully evolved formulas which it was thought would lay the slavery question to rest. Even when the question was revived, the party formed in opposition to the slave system took up a moderate and not an extreme position, declaring not for the abolition, but against the further extension of the "peculiar institution." And though the triumph of this party led to secession and civil war, it was not long before the old spirit reasserted itself. With what an extraordinary wisdom, with what practical good sense, the South recognized that the issue of secession had been decided, and took its place once more in our constitutional system. How short a time it was, after all, before the North recognized that it must leave to its defeated brethren a large measure of that local self-government for which they had contended.

Today, certainly no less, and perhaps more than at any time in our history, we need to remember our national tradition in this regard. Differences of opinion and of interest there must inevitably be amongst economic groups and amongst sections of our people. We cannot expect to exorcise them by some kind of sentimental benevolence. But even in the midst of the clash of interests, Americans will wish to maintain their sense of proportion. In the relations of capital and labor, for example, it is well for our employing class to take account of the fact that collective bargaining and trade unionism are world-wide phenomena so far as industrial states are concerned. But, on the other side of the shield, it is no less important for the forces of labor to recognize the responsibilities and the necessity of sober and practical action which go with increasing influence. And on the one side and the other, it is fundamental to disown any policy of violence. The judgment of public opinion in such a country as ours will surely be cast against those who do not recognize this fact.

In their political institutions the American people have constantly illustrated their love for the middle course. This is illustrated particularly in the nature of our political parties. They have never divided along sharp and clearly-defined lines. One party has never contained all the conservatives, and the other party all the progressives; and on the whole, despite the clamor of a certain number of our political theorists for a new political realignment, this system has worked well. It is an excellent thing that, at any given moment in the evolution of public policy, there should be room, amongst those in general and traditional sympathy with the administration in power, for more than one point of view. When Toryism has too completely dominated one of our two major party organizations, defeat has been inevitable; and it would be equally true that a party which proscribed all conservatives would find itself exposed to mistakes that might have been avoided. Not everything that is new is necessarily practicable or desirable. Nor is it a sin in America, on the other hand, to express the hope that the inequalities or inequities of American life may be in some measure ameliorated by the action of government. The American sense of balance is the best guarantee of constitutional government.

But there is a fourth element in the success with which the Americans have made their Constitution function over one hundred and fifty years. They have recognized the *necessity for constant adaptation* to new conditions. The die-hard Tories have played no dominating role in the life of the United States. There are, of course, in this country, as elsewhere, stupid people who imagine that the world is always the same, and who are not aware of the explosive force that lies in popular discontents that are not faced and to some degree remedied. There are Americans who still believe that they can command the process of social change to cease, as King Canute, with equal futility, commanded the waves to stand still. Their voices have been particularly loud in the last few years. They have even been amongst the judges of the Supreme Court of the United States. But they are not typical of the American way of thinking. Adaptation to new conditions is part of the tradition of American statesmanship.

Once indeed, American wisdom failed to operate on a great social question. The South, in the thirty years before the Civil War, confronted with a growing and world-wide feeling that Negro slavery was an anachronism, goaded to resentment by the superior attitude of Northern radicals, adopted a stand pat and die-hard position with regard to the "peculiar institution." It became the defender of a status quo that was out-moded. It came to value that status quo even more than union itself. The result we know. It stands as a solemn warning drawn from our own history to those who believe that our industrial and social order must be for all time just what it is today, who will not open their minds to the currents of contemporary opinion.

But the slave question is the only one that has involved this country in a destructive civil convulsion. The great alterations in our social body during the last hundred and fifty years have come about within the framework of the Constitution. Much of the credit for this fact must go to the founding fathers themselves.

For in drawing the great document we are examining this evening, they took care to state general principles, and to leave plenty of room for construction to adapt the Constitution to new conditions. I have pointed out, for example, that they were not, most of them, believers in universal suffrage. But they gave the right to vote in national elections to those who voted for the more numerous branch of the state legislature. As public opinion changed, therefore, it was easy for the basis of the franchise to be widened. No great political struggle was necessary. The development came about in the most natural and orderly manner.

What is still more important, they defined the powers of the national government in very general terms. The prevailing philosophy of the time (though by no means necessarily the philosophy of the fathers) was that that government is best which governs least. But it has been possible, none the less, to develop the powers of our federal mechanism to an almost unheard of extent. The Supreme Court of the United States, under the leadership of John Marshall, the partisan Federalist whom President Adams appointed to the bench in his last months of office, in the face of charges of packing from his Democratic opponents,—the Supreme Court, I say, under Marshall, applied those principles of broad construction which were the first steps in the development of federal power. There have been periods of action and reaction in this regard. But if you are inclined to feel that the checks on the growth of federal power are excessive, read Professor Corwin's "The Twilight of the Supreme Court." You will come to realize that through the power of appropriating money an immense scope can be given to federal action, that the commerce clause has been extended further and further with the process of time; and if you will supplement this interesting book with the perusal of the Court's decision in the Wagner Act, you will be aware that the process is still continuing. It is a good thing that, from time to time, there are decisions which compel reconsideration of the question as to just how far we wish to go towards what the fathers called a consolidated government; on the other hand, it is clear that in the modern world more and more questions must come within the orbit of federal, rather than state, authority; and our constitutional development takes full account of this fact. It is the great merit of our Constitution that it has adapted itself to the needs of our own time. It must continue to do so.

No doubt there will be some men who will not wish to await its orderly process, who, impatient and wrong-headed, imagine that Utopia can be brought about with the bayonet; but these men are but a handful in our national life, troublemaking at times, but not dangerous. More is to be apprehended from our national die-hards. The spirit of inflexible opposition to change is a greater menace to American institutions than radicalism. It would be particularly dangerous if it should ever come to dominate our judicial system. For, as I have pointed out, it is not easy to amend our Constitution in matters of widespread difference of opinion. We have depended, and shall continue to depend, for our adaptation to circumstances upon judicial interpretation. It is vital that our judges therefore be statesmen of wide views, not mere worshippers of the past; and it is a sign of our social and political health that we have come to recognize as never before the significance of the judiciary in our constitutional system. We have no reason to wish to alter its role, in principle; we find in it precious guarantees of liberties we hold most dear; but it ought never to become the citadel of Toryism, any more than it ought to be the mere tool of the executive. It is because the Constitution is a flexible document that it has endured one hundred and fifty years.

Will it continue to live for many generations to come? The future alone holds the answer to the question. But a qualified answer we may give. As long as the ideals which have formed America remain, the Constitution will remain. As long as liberty is cherished, as long as American majorities put away the temptations of arbitrary power, as long as the necessity of gradual progress is recognized, as long as the American instinct for compromise persists, as long as American government is penetrated, in all three of its branches, with this spirit, the Constitution will endure. And when these ideals have lost their virtue, if that day should ever come, the world will be the richer for the memory of the ordered freedom that they have sustained, and the poorer for the surrender of the institutions they have nourished.

9 ~

1918 and 1945:
Can We Learn from Experience?*

A CYNIC once remarked that the only thing to be learned from history is that men learn nothing from history. There is melancholy evidence of the partial truth of this unpleasant epigram; yet to believe it wholly would be equivalent to denying, not only for each generation, but for each individual human being, the possibility of learning from the collective life of our group, our community, or our nation. Certainly men and women of middle age today, who lived as adults through the last world war, cannot afford to believe that they have acquired no experience worth acquiring from that great conflict; nor can they do otherwise, in the midst of this Second World War, than look back and see if there is not, in the events of twenty-five years ago, some accumulation of knowledge that may be useful to them in facing the problems of our own time. The issues of the present struggle are so momentous, the problems which it raises so complex and far-reaching that we cannot hope to be free of error, and probably very substantial error, in attempting

* This article was written as the Second World War was drawing to a close.

to deal with them; but we might at least hope, and we ought at least to try, to abstain from the very same errors which bedeviled us a quarter of a century ago.

What were some of these errors? Let us examine them with a view to a little better attitude in the years just ahead.

One of the most deplorable aspects of the years 1919 and 1920 in connection with the making of peace was that the whole question of our proper role in international affairs became a matter of bitter partisan debate. It is not particularly important, a quarter of a century afterwards, to determine precisely who was to blame. There were certainly errors on both sides. It was an error, judged by its consequences, for President Wilson to appeal for a Democratic Congress in 1918; it was an error for him to ignore the Republican party as completely as he did in the make-up of his peace delegation; it was an error to challenge the Senate as sharply as he did in March, 1919; it was an error to adopt so unyielding a position on the question of reservations to the Covenant. But it was equally an error for the Republicans to appeal, as they did from an early period in the treaty debate, to the narrowest and most myopic nationalism; it was an error for the Republican leaders to permit themselves more and more to be dominated by the small irreconcilable group which was never representative of American opinion; it was an error to magnify the dangers and permit to be obscured the advantages which might flow from American participation in the work of the League.

These were the errors of the political leaders; they were as nothing compared with the error of the average American when it came to the discussion of the League Covenant itself. For the plain fact is that that part of the American people which really cared about the League was duped in 1920, in the literal sense of the word. When the Republican nominating convention met in Chicago in 1920, after a bitter battle in the platform committee, it adopted a plank which said nothing about the League and gave no reasonable ground for hope that a Republican victory would mean entrance into the League; on the contrary, it was perfectly clear that the irreconcilables in the party had had their way and that just as they had prevailed in the convention by the very intensity of their convictions so it was probable that they would prevail in the councils of their party after the election was over. The candidate nominated at Chicago made speeches on both sides of the question of the League; yet if these speeches had been viewed in the light of chronology and studied in relation to the pressures applied, it would have been evident that the drift of Senator Harding was away from any connection with Geneva.

But men find it easier to give way to partisan feeling and partisan predilection than to face the facts; and so it was that large numbers of others, and among them very eminent men, found it possible not only to vote for the Republican candidate, but even to persuade others to vote for him on the increasingly unjustified hypothesis that that candidate would bring about the ratification of the treaty and the acceptance of the Covenant. So far as clarity of purpose goes, the advantage was all with the irreconcilables; they knew what they wanted, and how to get it; whether one agrees with them or not, one can at least perceive that they moved intelligently toward their goal. This is much more than can be said for the persons who managed to persuade themselves in 1920 that the way to get us into the League of Nations was to vote for a candidate who had no interest in it, who had been nominated on a platform which avoided mention of it, and whose most ardent supporters loathed the very idea of Geneva. God forbid that we should get into such a mess again! Whether we do or not depends in part upon those who are, or who imagine themselves to be, our leaders; but the average citizen has his own responsibility, nonetheless. He ought to be able to recognize and rebuke the bitterly partisan view when he sees it; and he ought not to permit himself to be befuddled by partisan appeals to his fears, his habits, and his prejudices.

But lest the language I have just used seem too severe to some of those who joyously and confidently voted for Senator Harding in 1920, I want next to turn to some other matters, in which it appears to me that President Wilson himself was probably in error. It may well have been an error to attempt so much at Paris, to draft an international constitution in so short a period. The Covenant, in its broad lines, was drawn up in about a fortnight (though, of course, I do not mean by this to imply that it had not been the subject of much preliminary thought and that it had not been preceded by a number of tentative drafts which proved very useful to its final draftsmen). It was a rather complicated document; at any rate it was complicated from the angle of the average citizen. Its language proved to be, in some respects, unfortunately vague; in others, unhappily precise; and there was enough of it so that those who wished to object could find plenty to object to and could confuse and obfuscate the public mind with regard to its really rather simple principles. In all the debate on the League in America, almost no one thought of it in terms of the genetic, as an institution that might grow and develop and that might turn out to be useful wholly apart from the precise provisions of the Covenant; instead, a legalistic and technical debate sprang up which did little to clarify, and much to obscure, the great question of international association that was involved. Meditating on these events, one naturally asks oneself whether this time, if the idea of international association is to be sold to the American people, it may not be better to put as little down on paper as possible; in which case it will be much easier for the people to perceive the essentials of the problem of co-operation between the great states, and much more difficult for eminent lawyers, Senators, and partisans to conjure up all sorts of dangers and to raise all sorts of objections to this, that, and the other provision of a projected international instrument.

It is precisely from this point of view that I find it difficult to understand the enthusiasm of some of my friends for what is called the Culbertson Plan. Mr. Culbertson's is a highly ingenious mind; and it is sagacious and enterprising of him to bring forward a project which hits the American people where they live —in their aspirations for international peace. But if, at the present moment, it is not easy for the Russians and the Poles even to speak to one another, in the midst of a war in which their interests are very largely coincident, and if the question of a frontier between them so overmasters the emotions of both sides that they take it out in making venomous faces at one another when they ought to be fighting the common enemy, what is the chance that not only Russia and Poland, but an indefinite number of other states will sit down calmly and reasonably and agree to anything so beautifully logical as the Culbertson Plan? And assuming that, by way of a miracle, the negotiators of these various states did agree to it, is it possible to imagine a more vulnerable document than the one which would result? There would be objections here and objections there; and trying to put it all down on paper at once would immensely increase the risk of ending with no agreement at all. If, twenty-five years ago, our Senators found objectionable the Covenant of the League, if, as late as 1935, they boggled at such an innocent document as the World Court protocol, what would be the uproar in the Upper House of our Congress at such an international instrument as Mr. Culbertson proposes? Is it not better, is it not indeed one of the lessons of 1918, that this time we must see that international co-operation grows, rather than that it is made; and must we not put our reliance upon the growth of the spirit of common action, upon the *habit* of international deliberation, rather than upon some more specific international arrangement for the maintenance of peace?

But this by no means exhausts the mistakes of 1918. There was a fundamental defect in the Covenant, in my judgment, which is only too characteristic of the thinking of the American people as a whole. On the question of international peace, we have always desired to have our cake and eat it, too. This is certainly normal enough in human affairs; but it has so far proven to be impossible. Translated into more concrete terms in relation to the problem of international peace, it means that the American people have been ardent friends of concord but have never wished to make the necessary sacrifice to maintain it. In the last analysis, peace depends upon force, upon force directed against the potential or actual breaker of the public tranquillity. Now the Covenant failed to recognize this fact. It did, indeed, provide for certain penalties to be imposed upon a law-breaking state; but whereas it was reasonably precise with regard to these penalties so far as economic pressure was concerned, it was decidedly vague when it came to an actual use of physical power. It spoke confidently on the economic side of the "severance of all trade or financial relations, the prohibition of all intercourse between their nationals and the nationals of the Covenant-breaking state, and the prevention of all financial, commercial, or personal intercourse between the nationals of the Covenant-breaking state and the nationals of any other state, whether a member of the League or not." But when it came to the application of armed might, there was an anemic sentence which declared it to be "the duty of the Council in such case to recommend to the several governments concerned what effective military, naval or air force the Members of the League shall severally contribute." There was no pledge of any kind, no promise, merely a suggestion.

Now human experience indicates that the application of economic pressure as a substitute for war is not a very satisfactory answer to the problem of peace; and the plain fact of the matter is that on the only occasion when it was tried, in the truly international sense of the term—that is, in the case of the Italian conquest of Ethiopia—it broke down, and broke down precisely because the powers which attempted to apply it were afraid to carry it through lest they might be involved in war. The limited examples of the use of economic pressures by a single state offer no great encouragement to the hope that a boycott is a substitute for a bombardment. Jefferson's embargo certainly did not prevent war; and when in July of 1941 President Roosevelt severed commercial relations with Japan, it was the prelude, not to understanding, but to Pearl Harbor. All in all, then, we had better learn that we are not likely to win peace easily in this world; and the notion that by the application of economic pressure a great and powerful state can be brought to terms is a notion of which we should disabuse ourselves, a notion almost as naïve as that later one which was fathered by Secretary Kellogg and which assumed (with a romantic innocence that could hardly have been discovered outside of the United States) that if everyone only promised not to go to war, there would not be any war. The peace of the world in the future, if it can be preserved at all, may be preserved first by understanding among the great victor states and second by common action of these states against lawbreakers; but it will never be preserved without sacrifice. Our lesson on this point ought not to be confined to 1919 and 1920; for it is fairly clear that if the menace of National Socialism in Germany had been resolutely and courageously dealt with in 1935 or 1936 the world might not have been plunged into catastrophe in 1939. It was squeamishness about the use of force when force was the only practicable weapon that permitted the growth of German armament and the monstrous power of Adolf Hitler; and unless Americans are prepared in case of need to help keep the peace by force of arms, they may be pretty sure that it will again be broken.

But let us look further at some of our misconceptions of 1919 and 1920. Many of them lay pretty deep in our thinking—even deeper, perhaps, than any of our errors connected with the Covenant of the League of Nations. For one thing, we were, most of us, extremely naïve about the task that we had set ourselves. During the years of the war there was, in much public discussion and in much of our individual thinking, a kind of apocalyptic feeling about the struggle in which we were engaged. We fondly believed that when we had done with Germany, a new order of peace and justice would automatically dawn. We expected, and were perhaps in some measure led to expect, that the millennium would be near at hand when the German armies had laid down their arms. But when the armistice was signed and the cannon had ceased their thunder, the actual picture was far otherwise. We discovered that the best of all possible worlds was not just around the corner. We discovered that it had to be won, instead of its arriving automatically. We were a little tired; we soon became more than a little disillusioned. The trouble with us was that we had pitched our hopes too high; we had formed no sufficient conception of the magnitude of our task. The same thing, of course, can happen to us again. Perhaps it will. But surely, after the experience of the last quarter of a century, there can be no excuse for any man's thinking that the end of the war is the end of our problems. It is one of the encouraging things about the attitude of our young people toward this war that, so far as I can discover from the rostrum and the armchair of a college teacher, they do not expect to have solved everything in the world by beating Hitler and Hirohito. They know that this is only a part of the task of their generation and that, in one way of looking at it, is the easiest part. They are, I think, bracing themselves for a longer and a more arduous and a more ambitious enterprise; and we of an elder generation, who have a wider experience and, I hope, a no less firm resolution, ought not to complain if they do not accept the slogans and shibboleths with regard to the present war in the spirit in which some of us accepted the slogans and shibboleths of 1918. For there is no gospel more perilous than the gospel that James Russell Lowell expressed nearly a hundred years ago in the famous lines,

> Once to every man and nation comes the moment to decide,
> In the strife 'twixt truth and falsehood for the good or evil side.

The struggle for international decency, for an international order, for a better integrated and articulated world society, is not a matter of the next few years alone; and we may do extremely well in the war without coming anywhere near attaining any of the larger goals we have in mind. We must steel ourselves now and here against the cynicism which often follows on victory. It is entirely possible that in the middle nineteen fifties, shall we say, there will arise historical writers who will again demonstrate, as some of them demonstrated in the middle thirties, that, after all, our intervention in the present war was a monumental mistake; that a wise policy would have dictated our abstention from the conflict; and that the very imperfect world that will undoubtedly exist at that time is proof how very wrong we were in 1942 and 1943. These writers may forget that the choice facing the American people in these tragic days of ours was, like most human choices, a choice between evils; they may fail to understand because it will no longer be present to their imaginations and no longer an ingrained part of their most intimate experience what a world dominated by the spirit of National Socialism would have been like; they may forget that the liberties of many a proud and hopeful people, great and small, hung upon the issue of the conflict; and they may preach again the same doctrine of indifference which had so much to do with landing us where we are today. Let us resolve to have none of this spirit. Let us not expect to solve everything through victory. Let us hope for no immediate or even remote millennium. Let us take the longer view, which is that when we have won there will still be much to win. The more clearly we perceive this fact and the more ready we are to accept it, the more effective will be our role in the postwar world.

There is another point worth reflecting upon that is closely connected with this one. The adjustments that follow this war will inevitably involve far-reaching political compromises. They will involve give-and-take. They will mean that the postwar world is not, in every respect, and not in some most important respects, fashioned after the world of our dreams. Did we understand this in 1918? I think not. When the Peace Conference met in Paris, we were surprised and pained at the recrudescence of national selfishness, so surprised, in fact, that it hardly occurred to us that we were somewhat selfish ourselves; and we treated every compromise which poor Wilson made as if it almost inevitably involved some kind of compact with the devil. I well remember the distinguished editor of one of our oldest and most respected periodicals calling on this occasion for territorial settlements based on "absolute justice." This editor, I fear, was no more naïve than many of his readers. He was ready to believe —God save the mark!—that the complex questions of European boundaries could be solved in such a fashion as to correspond to some ideal norm. He could hardly have studied any of these questions very profoundly; but in that respect he was no worse off than most of his editorial colleagues.

Yet the spirit which he demonstrated then is alarmingly present now. There seems, indeed, in current public discussion to be almost as much attention paid to how we should correct the sins and weaknesses of our allies as to what we should do to the Germans. There are many excellent people in the United States who are exceedingly concerned about India and about what they call "imperialism" and who have not reflected very deeply on either. After all, the Indian question is one of the most complex in the world today; and it is not to be solved by some easy formula like "independence." There is the very grave question of the defense of India against external aggression; there is the apparently irreconcilable difference of views between the Moslems and the Hindus; there is the difficult problem of the native states; and even if we had the answer to all these questions, which we have not, it would still be doubtful whether it should be our prime concern at the end of the war to tell the British what to do about a matter with which they have had much more experience than we have had and in which they have been moving, as we would wish to see them move, in the direction of larger freedom for the people under their tutelage.

It is the same way when we talk of "imperialism." The most stimulating single comment which I ever remember having read on this vague but exciting subject came from Bertrand Russell's *Proposed Roads to Freedom*. Bertrand Russell has rarely been described as a conservative; yet he had perceived one fact that most "liberals" had not, and this was that sometimes the rule of a native oligarchy, in a backward state or country, is infinitely more disastrous to the well-being of the masses of that state or country than a more far-seeing outside tutelage might be. It may be, of course, that we shall help to find a better way of dealing with these questions than the way that has been found in the past; but if we start being absolute about the matter and insist upon trying to impose our views on others, we are in for disillusionment.

Or take, for example, the question of our future relations with Soviet Russia. The government at Moscow has stated rather clearly by this time that it proposes to fix its boundaries at the end of the war so as to include the territories acquired in 1939 and 1940, with a bit of Eastern Galicia and a bit of Moldavia thrown in. This means that the populations of the Baltic provinces, the Esths and the Letts and the Lithuanians, will be once again under Russian rule as they were before 1914. It means that the Poles will have to give up territories which they occupied (and to which their claim is highly disputable) at the end of the last world war. It means that Bessarabia, which is another difficult nut to crack for the ethnographer, will not belong to Rumania, as it did for a twenty-year period. Now what is going to be our attitude with regard to all this? Are we going to make ourselves the champions of all the littler nations that are here concerned? If so, to what extent? and by what means? Or are we going to recognize that the disposition of territory in Eastern Europe is primarily a Russian affair and that we may not be able to satisfy all our predilections for the weak or solve all these problems on our own preconceived basis of right and justice?

Does this sound like cynicism? I hardly think so. To begin with, these territorial disputes are not simple ones, and there is a case for the Russians in each individual instance. But even if we were not able to convince ourselves that this was so, an important fact would remain. We do not refuse to get along in this world with everyone whose moral standards are not so altitudinous as our own. We give and we take. The world would be a madhouse, if we did not. We must learn to do the same in international affairs. There are invasions of interests not to be tolerated. There may be affronts to our national ideals not to be borne. But we cannot act as if we were a combination of Sir Galahad and Socrates. We must be prepared to accept the fact that the world is not always a noble place, and we must put away the temptation, if we do not get our way about everything, to take our dolls and go home, as we did for a time in the years after Versailles.

This point is so important that I must press it home in one more paragraph. Coalitions are subject to an easy decay. This decay is hastened by the exaggeration of differing views on matters which may be of great importance to one member of the coalition and of much less importance to another. On the other hand, the way to hold a coalition together is to seek for that balance of interests, that compromise of opinion, which gives to each of the states concerned recognition of its essential claims. It is easy to pull apart; it is hard to work together. The essence of working together is political compromise. Compromise is impossible if every question becomes a moral issue. We must be prepared this time not to be shocked into isolation by the discovery that our quondam allies do not always agree with us and that not every question will be settled as we think it ought to be settled.

All this that I have written concerns general attitudes rather than specific problems. I am not apologetic about this. The essence of our postwar policy will be a matter of attitude. But lest I fall under the condemnation to which academicians are so often exposed (and to which they are so inordinately sensitive), the charge that they are impractical, I propose to be a little more concrete on some matters connected with 1918. At the signing of the armistice we had driven the Kaiser from power. We had brought about a revolution in Germany. We fondly imagined that because the Germans had set up a regime which was democratic in form we had dealt with our central problem. We were disposed to approve the Weimar Constitution and to forget to look beneath the surface. Now it is an open question today whether such a parliamentary regime as was set up in Germany with the ministry of Max of Baden early in October, 1918, would not have met the situation about as satisfactorily as did the more drastic changes of the months that followed. At any rate, one thing is certain. The precautions which we took in the political sphere we failed to take in the military sphere. The power of the German Army was not destroyed. On the surface the picture was a fair one, but a deeper view, and a study of postwar Germany, reveals that the influence of the military caste was hardly less than it had been before. Whoever reads Hans Fried's *The Guilt of the German Army* will find in that remarkable work all too convincing evidence of the manner in which the gentlemen of the General Staff worked from the beginning to rebuild the machine of war; of the manner in which they played a role in politics, a role more and more far-reaching;

of the part that they took in the triumphs of National Socialism; of the eagerness with which they awaited the opportunity once more to vindicate their talents and their claims to mastery.

It goes without saying that at the end of this war we shall wish to see an end of the present leaders of Germany; but we must not stop there, and we must not be too preoccupied with questions of political structure, in the narrow sense of the term. On the contrary, we must be very sure that the power of the General Staff and of the army is broken, and broken beyond repair for a long time to come. Walter Lippmann, always one of the most imaginative of American publicists, may have pointed out the way to do this in his proposals for an international control of German industry, especially such industry as is connected with armament; but whether or not his is the precise formula, we must certainly see to it that we do a better job this next time than we did the last. We must probably demonstrate our victory more fully than we did in 1918; we must not allow it to be said, as Hitler and his satellites are never tired of saying, that Germany was duped, but not defeated; if we have to march down the Linden to make it clear that we have won, we must march down the Linden; we cannot afford to take any half measures. On the other hand, while we will, on the basis of experience, have to be more rigorous so far as purely military matters are concerned, we shall have to be more flexible and more intelligent when it comes to such questions as war debts and reparations. The crude expression of a very limited truth that formed itself on the lips of Calvin Coolidge, "They hired the money, didn't they?" hardly seems adequate today. Twenty-five years ago we insisted that in the common cause our allies not only must make the major sacrifice in lives, but also must not expect any substantial assistance from us in money not to be repaid. Of course with time we modified our original stand, so that it is possible to say, at any rate from the view of semantics, that we canceled a part of the war debt. But that we immensely complicated the problems of the twenties by the attitude that we assumed can hardly be doubted. Our attitude with regard to the war debts naturally increased the pressure which our debtors exerted on Germany for the payment of reparations; this pressure resulted in the invasion of the Ruhr, that ill-timed adventure of 1923 which helped to wreck the Germany economy, discredit the German republican government, and so prepare the way for the catastrophic career of National Socialism.

Today, there is some reason to think that we may be wiser. The lease-lend policy is, in germ, a very different policy from that of twenty-five years ago; and there are many more Americans now than there were then who are wise enough to reflect that the dollars that we are pouring across the Atlantic and the Pacific are the means of saving the lives of many thousands of American boys, that they cannot possibly balance the sacrifices which the Russians and the British are making in the common enterprise of beating Hitler, and that we cannot deal effectively with the problems of the postwar era if our principal concern is merely to get our money back.

There is one other very concrete and practical lesson which we may conceivably have learned from the errors we committed a quarter of a century ago. The currents of economic nationalism that began to flow so strongly at the end of the war had at least one of their sources in the United States. We came out of the war a creditor nation; we came out of the war with a very definite interest in the prosperity and the restoration of Europe. Yet what was one of our first moves in the economic sphere? It was, by a high tariff, in the Fordney-McCumber bill, to impede international trade; and the combination of high tariff with insistence on the repayment of the war debts constitutes, as many persons see clearly today, one of the most grotesque chapters in the history of our international relations. By our own action we stimulated similar action elsewhere; and the whole vast network of obstacles to the restoration of international trade owed a great deal of its growth to the attitude of the United States.

Behind all this was a fallacy which still appears and which may distort our views of policy after the present war as it did after the last one. It is hard to realize that we have an interest in the restoration of prosperity outside the United States; the parochial and nationalistic point of view is the very opposite; yet the experience of our time seems to show quite clearly that a breakdown in the economic system of one country communicates itself to others and that the restoration and expansion of the economic system of one country also communicates itself to others. Some limited minds today are concerned about the future because they think we will give away a lot more to others than we ought to give away; they declaim against "a quart of milk for every Hottentot" (whoever mentioned the Hottentot, by the way?), and they are nervous lest the well-known altruism of the American people express itself in a disastrous generosity. I must confess that, in general, I perceive very little reason for this apprehension in the past experience of the United States. The difficulty we experienced in the period after the last world war was certainly not that we were overwhelmingly concerned with the welfare of others: on the masthead of a well-known newspaper immediately after the armistice appeared the well-remembered slogan, "Get the boys home toot sweet"; much of the argument against the League was nothing but a bare-faced appeal to national selfishness; our tariff policy was framed in the same spirit; our attitude toward the war debts was of a piece with all this; and nothing that we said or did suggested an extravagant and improvident benevolence.

No, that is not what we have to worry about after the war. The danger lies in another direction. It lies in the fact that we may not recognize that it is to our *interest*, looking at the matter broadly, that the world recover from its spree and that we help it to recover; it lies in the fact that we may foolishly believe that we can once more live to ourselves alone and remain unaffected by the political and social convulsions outside our borders that would almost certainly follow on such a course. This, at any rate, is the lesson of experience; and it is experience that ·I am discussing in these fugitive observations.

Now it is admitted that, if we are to be benevolent, we ought to be intelligently benevolent. We were certainly not that in the twenties. The loans that poured out of the United States into the treasuries of Latin-American and European states were often justified on the broad grounds that I have just stated; but they were not geared to other parts of our economic policy, and they were not part of any general, comprehensive, or intelligent scheme for world restoration. They were futile and unwise: (1) because we had not done our part in the erection of a system of international security, (2) because we had not done our part in the freeing of international trade, and (3) because we had no coherent idea of what we intended to do with them. There is a chance that we will do better this time, as indeed we are doing better, in my judgment, through the Export-Import Bank; but we will do better only if we heed the reason of experience and relate our lending program to the other dominating realities of international intercourse.

And now there is a final point, and it does not have to do, I confess, so much with 1919 as with 1929. It may be that a quarter of a century ago we could have committed some of our errors with impunity if we had really known how to run our economic machine and to keep it running with some approach to success. The men from whom we took our counsel in the twenties understood all the problems but the biggest ones; they were wise in many respects but without wisdom where it mattered most. For, in many instances, they did not know how, they hardly tried, to take precautions against the world depression. And it was the depression that mattered, and mattered terrifically. The late twenties were a period of optimism in international relations as they were a period of optimism in finance; and it was the crash of 1929 that changed the international as it changed the national scene. Out of the depression came Japanese militarism and German National Socialism; on the depression these obscene movements throve; and the restoration of prosperity through armament was their prescription for ending their peoples' troubles. It may well be, as we contemplate the future, that we will discover that the problems of a stabler international order are closely associated with the problems of a stable internal order and that we shall have to grapple effectively with some of our most important domestic problems if we intend to grapple effectively with the foreign ones. Such, at least, would seem to be the lesson of the past; such would seem to be the teaching of experience.

Is it too much to hope that this and the other lessons I have mentioned will be learned? Is it too much to hope that man can deal with the society of which he is a part in a scientific spirit, analyzing his errors and seeking to avoid them? It may be so. But the issue is a transcendent one. And it is so especially for the generation that saw the last war. They are the first generation in nearly two hundred years which, at fifty, has witnessed two cyclonic struggles. They have a chance at helping to rebuild what they have done their part to destroy. Will they be equal to the challenge?

10 ~

Diplomacy and
Popular Government*

I MUST first take this occasion to acknowledge the honor done me in electing me as a corresponding member of this venerable and distinguished society. I should in any case be grateful; but as a Massachusetts man, born in Boston, and one who never penetrated beyond the Hudson until I had been thoroughly educated at Harvard, I feel particularly happy at this recognition. My long period of teaching in what some Massachusetts people, including my own grandmother, used to describe as "the West" or "out there" (I am speaking of Rochester, New York) has not dimmed my loyalty to my native state and city, and it is a pleasure to come back here under these happy circumstances. I have chosen for my topic "Diplomacy and Popular Government," a title perhaps more ambitious than the exposition which I shall attach to it. There has been much writing on American foreign policy, but it has to a large extent been purely narrative. What I want to do is to treat a small segment of the subject philosophically and to raise some questions as to how a demo-

* Paper delivered before the Massachusetts Historical Society, November, 1952, and printed by permission.

cratic state such as ours, or perhaps I should say how our democratic state, actually conducts itself in the field of diplomacy.

First of all, I want to make the point, the central point, that our diplomacy has for the most part proceeded from the people, and in analyzing it we may, and should, start from this assumption. It is, however, an assumption that should be supported by evidence. The first thing to stress is that America has until recently never had a professional diplomatic class and that this class, when it came into being, was much less influential than in most European countries. The State Department was a very small organization during the greater part of the nineteenth century. Though there were occasional long-time workers in it like William Hunter and Alvey A. Adee, it is difficult to trace the influence of these men on policy. The Secretaries themselves made the decisions, or, if they did not make them, the Presidents whom they served made them. As for our representatives abroad, they were usually carefully controlled by their instructions and rarely exercised a decisive influence on policy. In the twentieth century the progress toward professionalization has been more rapid. But my investigation of the secretariats of Charles E. Hughes, of Frank B. Kellogg, and of Henry L. Stimson convinces me that these men, and occasionally some one or two individuals close to them, were the true makers of policy. Certainly instances can be cited of policies evolved in the department and coming from below. But their acceptance or rejection would naturally have to depend upon the Secretary himself.

The next point to be made is that the Secretaries, and the Presidents whom they served, were almost invariably men with political rather than diplomatic training. John Hay was the only genuine professional in the entire list, though some others, like James Monroe and John Quincy Adams, had had professional experience when they assumed the office. As a result of their origins these men were more likely to think in terms of interpreting the public will than did the aloof figures who often operated in European chancelleries. Moreover, they were controlled by a President who was, inevitably, much concerned with the political effects of his action. Woodrow Wilson once said that the essence of the Presidential task was interpretation. The statement may be exaggerated. But there is certainly much force in it, nonetheless. Inevitably our foreign policy has been shaped by opinion, by democratic opinion, to a degree that is not true abroad.

In a sense, it has had to be. For though there have been periods when the people of the United States have been indifferent to foreign affairs, they have rarely been indifferent when great interests were at stake or great emotions aroused. One of the most vigorous debates in the history of the early years of the republic came over the Jay treaty. The foreign policy of the Jefferson and Madison administrations was exhaustively discussed in Congress. The annexation of Texas was a great political issue. The list might be extended indefinitely. No informed student of American foreign policy will make the declaration —often heard—that Americans have only recently taken foreign policy seriously.

Furthermore, they have always insisted upon the right to know. Treaties, it is true, were considered in secret in the nineteenth and thus far in the twentieth century. But from the indiscretions of two Senators with regard to the Jay treaty of 1794 down to our time, the secrecy has been most imperfect. Even in relatively early days the contents of treaties were often published in *Niles' Register* before the treaties themselves had been ratified.

Very early in its history the American government published a great deal of its diplomatic correspondence. Much of this is hidden from the gaze of the layman in the Congressional *Documents*, but it is there nonetheless. And public declarations of policy go back as far as the Farewell Address and the Monroe Doctrine. Thus the American people have always had an important part in the formation of their foreign policy. What I wish to do here is to show how that influence is exerted in practice.

I shall take two particular lines of development as the basis of my examination—the Monroe Doctrine and the development of the idea of collective security—and try to relate them to certain broad generalizations with regard to the way in which the American people have expressed themselves in the field of international relations. I hope these generalizations may have a wider suggestiveness than the subjects with which they deal, important as these subjects are.

In the first place, let it be said that there seems to be, under popular government, a strong tendency to state the objective of foreign policy in terms of general principle. It is not strange that this is so; for, if the people are regarded as the ultimate tribunal in the determination of our diplomatic action, the case for this or that choice must be stated in broad terms. The mass of men cannot be expected to be expert in the field of international affairs; they have neither the time nor the inclination to study a problem as a scholar would study it; they must in the nature of the case pronounce their judgment on wider grounds. The question that flows from this fact is whether in the main an excessive ideological preoccupation characterizes a democratic foreign policy, whether the national interest is sacrificed to shibboleths or distorted by excessive concern with what—when we approve of them—we describe as principles. It is a question of great moment at the present time, when the United States is ranged against another great power, sharply differing from it in its view of the future, in its economic and political conceptions, and in its scale of human values. But since I am, as a historian, more concerned with the past than with the future, I shall turn my attention not to prophecy but to some analysis of the past in terms of the two great doctrines that I propose to examine.

Let us take a long look at the Monroe Doctrine and at its development, not from the annalistic point of view but with the purpose of discovering just how the American mind operates in the field of foreign policy.

There is an old maxim that all generalizations are false, including this one; and this maxim ought to make us think twice about the Monroe Doctrine. The Doctrine was promulgated by James Monroe in 1823. It declared that the extension of the political system of Europe (a system which the President did not trouble to define and which was not the same in all of the Continental states) would be dangerous to our peace and safety, and it stated furthermore that "our southern brethren" (that is, the newly independent republics of Spanish America) could hardly be expected to adopt it of their own accord.

In the context of the year 1823 a skeptical mind might well doubt whether European intervention in South America was necessarily and inevitably dangerous to the peace and safety of the United States. One can understand easily enough how the occupation of the island of Cuba by a strong power, and particularly by a power with antislavery leanings, such as Great Britain, might seem a threat to the Americans; but beyond this it is not easy to go. The time was to come when the idea of an interoceanic canal gained increasing currency and when communication between our Far West and the East by the way of Panama or Nicaragua would be important and the control of any means of transportation across Central America by a foreign power would be a matter of grave concern to this country; but in 1823 that time was about a quarter of a century distant. Still more, it is hard to see how, let us say, a monarchy in the Argentine (there were schemes for such a monarchy) would have directly menaced the United States or why a nondemocratic government, let us say in Chile or in Paraguay, would alter in any fundamental respect the position of the United States in this hemisphere. If one considers the Monroe pronouncement as an abstract proposition, therefore, it was by no means beyond all question; nor is it any answer to this criticism to say that Monroe's vision extended to a remote and very different future; we know as a matter of fact that it did not.

Nor was Monroe correct in his view of our southern brethren. That atrabilious but able and devoted statesman, John Quincy Adams, had some years before raised in his diary the question whether the Latin-American revolutions really resembled that one of 1776, whether their objectives were the same, whether their future development would be along similar lines, whether, in short, there was a clear ideological affinity between the former dominions of Spain and the United States of America. And, though Adams accepted and played a part in the formulation of the message of 1823, though indeed he endorsed its general principles, he was clearly less influenced by this notion of political affinity than was his chief. Today, looking back over a hundred and twenty-five years and more, we can see that democratic government has by no means run as smooth a course in the lands to the south as it has in the United States, that there are today only a few Latin-American states which have maintained the democratic way of life unflinchingly, and that Monroe's generalizations as to the New World were distinctly vulnerable.

Do not think that I am about to show that the fifth President's pronouncement was all nonsense; not at all. On the contrary, I am concerned to indicate how it was shaped by the American people and their governors; how it became increasingly useful in practice; how it was adapted to circumstances and modified by occasion; how this convenient general tenet (of doubtful philosophical accuracy) became a most useful instrument for the conduct of policy.

In examining the history of the Doctrine from this point of view, we must, however, begin by pointing out that it was a long time before the words of Monroe took root. They were designed for a specific occasion, and the idea that they embodied was by no means accepted in its fullest implications as soon as uttered. On the contrary, before long a partisan debate broke out which, while it did not center precisely on the Doctrine, illustrates the practical tendency of the American mind and the popular reaction against dogma which acts as a foil to the popular attachment to dogma. In the administration of John Quincy Adams an attempt was made to hold a Congress of the American states at Panama, and to that Congress the Adams administration wished to send representatives. The President had no extended purposes in view; he did not desire to turn the message of his predecessor into some project of close association with the republics of the South; his purpose was much more limited. Yet a great hue and cry was raised by his opponents; and not a little of this hue and cry was directed at depreciating and questioning the declaration of December 2, 1823. The motives behind this criticism were most obviously partisan; the anti-Adams men were already maneuvering with the election of 1828 in mind. It is worthwhile pondering the fact that what was to become a cherished national dogma was thus subjected to factious criticism only a few years after it had been enunciated.

Partisanship runs through a great deal of the foreign policy of this democratic nation. It is a luxury we cannot indulge in, in my judgment, in the times in which we live. But it is fair to say of the foes of the Adams administration that, from their point of view, they were engaged in innocent play; no fundamental national interest was involved; indeed the Panama Congress itself was to turn out a fiasco. They even had hold of a bit of truth in fact, for it must always be a question how far a general principle is to be accepted and how far it is qualified by expediency. This is one of the gravest problems of statecraft for all but the convinced doctrinaire. Men often do good from questionable motives; in challenging the validity of Monroe's pronouncement the men of 1826 were posing a problem of attention.

It is also worthy of attention that the Monroe Doctrine, when next invoked in a big way, showed the influence of the Panama debates of 1826. James K. Polk, who re-enunciated it in 1845, had been in Congress at that time. In 1845 he declared that it applied with greatly increased force to the North American continent. This might well seem to the historian one way of attenuating Monroe's principles, and this judgment seems all the sounder since Polk remained relatively indifferent to Anglo-French action against the Argentine in 1846. Nonetheless, despite the President's caution, the Whigs pooh-poohed the new declaration, and Calhoun, often out of step with the Democrats, made a great speech in 1848 in which he clearly stated that it was not wise to tie oneself to a shibboleth and that the nation must be free to act as it deemed wise in every emergency, unbound by any formula.

All this is to me very interesting indeed; what it illustrates is that, despite the tendency under popular government to tie oneself to generalities, there is a converse impulse which ends to loosen the tie. The American politicians who in 1846 and 1848 challenged President Polk were expressing, as the President himself was, something significant in the public opinion of the time.

It is no coincidence that the wider acceptance of Monroe's declaration coincided with genuine national interests. The question of an interoceanic canal began to assume practical importance in the late forties; and one aspect of this question was the increase of British influence in Central America. The Whigs, in power from 1849 to 1853, sought to deal with the problem on purely practical grounds; they sought to arrange a practicable settlement of the problems raised by the British possession of Belize, by British interest in the Bay Islands and in the Gulf of Fonseca. But the Clayton-Bulwer treaty, by which they sought to make a reasonable settlement of the matter at issue, was not long acceptable. Suspicion of British purposes persisted; the Democrats invoked the Monroe Doctrine, and by 1857 both parties were giving it a qualified adhesion. The popular instinct which made this adhesion possible was, it seems to me, sound; and the invocation of a general principle was a most effective way of promoting a national interest.

The Monroe Doctrine, however, attained a true national status in the case of the French invasion of Mexico and the setting up of the puppet monarchy of the Austrian Archduke Maximilian. It can hardly be denied that here was a genuine threat, both on ideological and realistic grounds, to the position of the United States. As soon as the hands of the American government were freed by the victory of the North in the Civil War, a widespread demand arose for action against the French; there was now no question of party; Democrats as well as Republicans joined in the clamor. Fortunately, the situation did not suggest the necessity of war; the Mexicans themselves were taking good care of their own problem by a heroic resistance to the troops of Louis Napoleon, and the embarrassments of the Emperor at home provided an added motive for the abandonment of what was, perhaps, from the beginning a quixotic enterprise. The problem was brilliantly handled by Secretary of State Seward, who at once stepped up his tone with the French government, while carefully abstaining from any rash or immediate provocation. In his various diplomatic steps, the Secretary of State was faithfully interpreting American public opinion; his tone and his method are classical examples of the operation of diplomacy at its best under popular government.

The invoking of the Monroe Doctrine to justify exclusive American control of an interoceanic canal (which meant, of course, the abandonment of the arrangements of the Clayton-Bulwer treaty) it is not necessary to discuss in detail, but a great deal of light is thrown on diplomacy and popular government by the famous Venezuela episode of 1895. In that year, after an attempt to deal with the matter by direct negotiation, Grover Cleveland aroused the nation by demanding of Great Britain that it arbitrate a boundary dispute involving territory between British Guiana and Venezuela and even went so far as to threaten to appoint a commission to draw the line itself if the British government refused to yield to the American demand. For a time there was a tremendous expression of popular feeling, but the matter was finally settled by an arbitration agreement. What is hardly realized, however, is that in that arbitral agreement the case was already substantially prejudged in favor of the British claims; the Cleveland administration, by accepting the principle that fifty years of occupation would be regarded as giving title by prescription, was in effect conceding a very large part of the British claim. Despite the momentary popularity gained by the twisting of the British lion's tail, President Cleveland soon realized that he had gone too far; and it was presently made clear that a considerable segment of American public opinion was by no means disposed to support the President if the outcome of that support were to be a war with Great Britain. This segment of opinion was, it seems to me, expressing a sound point of view, for it was, in my judgment, a matter of no great importance to the United States who controlled large areas of almost uninhabited territory in the hinterland of Spanish America. True, the mouth of the Orinoco was also involved, but there seems no reason to believe that the British had the slightest idea of seeking control of that river or of erecting a naval station upon it. Cleveland had gone much too far; and it is a measure of the good sense of many Americans, and also of his own, that before long he realized that fact.

But there is another point of major importance involved in the Venezuela episode of 1895. It is frequently contended that a popular government cannot retreat from a position that it has once assumed and that the tendency of open diplomacy of the

Cleveland type must be to create embroilments which a more discreet handling of the issue might easily avoid. This criticism, if sound, would be no less than damning; but it does not happen to be sound. It was clearly demonstrated in this case that a way out of an embarrassing situation can be found, at least on occasion, and that the American people have a fund of good sense on which it is often possible to rely. The retreat that the President executed was not a secret maneuver; the basis of the understanding with Great Britain was embodied in a public document; and yet American opinion accepted that understanding with little difficulty. Nor is this the only case (the matter might be embroidered at length) in which high-sounding declarations have been qualified in practice; everyone remembers that the election of 1844 was fought on the cry of "fifty-four forty or fight" but that after the election President Polk compromised with the British government on the line of the forty-ninth parallel as the northern boundary of Oregon. We shall have more to say of this matter.

In the first decade of the twentieth century there took place a new extension of the Monroe Doctrine. This is the famous Roosevelt corollary. By this corollary the President laid down the principle that if a state of the New World flagrantly misconducted itself or if in a given case frequent revolution resulted in a "general loosening of the ties of civilized society" the United States, in order to prevent intervention by others, might itself be obliged to intervene. In pursuance of this doctrine, there took place, first, a customs receivership over the Dominican Republic and later actual armed intervention in the affairs of the states of the Caribbean, in Nicaragua, in Haiti, and in the Dominican Republic itself. The climax of this policy, it ought to be observed, and two out of three of the interventions under it took place in the years of world war, when American public opinion was much occupied with other matters. None of the actual occupations of foreign territory came about as a result of any popular demand; all illustrate the manner in which policy may, in some instances, be framed by professionals rather than by the pressures of mass opinion.

I do not wish to make myself the defender of the Roosevelt corollary; though it is perhaps fair to say that in the conditions of the first decades of the twentieth century it was necessary to watch with special vigilance an area which controlled the passages to the Panama Canal, especially in view of the growing naval power of Germany. The point I wish to make has nothing to do with this; personally, I believe it unlikely that there was any real danger from the First Reich at that time. The point to be stressed is that this policy, largely discredited, was abandoned after the war; and the abandonment was in part due to the criticism which came from many quarters with regard to it. It had never been generally popular; the Democrats had criticized it from the beginning; when President Wilson applied it, it came under fire from the Republicans, among others from that great idealist Warren Harding; and when the Coolidge administration, having gotten out of Nicaragua, marched in again, it was the Democrats who once more took up the role of the critic. Now partisan criticism may, it is true, come from ulterior motives; but it is almost always a sure sign that there is some discontent to be exploited, some prejudice to be ministered to. I think it fair, therefore, to reiterate my observation of a moment ago that the policy of intervention in the Caribbean was never a popular policy, was never wholeheartedly accepted by the American people.

In the twenties and the thirties there took place a remarkable alteration in the attitude of the United States toward the countries to the south. There is no doubt that, for once, that change owed much to one of our professional diplomats; the name of Sumner Welles will always be associated with the good-neighbor policy. But in the twenties Welles was in the State Department for only a half of the decade; and there are clear evidences that the attitude which he embodied had deeper roots than lie in the personality of a single individual. In the retreat from the Roosevelt corollary he had the support of Secretary Hughes, and in the years 1921 to 1925 the United States withdrew from both Nicaragua and the Dominican Republic, though from the first, as I have said, only temporarily. But the Coolidge administration, under a very uninspired Secretary of State, moved in the same direction; the second intervention in Nicaragua was a brief one; and by 1928 the famous Clark memorandum, not yet published, dissociated the Monroe Doctrine from the maxims of the ebullient Theodore. This retreat took a more striking form in the thirties: at the conference of Montevideo in 1933, the United States pledged itself against intervention in the affairs of the states of the New World, and this pledge (a bit qualified in 1933) was reiterated in 1936 at the conference of Buenos Aires. Furthermore, and the fact is indeed an extraordinary one, the protocols of Montevideo and Buenos Aires were ratified unanimously by the Senate of the United States, a striking evidence of the degree to which they were supported by American sentiment and of the inexpediency of any partisan opposition to them. In these same years of the early thirties the Clark memorandum was published to the world; the Platt amendment, which conferred on the United States a right of intervention in Cuba, was abrogated; the marines were withdrawn from Haiti; and by 1934 not a single American soldier remained on the soil of any of the independent states of Latin America.

All this was sound policy, as it seems to me; the reasons for the Roosevelt corollary, its partial justification on strategic grounds, had disappeared with the defeat of imperial Germany; and for a time the New World was unthreatened by the ambitions of the Old. The threat, however, was to be renewed, and this time it was met in a new way. The emphasis was shifted; instead of a somewhat arrogant assertion of a right to protect the two continents from aggression was substituted a co-operative policy. This policy involved, using words in their broadest sense, a kind of internationalization of the Monroe Doctrine— not a formal internationalization but a substitution of co-operative for unilateral action. If the American people had been unduly attached to a formula for a formula's sake, there should have been some opposition to this policy, but no such opposition appeared. It was possible for the Roosevelt administration to bind the Latin-American states to the United States by closer bonds. At Buenos Aires the principle of consultation in case of threatened attack was accepted; at Lima in 1938 it was given a more precise form and the machinery provided to apply it; and, when the Second World War burst on the world, the solidarity of the American states was strikingly demonstrated though it was not perfect. This solidarity was no doubt a recognition of common interests and of a common danger; but who can estimate the importance of the assumption (questionable though it may be) that the institutions of democracy were similar in both North and South America? If there was an ideological assumption in the Monroe Doctrine and in the good-neighbor policy, it was an assumption that strengthened and fortified, rather than weakened, the practical purposes of American diplomacy. It was not theory perverting the course of action but theory giving it fuller meaning.

The policies followed during the Second World War illustrate also how useful the Monroe Doctrine might still be. In the thirties, as the good-neighbor policy took form, one heard less and less of the famous dogma; but in the early forties it was suddenly revived. President Monroe would have been astounded to learn that Greenland came within the scope of his famous declaration; but so it did. He would have been less surprised, perhaps, at the enunciation, or rather the re-enunciation, of the addition to the Doctrine which put a veto on the transfer of European territory in the New World from one nation to another and at the formalization of this principle in the Declaration of Havana; and he would doubtless have approved the doctrine, also laid down at Havana, that an act of aggression against any American state would be considered an act of aggression against all. He would have agreed, I am sure, that every one of these policies served the real interest of the United States.

The rest of the story of the Monroe Doctrine, and its transformation, belongs more properly to the history of the idea of collective security, and to that idea I shall shortly turn. But let us first take a backward look at the ground that we have already traversed and see what generalizations I have sought to establish. The case runs something like this. Bold and sweeping assertions of general principle are likely to be characteristic of American foreign policy; they have a close relationship to the nature of popular government; they have an immense appeal to the average citizen, who is no expert in detail. It is by no means a fact, however, that they necessarily win universal and immediate acceptance; indeed, they are likely at first to be the subjects of partisan attack. This partisan attack may well proceed from ignoble motives; we will all agree that there can be too much partisanship in foreign affairs, but it serves the useful purpose of provoking an examination of the important question whether the doctrine that has been formulated serves the true interest of the United States. In the course of time, the dogma itself will gain strength as it does in reality serve these interests. Even then, however, it will be placed in a practical context; it will be applied with some regard to the risks involved; and it will be given a new color and form as the world situation itself changes. There is little to suggest that the American people will become doctrinaire in their attachment to any principle. This flexibility constitutes one of the strengths of their national temperament; and it is, indeed, one of the incidents of popular government. Both sides of a question can always get themselves represented in a democracy; and the result is often an extremely satisfactory one. I am not saying, of course, that blunders will never be made;

but these blunders seem by great odds subordinate to the wisdom of a diplomacy dependent upon the mass of the people.

Let us then turn to the doctrine of collective security, to the idea that an act of aggression by any state constitutes a threat to world society and must be proceeded against accordingly. This conception, I need hardly say, owes much to Woodrow Wilson. He did not originate it; he does not occupy quite the place with regard to it that President Monroe does with regard to his famous declaration; but he was one of the first Americans to perceive its importance, and he advocated it publicly before the end of his first term of office. He made the establishment of a system of collective security a *sine qua non* of the peace adjustments to follow the war as early as the seventeenth of January, 1917; and he made it a principal, shall we say the principal, objective for this principle at Paris; he gave his evenings, after weary daylong negotiation, to the drafting of the Covenant of the League of Nations; he returned to America to fight for it; he broke himself in the struggle to make his views prevail.

We all know what happened. Just as John Quincy Adams found that a very mild attempt to act in the spirit of Monroe's message evoked partisan opposition, so in this case Wilson, in propounding new doctrine, found himself involved in a partisan controversy. The President himself was not in any sense conciliatory; and the net result was the failure of the treaty of Versailles and American aloofness from the League of Nations itself.

It is no part of our present theme to discuss the various problems concerned in the defeat of the Wilsonian dream or attempt to fix the responsibility for the unhappy events of 1919 and 1920. But there are several things about it that we must say. In one sense Wilson was almost prophetic. In his tour through the country in the fall of 1919, preceding his final breakdown, he more than once declared that if the United States did not associate itself with the other nations of the world for the preservation of peace the next generation would be compelled in its turn to go forth to battle for its own safety and the freedom of the Western World. Yet it is not strange that in 1920 the people of the United States were not inclined to accept this view. A great power for evil had been defeated; the only other really great power on the continent of Europe was in the throes of revolution and could hardly threaten the peace for a considerable time to come; and the idea that the American government was to constitute itself the policeman of the whole world was one so ambitious and so extensive as to raise some doubts in the minds of the most idealistic. The country was not spiritually or morally prepared for such a commitment; and even those of us who saw with pain the repudiation of the Covenant must by this time have come fully to recognize the fact. In truth, it is doubtful whether Wilson put forward his idea at a propitious time. In 1920 a return to normalcy seemed possible, certainly it seemed possible to those whose vision was restricted to the immediate scene. It was natural that the opposition should capitalize this fact; and, though we may deplore the spirit in which much of the debate was conducted, we can understand that genuine issues lay behind the partisanship.

Yet the struggle over the League made its impression on the American mind. The idea that aggressive war was immoral took root, and indeed we may fairly say that it influenced American policy. One of the best illustrations of this fact is the Kellogg pact for the preservation of peace, negotiated in 1928. This pact, to Europeans, seems the height of political naïveté, the extraordinary product of a diplomacy based upon the simplicities of popular judgment in a country unsophisticated in the ways of the world. It consisted merely of a pledge on the part of the signatories not to resort to war as an instrument of national policy. It was indeed a sign of political immaturity that such a pact as this had the overwhelming support of public opinion, that Secretary Kellogg was prodded into it by a wide popular demand. International politics is a tough and hard game; and anyone who imagines that high-sounding declarations are of its essence and can replace the sterner instruments of peace—arms and men—is much in need of further instruction. But those who promoted the pact, or at least some of the more farseeing of them, had a more practical view of the problem than zealots like Samuel Levinson, with whom the idea seems to have originated, or mountain statesmen like Borah, who gave it his hearty support. They believed that once such a declaration was made it would have to be implemented—that the United States, having signed such a document, would have to act in defense of the peace when the threat came.

It cannot be said, however, that the American people assimilated that conception for some time to come, and it was they alone who could give it vitality. In the Manchurian crisis of 1931 Secretary Stimson would have liked, apparently, to take some measures against Japan, to act with the League in enforcing the principles of the Covenant. Although he did not meditate the use of armed force, he did at least think of the possibility of an economic embargo. But this idea was vetoed by President Hoover, and there are few signs that it had any deep-rooted support in public opinion. Perhaps the world would have been better off if things had been different; that is not, however, a question for the historian. It was much the same when in 1935 Mussolini challenged the League by the conquest of Ethiopia; American opinion was by no means ready to take up the challenge that the Italian dictator had thrown down. The dispatches of Secretary Hull show an almost nervous fear of doing something effective, an almost jittery concern for the political aspects of the matter, and perhaps it ought to be said that only if the doctrine of collective security were wholeheartedly accepted was there reason for America to take up this particular challenge, which touched no vital economic or security interest. At any rate, nothing happened; in this case, as in the previous one, the people of the United States apparently did not feel that their vital interests were concerned.

It was, after all, far different with the rise of Adolf Hitler. As Hitler's sinister purposes became revealed, American opinion altered. It was led, of course, by a great President of the United States. But anyone who has studied the course of events in 1939 and 1940 in detail can hardly escape the conclusion that Franklin Roosevelt led because there were plenty of followers. He was the last man in the world to adopt hopeless causes, and his attitude toward the general problem of collective security is shown by the complacency with which he accepted the neutrality legislation of 1935, 1936, and 1937 (legislation based upon quite a different theory) at a time when the drift of public sentiment was in the direction of what we have learned to describe as "isolationism." The bizarre theory that Roosevelt dragged us along a course which we scarcely understood, that he plotted and schemed to bring about hostilities, has been adopted by some reputable historians, but it is not likely to stand the test of historical analysis or of the soberer judgment of the future chroniclers of the nation. Behind the President stood the American people.

And so in principle the old ideas of neutrality were discarded, and a kind of quasi belligerency took its place. The repeal of the statute forbidding the shipment of arms and materials of war to belligerents might have been regarded as merely a return to the ancient principles of international law; but the bases-destroyer deal of September, 1940, however draped in the gauzy garment of legality, was surely defensible only on a new theory of national action. Still more, the lend-lease enactment of 1941 was justifiable only by reference to new principles of policy. Let it be remembered, too, that in this same period the administration was extending loans to China in its struggle against Japan.

I do not mean that the acts which I have just been mentioning are a full expression of the doctrine of collective security. They were based not so much on theory as on interest, on the fear of a victorious Germany and of a victorious Japan. But they led away from the old notion of neutrality; they expressed a tendency toward a new doctrine. That tendency was fortified as the war proceeded; and before its end the new doctrine had been placed in the way of wider acceptance. Preceding the Charter conference of San Francisco was the Pan-American meeting at Mexico City which brought forth the Declaration of Chapultepec; and the Declaration of Chapultepec laid down the principle, already stated in the Act of Havana, that an act of aggression against any one of the signatory powers was an act of aggression against all and proceeded to implement this principle by cataloguing a series of measures which the contracting parties were to take in case of a breach of the peace. This was in February of 1945. Soon after came the Charter of the United Nations. Here, more sharply defined and in more concrete form, was the doctrine for which Woodrow Wilson had contended a quarter of a century before; but this time its reception by the country was very different indeed. This time no cantankerous debate awaited the instrument in the Senate of the United States; the vote by which the treaty was ratified was 87 to 2; and this vote may be said to reflect the overwhelming sentiment of the American people. This time they were much disposed to accept what had been received with relative indifference in 1919; and so the idea of collective security was written into the law of the land and was embodied in the treaty law of the United States. Since 1945 there have been increasing signs that this idea is taken seriously. The most important and sweeping declaration ever made by a President of the United States is the declaration of President Truman that the United States stands ready to assist any nation which is menaced by outside aggression—a declaration which was speedily implemented by the grant of assistance to Greece and Turkey. In the same year, the Conference of Rio re-enacted the guarantees contained in the Act of Chapultepec. In 1948 came the Vandenberg resolution, an invitation to the administration to negotiate a pact with the nations of Europe; and in 1949 the North Atlantic Pact was duly signed and ratified. Since then the United States has responded directly to an act of open aggression by its assistance given to the government of Korea, and Secretary Acheson has negotiated a defense agreement with the nations of the Pacific. All of these steps represent an attempt to give practical substance to the general principle we are examining.

Many interesting points can be made about this development. In the first place, it is to be observed that every one of these steps had the sanction of an overwhelming majority of the Congress and, one must thus infer, of public opinion. The Convention of Rio was ratified unanimously by the Senate. The North Atlantic Pact was approved by a vote of 83 to 12. The bill for aid to Greece and Turkey was enacted by a Republican Congress and by substantial majorities. The President's response to aggression in Korea has been endorsed by very wide segments of opinion, by General MacArthur, on the one hand, and by the thick-and-thin supporters of the administration on the other. In the current Presidential campaign, both candidates have not hesitated to state that Truman's action was wise and desirable. Both have insisted that there must be no capitulation to the aggressor. All of these things demonstrate how the idea of collective security is being assimilated into American opinion.

But there are already clear signs that, as was the case with the Monroe Doctrine, the new doctrine is not going to be interpreted in some dogmatic and rigid fashion which might lead to difficulty. For example, the Convention of Rio, while pledging the various signatory states to common action against a peace-breaking state, does not require of the parties that they go to war. To ask this of all the states of Latin America without regard to the interests concerned might be a bit Utopian, and it has not been done. The Atlantic Pact, however, explicitly mentions armed force as one of the elements involved in the enforcement of its obligations. The transcendent significance of preserving Western Europe from attack has been clearly recognized in the language of the treaty. The Truman Doctrine, on the other hand, was phrased in very general terms, terms that commit to no concrete type of assistance.

There are critics of the doctrine of collective security who predict all kinds of baneful consequences from its growing vogue. George Kennan, for example, one of the ablest and most articulate of American professional diplomats, is much worried by the fear that in practice collective security will bind the United States to all-out war, that the necessary consequence of the doctrine is that evil must not only be punished but completely put down, and that, in the logic of things, action against aggression can never be stopped short of unconditional surrender on the part of the aggressor.

The course of events in Korea seems to refute this idea. There were, it is true, partisans of all-out war after our entry into South Korea. Of these the most eminent, the most vocal, and potentially the most influential was, I suppose, General MacArthur. Yet the General's views of sound policy in this matter were by no means accepted by the American people. He came home, he was acclaimed as the great soldier that he undoubtedly was, and his views were ignored. As time went on, the eloquence of his speech to Congress was followed by more plaintive utterances, and, before very long, he abandoned the Korean issue to utter jeremiads against the general wickedness of the Truman administration and the corruption of the times. By July of 1952 he was unable to command any important support in his campaign for the Presidency, and he has now withdrawn to labor arduously (so I hope we may assume) to spread the products of Remington Rand throughout the world. We hear little of all-out war, or total victory, in the Far East; and neither of the candidates of the two great political parties in 1952 appeared likely to endorse any such policy. Instead, we are engaged in negotiation in Korea, and, though we still maintain in theory that the unification of all Korea is the objective of American policy, we are making it fairly plain that we would be satisfied with a settlement that deprived the aggressor of any of the fruits of his aggression. The whole Korean episode seems to refute the melancholy assumptions of Mr. Kennan.

Another aspect of the actual application of the collective security idea bothered Kennan. He calls attention in his Chicago lectures to the great difficulties that are involved in the working of any alliance and suggests that these will be multiplied by the adoption of this new principle. That alliances work with clock-like precision and unqualified smoothness is not to be contended, or indeed to be expected. But here again the American people seem to know how to reconcile themselves to reality. In the Korean case, they have on the whole recognized the difficulties involved in bringing to bear the power of a great number of nations in a given theater of war. They have certainly not expressed widespread discontent with the rule played by our associates. They even seem to recognize that, where common action is necessary, mutual regard for the interests concerned is prescribed by the very circumstances of the case. And, unless we believe that all-out war in the Orient was precisely what the doctor ordered, we can say with some assurance that in practice the influence of our allies has been on the whole a healthy one in the Korean struggle.

The doctrine of collective security is too new for us to generalize confidently about it in the broad sense or to predict its future. But, from what we can see today, the ideological and the practical are likely to be mingled in its application. Without it, without the place that it has come to occupy in the American mind, it is doubtful whether the American people could have been brought to that epoch-making breach with the past that is represented by our present policy of alliances and regional understanding. Without it, something of the moral strength of the American position would have been undermined. Without it, the nations of Europe might well have been abandoned to the ambition of the Kremlin. And, in the future, it seems probable that it will continue to serve the interests of the United States, while yet expressing a lofty aspiration. This great self-governing nation entered on the stage of the world, in the diplomatic sense, little more than fifty years ago. Yet its popular government has not prevented it from making many decisions fully as wise as those that have been made by dictators; and the preoccupation of the body of the people with broad general ideas has not prevented the wise application of these ideas in practice.

After all, let us contrast American diplomacy with that of the dictators. Think of Germany under the leadership of Hitler, blindfolded and in chains, led to its own destruction; think of Italy, led far from the course of sound policy by the senseless ambition and vanity of Mussolini; think of the Japanese, dominated by a small military clique which utterly miscalculated the national strength and the national interest; and then think of the United States. Errors, of course, there have been in the diplomacy of this great self-governing nation; but they have been minor compared with those of the autocrats. In seeking its own interest, the American people have, in fact, both in the Monroe Doctrine and in the doctrine of collective security, been serving the interests of others; they have been moving toward a world in which barren and inflamed nationalism will yield to larger views. And they have been moving along practical lines. What more needs to be said about the relationship of diplomacy to popular government?

II ⌁

William H. Seward
as Secretary of State *

ONLY a short time ago I wrote to a number of scholars in the field of American diplomacy asking them to express a judgment, in terms of academic grades, on the Secretaries of State of the United States from the foundation of the government to the present time. I collated the results, and was thus enabled to arrive at a collective judgment as to the place of each of these men in the development of our foreign policy. The palm went to John Quincy Adams. But the second place went to William H. Seward, and that by a very substantial margin. In the brief commentary upon which I am now about to embark, I want to examine the reasons, as I see them, why to this son of Union was accorded so high a place amongst the directors of our foreign affairs. And I may say, before I begin this examination, that I heartily concur in the judgment which was rendered.

Seward came to the great office which he held from 1861–1869 without a scintilla of experience in the field of international politics. Adams had been minister to Prussia, to the Netherlands, to Russia, and to Britain when Monroe chose him as Secretary in

* Reprinted by permission from *Union Worthies*, VI (1951), 10–17.

1817. He was, technically speaking, the best prepared man who ever directed the State Department. But the fact that the great New Yorker stands second underlines an important principle. It is not technical excellence that the country needs most in the direction of the complex problems of international life. It is, on the contrary, that quality that can best be described as political wisdom. Look at the list of American Secretaries as a whole, and it will be found that the most eminent figures in the list were by no means those who had had the greatest diplomatic experience. They were, on the contrary, with the possible exception of John Hay, those whose preparation was in the political arena rather than in the chancelleries of Europe. And the reason for this goes to the roots of the matter of American foreign policy. For the conduct of our foreign affairs has never been, as it has often been in Europe, a matter of independent action, with only an occasional reference to the electorate. In America, foreign policy has been formed by the people; it has not been an esoteric matter, but has again and again come up from the electorate, rather than down from the State Department. It has required, in other words, the gift of political interpretation and understanding of the popular mood, the popular aspirations, and the popular will. In 1861, when Seward took his post as Secretary, he had already had a very large political experience. He had been Governor of New York and a Senator of the United States since 1849. He had been a shrewd politician, and yet a man with a statesman-like grasp of the issues of the day. He knew how to deal with politicians, and to know how to deal with politicians is not a bad training for dealing with diplomats. Indeed, once again, it has often been a better training than any other.

Seward, it is true, made mistakes at the outset of his service in the State Department. The fantastic idea of provoking foreign complications in order to unify American opinion at home, and perhaps prevent the coming of a civil war, an idea embodied in his "Thoughts for the Consideration of the President," was quashed by President Lincoln in the early days of his term. The challenge to Spain with regard to the introduction of Spanish rule in the Dominican Republic, issued in the first months of office, was one which could hardly be more than *brutum fulmen* at a time when the very integrity of the Union was menaced. Some of the first of Seward's notes to Britain were unduly truculent in their form and spirit, and were wisely tempered by the Chief Executive. But these things only set in a more flattering perspective the administration of the State Department under the great New Yorker. After the first few months he made very few mistakes indeed. He learned quickly how to deal with the great problems which came before him, and the momentous issues of the war period were handled with rare skill after only a short apprenticeship.

I have said that American foreign policy must be closely integrated with American public opinion. No one understood this better than did Seward. It was with him that there first began the publication, the systematic publication of a large part of the correspondence of the State Department, either contemporaneously with the course of policy, or only a little while after policy had been formed. The great series which was first put forth under the name of "Diplomatic Correspondence of the United States," and which later became known as "Foreign Relations of the United States," begins with his administration.

In this correspondence in the years 1861–65 one fact stands out above all others. One of Seward's salient characteristics was optimism, and faith in his country. Never was such a quality more badly needed than in the days of the Civil War. Grim as the struggle was, Seward's faith in victory never faltered. His despatches at all times breathed a lofty confidence in the outcome of the struggle. He was never appalled at the thought of a possible European intervention. He was never frightened by European protests at the blockade, or by European flirtations with the representatives of the Southern states. He cast his diplomatic correspondence in such a mold as to elevate and solidify Northern public opinion. Many of his most important state papers were aimed at the maintenance of morale at home as much as at the accomplishment of some specific result abroad. We cannot measure their effect in any scientific way, of course, but it seems fair to say that they were an important factor in producing that hopeful view of the whole struggle that eventually conducted to victory.

But a Secretary of State must deal with practical issues rather than with the issuance of national manifestoes. Seward met the practical issues of the war period with the greatest skill, and one of the most striking examples of this skill is to be found in his handling of the case of the *Trent*. You will remember the essential circumstances. Mason and Slidell, commissioners sent by the South to Europe, were seized upon the British mail-packet, *Trent*, by an American warship, taken off, carried to Boston, and imprisoned in Fort Warren. The country blazed with approval of the commander who had detained them. The act aroused much indignation in Great Britain, however, and a demand for the surrender of the two men was not long in being forwarded to Washington. The situation was a critical one. To deny the British demand was not only to run the risk of serious trouble, but also to fly in the face of the prescriptions of international law. There seems today little doubt that the British were right, and that the United States was wrong. But to surrender Mason and Slidell was to run the risk of tremendous popular resentment at home. Never is a diplomat more severely tried than when, in the face of great popular excitement, he is obliged to yield to the demands of a foreign nation. To deal with such a situation successfully required not only courage but adroitness as well. The Secretary was equal to the occasion. He favored in the cabinet the surrender of the commissioners. On this point he was clearer than was the President himself. But when it came to writing the note in which the surrender was conceded, he managed to put the matter on grounds that flattered American pride, and made his action seem a defense of vital American interests. There was, perhaps, more ingenuity than forthrightness in the argument that he managed to make. He contended that the United States, in seizing the commissioners, without taking the *Trent* itself before a prize court, was violating the fundamental American principle of the freedom of the seas. "If I decide this case in favor of my own government," he wrote, "I must disavow its most cherished principles, and reverse and abandon its essential policy. The country cannot afford the sacrifice." There is, no doubt, much bombast and much doubtful argument in Seward's note. But from the practical political point of view it was a document of the first rank. It suited very well the necessities of the situation. And it put an end to the danger of a serious clash with Great Britain.

But Seward could be as firm in maintaining what he deemed to be a just position as he could be clever in extricating himself from a diplomatic difficulty. It may be that in some respects he was firm to the point of bumptiousness. It is certain that his position on such a question as the recognition of the belligerency of the South, and still more his position on the intervention of the European powers in the American domestic struggle, made it perfectly clear that the United States intended to carry through until the Union was restored. It may well be that there was never any serious danger of hostile action, of an attempt to break the Northern blockade, for example, on the part of the British or the French, but there was certainly some danger of a European démarche in favor of the South, and the mere offer of mediation, had it been made, might have had an adverse effect on American public opinion. By forestalling it, by making it clear beyond all peradventure that the United States would have nothing to do with any peace by compromise, the Secretary performed a conspicuous public service.

Seward saw in a very sound perspective the importance of the slavery issue in its relation to European opinion. When the question of Emancipation was first brought forward in the cabinet by President Lincoln in July of 1862, it was the New Yorker who pointed out that the freeing of the slaves at just that time might well be regarded as a manœuvre of despair on the part of the North. It would be well to wait, he argued, for a Northern victory. And wait the administration did. The First Emancipation Proclamation was issued after Antietam. Once it was put forth, the Secretary never ceased to emphasize the significance of what had been done. "The interests of humanity," he wrote to Adams, "have now been identified with the cause of our country." And to Dayton, our minister in Paris, he declared, "Are the enlightened and humane nations, Great Britain and France, to throw their protection over the insurgents now? Are they to enter directly, or indirectly, into this conflict, which, besides being exclusively one belonging to the friendly people of a distant continent, has also, by force of circumstances, become a war between freedom and human bondage? . . . Is this to be the climax of the world's progress in the nineteenth century?"

In such a passage as that just quoted one gets not only the best of Seward, but the best of American diplomacy. For it is characteristic of American foreign policy on the highest level that it identifies itself with great moral issues, and makes those issues vivid and controlling.

In one important problem that extended far beyond the years of war Seward identified himself with principle in a fashion that was highly significant. This was in the case of the French intervention in Mexico. As is well known, the Emperor Napoleon III took advantage of the distress of the United States to set up an Austrian Archduke upon a Mexican throne. This project was already incubating when the Civil War broke out, and it was advanced towards realization in the years of the war itself. In the summer of 1864 the Austrian Archduke Maximilian

sailed for his shadowy kingdom. During these three years the
Secretary of State pursued a course at once based on American
traditions and ideals, and at the same time properly cautious.
Having learned from his early challenge to Spain that the
Monroe Doctrine was not highly regarded abroad, he never mentioned it by name in his voluminous correspondence. For some
time he suavely assumed that the rumors of monarchy were ill-
founded. When he could no longer do this he made it clear that
the United States was in principle opposed to the establishment
of a monarchical government in the New World. At the same
time he deftly dissociated himself from the resolution of the
House of Representatives passed unanimously in the summer of
1864 in which the whole Mexican project was condemned, declaring that this resolution had no binding force. But when the
war came to an end, and freed his hands, he proceeded in a remarkable series of notes to increase the pressure on the French
government. The situation was in some respects a dangerous one.
National resentment against the intrusion of the French in the
New World was substantial; and it was necessary to control it,
while at the same time using it as a means of pressure on the
Court of the Tuileries. This was precisely what Seward did.
He temporized for a little; began to step up his tone as he became aware of mounting opposition in France to the whole
project, and of the anxiety of the French foreign minister to
avoid a breach with the United States; edged Drouyn de L'Huys,
the French Foreign Minister, from one position to another until
he finally secured the promise of the evacuation of Mexico in a
fixed period of time. No doubt in the latter part of this correspondence he was writing in part for domestic consumption;
even so he was none the less maintaining and consolidating an
important principle of American diplomacy. Though, as has
been said, he never mentioned the Monroe Doctrine by name,
it was in these years following on 1865 that it became a na-

tionally accepted dogma, and it was by his action more than
that of any other man that this came to be the case.

There is another aspect of Seward's secretariat that deserves
some emphasis. Seward was by temperament an expansionist.
His optimism and his democratic faith set no bounds to the
growth of the United States. His anti-slavery principles came
in conflict with this side of his character in the fifties, but, once
the Civil War was over, the situation changed. It was due to him,
of course, that in 1867 Alaska was purchased from the Russian
government. It is to be noted that he was able to secure the acceptance of the treaty which brought about this cession from a
Senate that was in bitter opposition to the administration, and
from a chairman of the Foreign Relations Committee who was
by no means of the same mind as the Secretary with regard to
the problems of reconstruction. It is also to be noted that at the
time to many people Alaska seemed of very little value, and was
derisively described as "Seward's icebox." Time has, however,
vindicated the wisdom of his action. By the year 1900 Alaska
had yielded in fish, furs, and gold nearly $150,000,000, and the
revenue tax on her seal-skins had brought in a sum larger than
the purchase price; and, on the strategic side, no one today will
doubt the importance of this great outpost towards the Orient.

Had Seward had his own way he would have gone farther;
he negotiated a treaty for the acquisition of the Danish West
Indies; he flirted with the idea of the incorporation of the Dominican Republic into the United States; he advocated the annexation of Hawaii. The public opinion of his time was not
prepared for such extensions of territory; yet two of the three
projects just mentioned were later to be translated into reality.

One other of Seward's abortive negotiations was to be vindicated by time. The solution by arbitration of our numerous controversies with Great Britain arising from the Civil War was
foreshadowed in the Johnson-Clarendon convention. For reasons

having nothing to do with its merits, the Senate rejected this important compact, but the principles on which it was based were followed in the famous arbitration of the *Alabama* claims in the Grant administration. Seward had set the right tone for the solution of the problem, though his leadership was rejected.

How shall we sum up what we have just been saying? Seward came to the State Department untried; his political gifts soon enabled him to adjust himself to his new post; he was able to sense the feeling of the nation, and to make confident appeal to it; at the same time he knew how to guide and control it; he was aware of American political ideals, but he was also intensely practical; he was capable of decisive action; but he knew, too, when to temporize and even concede. He had faith in the future of America, and in the future of democracy. He justly mingled the appeal to reason and the appeal to feeling. It is by the arts that he practiced, by the balance that he maintained, by the high purposes which he pursued, that the people of the United States will be best served in the field of diplomacy.

IV ~

PRESIDENTIAL ADDRESS

TO THE AMERICAN

HISTORICAL ASSOCIATION

12 ～

We Shall Gladly Teach *

A LARGE proportion of the members of the American Historical Association are college teachers. Yet in seventy-odd years of the history of this organization no presidential address has directly dealt with the central function of our profession. We have had committees to deal with the question of history in the schools; we have recently shown an acute awareness of the important fact that we have, over the long pull, become increasingly out of touch with secondary education and that something ought to be done about it. In the university world, as we face increasingly complex problems, we are perhaps more aware than we used to be of the significance of classroom activity in stimulating the young people of our land. But still the fact remains that no President of the Association has ever addressed himself directly to the problem of college teaching. I propose to do this.

It is not perhaps strange that things have been as they are. Like

* Presidential address read at the annual dinner of the American Historical Association, Sheraton-Jefferson Hotel, St. Louis, Missouri, December 29, 1956. Reprinted by permission from *The American Historical Review*, January, 1957.

most people, we philosophize too little with regard to the profession which we have had the happiness to adopt. We are engaged in highly agreeable work—paid, as Carl Becker used to say, for doing precisely the thing which we most want to do. We occupy positions of some prestige in the societies in which we live. Though many of us carry heavier burdens than we ought to carry, from the standpoint of our intellectual growth, and have less time for meditation and reflection than we ought to have, we enjoy a certain freedom from routine that is immensely satisfying; we live for the most part in an atmosphere free from external constraints; and we are not subjected to the painful necessity, obvious in the case of the administrator or the businessman, of making significant day-to-day decisions on which the fortunes of others may depend. It is no wonder, therefore, that we do not ask ourselves, as often as we might, the central questions as to just what we intend to accomplish by our labors and, more specifically, how we are to view our function as teachers and make that function more effective.

In answering these questions, or in trying to answer them, I intend to take no narrow view of the place of the historian. There are eminent men in our profession whose gifts do not lie in the classroom. There are certainly other ways of serving God than by talking to undergraduates, or even to graduates. There are values to be communicated artlessly as well as by taking thought. It is possible to do a big job in the world without ever asking why, to fire young men and young women by one's gifts of enthusiasm, of industry, of inquiry, not so much purposefully as by the very force and range of one's mind and character. Yet when all this is said, it still seems to me that we are under some compulsion to inquire whether, in this year of grace 1956, we have thought enough of the problem of teaching, of its social significance, and of the central concepts which ought to play a part in our instruction.

The problem is particularly important at the present time. We know, in the first place, that the colleges are going to grow portentously in the course of the next decade. The Report of the Committee of Fifteen on the Graduate School of Today and Tomorrow, published by the Fund for the Advancement of Education, which I commend to your attention, estimates that the number of college students, now about 2.7 million, will reach 3.2 million by 1960, and 6.4 million by 1970. To serve our present students, we have 190,000 college teachers. If the present teacher-student ratio is to be maintained, we shall need 250,000 college teachers by 1960, and 495,000 by 1970. We have here an urgent problem that we must face and that, even with the best will in the world, we will have great difficulty in solving.

In the second place, we shall have to admit (some of us reluctantly) that the trend in the American academic world is more and more vocational. This is not entirely to be deplored. The American college is one of the great mechanisms by which we maintain social fluidity, and social fluidity is one of the deepest values of American life. The application of the scholarly attitude to problems outside the traditional and older disciplines is also one of the distinctive features—and one of the useful features—of our society. Nonetheless, a subject like history is in a somewhat exposed situation in this kind of educational world. Where its values are practical and immediate, they are likely to be appropriated by other disciplines; where they are more general, they may well be neglected or depreciated. We have seen a process of decline in classical studies; we have seen and are seeing such important branches of history as medieval history threatened; we may see the area of interest further narrowed.

But there is a bigger reason than this why we should occupy ourselves with the problem of teaching. We have tended, as it seems to me, to exalt the written over the spoken word in the practice of our profession. Both carry their special messages, but for most of us the possibility of reaching large audiences through what we write is not great. Our best chance of making some impact on others will come through the influence we can exert in the classroom, through the enthusiasms we kindle, through the interests we arouse, through the wisdom that history teaches and that we can strive to disseminate. Here, as I see it, for all but the greatest and most imaginative scholar, is our greatest chance of usefulness, our largest hope. The young men and women who participate in our instruction are eager and anxious to learn from us; they are capable of benefiting by our multiplied historical experience; they may be warmed by our personalities and fired with a generous view of life and a wider view of knowledge. Are we making the most of our opportunities? These questions I cannot fail to ask, nor can I fail to try to answer them.

But let us not misunderstand one another. I intend, most certainly, no depreciation of what is called, sometimes a little exaggeratedly, productive scholarship. For the college teacher, instruction and research are both fundamental. They ought not to be separated. There is no real dichotomy between them; they are two faces of the same problem. It should be clear, even to to the most enthusiastic teacher, that research is, in some sense of the word, indispensable to the effective practice of his profession. We need to be ever-inquiring if we are to be effective teachers. It is easy to let our instruction degenerate into routine; to give the same lectures year after year, with the same stale jokes in the same context, with the same unexplored generalizations drawn from the same available secondary works, and with the same sometimes soporific effect upon the innocent victims of our instruction. To be worthy of our calling, we must possess, first of all, the instinct to go on learning. When a teacher has ceased to ask questions, when he has ceased, in other words, to cultivate the spirit of research, he has ceased to be effective. Many years ago Professor Robert Matteson Johnston of Harvard put the matter cogently in one of his seminars. He said of the classroom teacher that we learn by example in this world. A good teacher is an example of a man thinking, and somehow or other the example of a man thinking may, by the grace of God, communicate itself to some of those around him. Our subject is a vast one—since it concerns the totality of human experience, the vastest of all themes. Each of its parts, the intellectual life of man, his systems of economic and political organization, his religion, his arts, his science, and all the rest of it, is interrelated. We can never know enough to teach as we would like to teach. We must always be acquiring new insights, asking new questions. Furthermore, we are in grave danger of imprecision. It is, of course, the mark of a poor teacher that he never generalizes, that he confines himself to mere episode, mere narrative. But it is also the mark of a poor teacher if he generalizes wildly, with inadequate data. Research is the means by which we discipline ourselves, by which we make ourselves more careful, more accurate, and more profound.

It is possible to go further. There is an intellectual excitement in the process of research that can be communicated to others. To make it clear that it is fun to learn, fun to explore, fun to "follow knowledge like a sinking star," is to perform a service. In the complex world of today it has become more than ever necessary to penetrate deeper into the facts. Every practical question, as well as those not practical, is a question of scholarship. It ought to be interesting and challenging so to regard it.

There is, then, no quarrel between the man who emphasizes teaching and the man who emphasizes research. But before we leave the latter subject, we may perhaps for a moment examine the question whether our present attitude toward research has not led us into some pitfalls and created for us some problems. Scholars—such as we profess to be—ought to be imbued with the spirit of humility; and one of the questions that we may ask ourselves with propriety is whether, in our zeal for research, we have not lost, or may lose, or are in some danger of losing, the art of communication with large numbers of people by concentrating our attention on communicating—not always in a very attractive style—with a few people. What we write for each other is useful; it extends the boundaries of knowledge—sometimes—and it helps us to see old problems in a new light, or to discover new problems. We usually praise each other's works in the historical reviews, and this is undoubtedly good for our collective egos. But is this enough? How able are we, I ask again, to communicate with an important audience? How far in the long run are we able to make our noble subject better understood in a big way? Is it not significant that so many of the Pulitzer prizes in history and so many of the book-of-the-month club books on history are written by nonprofessional historians? Is it not significant that so many of us do not get beyond our doctor's theses and that these often require—or at least ought to have—extensive revision before publication? To do research supremely well might perhaps be enough satisfaction for any man. But, if we view the matter squarely, we see that there may well be a question whether our social contribution is everything that we would like to have it.

There is another aspect to the question on which we may well reflect. We have often been told that advance in the natural sciences has owed much to plain natural curiosity. Research that has no practical relevance, that is perhaps only remotely related to the existing body of knowledge, that derives purely and simply from a desire to know more about the nature of the universe, may lay the foundation for significant progress of a much more concrete character. An abstract thinker like Einstein may, through his speculation, have an enormous influence upon the application of science to life. No fact about the natural world is so insignificant that it cannot conceivably be related to a broad pattern of profound value. Oftentimes, by analogy, we are told that all historical research is valuable, irrespective of its perceived implications. But is the analogy sound? Is it really true that, in our own field of history, one subject is just as important as another? Do we, in our graduate work, reflect sufficiently on the relationship of this or that particular field of research to the larger pattern of the past? Of course we need not, and should not, in our explorations, seek immediate utility. To do this would be to constrict and limit our field to an intolerable degree, to turn a universal discipline into a mere handmaiden of other subjects, especially those most immediately concerned with the contemporary world. But is it unreasonable to ask, when we undertake or suggest a piece of research, that it should bear some relationship to a broad pattern, that it should be more than an isolated intellectual adventure (appealing as that can be), that it should be also a contribution to some larger conception of the past? There is another way of saying the same thing. Some of the most fruitful research is often the asking of questions about matters with which we are already familiar (the age of Jackson, for instance, or the age of reform) in an attempt to develop new insights rather than to explore the hitherto unexplored. Such researches may or may not be wholly justified in terms of the interpretation which results. But they are decidedly stimulating. They proceed, as pedestrian research usually does not, from a kind of intellectual audacity very far removed from the exhaustive interpretation of some subject which scarcely ties in with any broad conception of history.

We should do better, perhaps, if, in the direction of our students, we gave more consideration to the possibility of reinterpretation of fields already covered as compared with digging away at obscure facts, in an obscure area, in an obscure way. Do we really need to know, to borrow from Carl Becker, "whether Charles the Fat was at Ingelheim or Lustnau on July 1, 1887?" It is a fair question whether we do not sometimes kill the very spirit that we wish to foster, the spirit of exciting and excited inquiry into the past, by directing our students' attention to matters which fail to challenge them and turn what ought to be a highly intellectual adventure into a dreary kind of grubbing. And by the time the victim has completed his study, he may have lost all sense of the grandeur and scope of history, and he may find it difficult to think in bold or even in general terms of the vast pageant of the past.

Years ago, when I was an undergraduate at Harvard, the Reverend Samuel MacChord Crothers delivered an address to the honor students on what he called "The Retrospective Re-education of Doctors of Philosophy." I have been unable to recapture this address. But the title itself suggests well enough what he was talking about. He was pleading for the large view, for the broad understanding of a subject, as compared with the intensive cultivation of a small area. He was resting his case on the stock definition of a specialist as a man who knows more and more about less and less.

But let us return to the subject of teaching. We agree that the best teachers must also be scholars, that they must always be asking questions, always expanding, deepening, and broadening their own knowledge. We agree, I hope, that they must always be looking for insights as well as for new facts. But we are only at the beginning of our inquiry. How shall we make certain that they know how to teach, and what values are we to expect them to communicate?

The answer to these questions lies on two levels. It involves, in the first place, a matter of selection and training. It involves, in the second place, the deeper values which give history its dignity and meaning.

Is it not possible to improve our methods of preparation for a teaching career in history? Are we getting the right people? Are we training them in the right way? Are we fixing for them the right standards?

There is certainly no easy answer to the first of these questions. Undoubtedly, part of the problem is financial. We need more fellowships for graduate study in history; we need higher standards of compensation for our profession in general. But there is another facet to the matter. We cannot ourselves treat teaching casually, or as a mere interruption of something more important. The quality of our students will depend in no small degree upon the personal enthusiasm for our subject that we can communicate. The more glow there is in our instruction, the more successfully will we recruit the teachers of the future. If our work is central to us, it will become central to them. We need, too, to be less obsessed than many of us are by grades acquired in the course of an undergraduate career. Some of the very ablest graduate students will turn out to have very unpromising undergraduate records, just as some of the top men in law or medical school will. Young men and young women mature at different speeds. They are not finished at commencement. Furthermore, some of those with the most formidable number of "A's" may lack entirely the fundamental gift of communication or even a genuine "feel" for our subject. They may be mere prodigies of memory, without originality or that sympathetic attitude toward others which has so much to do with success in the classroom. Once a college student has had his enthusiasm aroused, he may show unexpected power and atone for deficiencies in his undergraduate career. But the dull dog who thinks only in terms of marks and attained them without much else to commend him is very likely beyond redemption. We need to think more of the total personality and less of the score sheet and the aptitude test in selecting and encouraging our graduate students.

After we get our graduate students, what then? Can we not in the first place pay a little more attention to teaching in our training for the doctorate? As matters stand, we often give candidates for the Ph.D. an opportunity to earn a little money on the side by classroom instruction. And then, too often, we forget all about them and leave them completely on their own. They deserve better of us than this. They deserve to be watched, to be improved, to be understood and evaluated.

On the lowest level the problem is a technical one. There are a few things to be learned, no doubt, with regard to method. To speak slowly, and so that you can be heard; to make the big facts stand out from the subordinate ones, in other words, to develop the gift of emphasis; to avoid ponderosity and flippancy alike; to talk, not to read; to present a subject as a related whole —these and similar matters are no doubt worth a little attention. Errors with regard to them can be pointed out effectively, if we take the trouble to visit the classes of our graduate students and see what it is they are doing wrong.

But there is a deeper aspect to teaching. Students must be made to feel that this work is not merely an honorable way of finding the funds for their graduate education, but that it has central significance, that the success they have in it will have something to do with the recommendations we give them and with their professional success. We must genuinely know what they are like and be able to answer with positiveness and, it is to be hoped, with enthusiasm when we are asked about them for jobs. Let us make an end of this miserable matter of recommending for teaching positions young men and young women of whose capacities as teachers we have little exact knowledge and who, whatever their learning, lack the gifts required of them in our noble calling.

I would, as a matter of fact, go further. For every promising graduate student, it seems to me, the preparation of a lecture, or a series of lectures, should be a part of training. I do not mean a highly specialized report such as we get in some of our seminars; I mean a lecture of the kind that he will have to give when he enters the world of teaching. The best of the graduate students ought to have a chance at the undergraduates. If this is not feasible, then there might well be a graduate seminar in which the participants lecture to one another, with subjects of the scope they will present in the classroom. It would do no harm, either, if they learned to conduct a discussion and demonstrated their ability to conduct such a discussion in a stimulating manner, indicating that they had grasped the essentials of a significant problem in a way that showed real insight.

This brings us to the general examination. The idea of the general examination is, in my view, highly meritorious. Here, indeed, is a kind of provision for a wide range of knowledge, as compared with the intensive cultivation of a small field. There are, however, some criticisms to be made of it. One is that it sets an exaggerated value on memory alone, on the ability to memorize large bodies of facts and present them to an admiring audience in a relatively brief space of time. After all, a well-trained person is under no very great difficulty in getting more and more facts as he goes along. Of course the power, the capacity, to absorb and retain is valuable. But let us not rate it too highly. There is plenty of time ahead in which to learn. And there are some students who show up badly in an examination which seems to them crucial, but who have very great merits indeed. At any rate, let us not think that a man ought to be judged on this one test. There are many qualities that go to make a successful teacher besides memory. Enthusiasm, insight, the humane spirit—all these are essential.

If we think of the general examination in terms of teaching, there are perhaps other criticisms that will occur to us. Should the fields chosen not be integrated in some degree with what are the most likely teaching programs for the candidate? Should they not sometimes (and oftener than they do) fall outside the field of history? Is it possible, for example, for a man to teach American history well if he has not had a good grounding in economics? Is it not desirable, in connection with work for the degree, to have every candidate familiarize himself with the philosophy of history? It is not that Brooks Adams in *The Law of Civilization and Decay*, or Spengler with his demoniac worship of power, or Croce with his inveterate relativism have any of them reached the ultimate in historical speculation. But is it not particularly worth while to bring students into contact with men who have thought in broad terms with regard to the significance of historical materials?

Finally, with regard to our technical problems, should we not revise the work for the master's degree and make that degree more meaningful in terms of capacity to teach? We shall, in all likelihood, not be able to supply the market with Ph.D.'s of sufficient numbers and high quality. Should we not give some thought to a master's program directly related to instruction at the college level?

And now we come to the ultimate problem which transcends all questions of method. How is the historical scholar to be both broad and deep? How is he to maintain standards of precision, of exactitude, of faithfulness to the spirit of research, and at the same time spread himself over a large range? What is he to do in a world in which the body of historical literature is continually accumulating at an awesome rate? What is he to do, particularly if he is an American historian in the modern field, in a world in which important political transactions are carried on over the telephone, in which international dealings are frequently on a verbal basis, in which the records of business concerns are portentously voluminous, in which the mass of the data grows and grows? How is he at the same time to be "definitive" and to keep his eye on the large and fertilizing conceptions which make history both interesting and valuable?

The answer to this question, as I see it, is something like this. We cannot teach any broad course to undergraduates and live up to the standard of precise scholarship which we would wish to attain and for which we must strive. But what we can do, and what we should be trying to do, is to set a pattern with regard to the past that has value for young men and young women. It is for us a cardinal responsibility to find that pattern; it will be one thing for one teacher and something else for another— but some *Weltanschauung*, some fundamental intellectual and

moral attitude, that we must have. For history is in the last analysis a point of view; and the undergraduates who listen to us,
long after they have forgotten the facts we communicated to
them, will remember the point of view.

I venture, therefore, in what follows, to illustrate this general
theme. I do so not in the spirit of one who lays down the law
but in the spirit of one who makes some suggestions that may be
of use to others. And my illustrations will, of course, be chiefly
drawn from that American history which I know best.

Now the first thing to be stressed, it seems to me, is that we
shall do less than justice to our subject if we think of it in the
narrow terms of its practical usefulness in solving the problems
of the present. History is useful in this sense, and we have certainly no reason to be ashamed of this fact. There is scarcely
another discipline, even the sciences, that is not enriched and
deepened and better adapted to the handling of a contemporary
issue by some study of the past. There is more recognition of
this fact than there used to be. The best political scientists are
steeped in the historical study of American institutions. The
best economists know full well that they cannot grapple with
the problem of deflation or reflation, or of wages and prices,
without some thorough grounding in the years that are gone.
The best students of international relations—at least so I hope—
realize that you cannot understand American foreign policy if
you understand only the last ten minutes of it or fail to pay regard to the complex of ideas and habits and institutions that have
helped to form the international mores of the American people.
If our subject has been captured by others, and more and more
used by others, this is occasion for rejoicing rather than jealousy.

But we cannot conceive of history in these narrowly empirical
terms. To do so not only would leave no important place for the
medievalist, or the classicist, or the student of the age of rational-
ism, to choose just a few examples, but would be—and this is
far more important—a gross perversion of the very heart of our

calling. We—and we alone with the philosophers—still place our faith in, and rest our profession on, the ancient Latin maxim, "humani nihil a me alienum puto." We alone, and the philosophers, must assert in an age of increasing specialization the majestic doctrine that it is man's duty to know and inquire with regard to everything that concerns him. We alone, with the philosophers, have an opportunity to communicate to our students that sense of excitement which comes from the very broadest view of human activity.

It is difficult, to be sure, to reconcile this view with the tendency toward segmentation that exhibits itself in academic programs, so far as departments of history are concerned. But the opportunity is there. Take, for example, the field of diplomatic history. This field has been largely concerned with the documents, in the narrow sense of the term. But surely more can be made of it. In the last fifty years the study of the past has been much enriched by the changing fashions of our times. Economic history has followed on political history, social history on economic history, intellectual history on social history. Surely it is time for the historians of foreign policy—and there should certainly be such—to refresh and invigorate and enlarge their narrative by giving it a broader focus. How can we talk of the events of the 1930's without giving more emphasis than we have given to the great depression, and how can we talk of the diplomacy of the 1950's without relating it to the economic changes of the last two decades? How can we discuss the isolationism of the nineteenth century without relating it to the field of ideas? How can we discuss intelligently the diplomatic relations of the United States with Great Britain unless we understand the cultural complexes that have tended to unite—or divide—the two nations? How can we deal intelligently with the questions of the Orient unless we try to get some insight into the Oriental way of thought? The opportunity lies ready for the next generation to rewrite the diplomatic history of the United States in broader

and more meaningful terms than ever before. And what could
be said of diplomatic history can most certainly be said of political history, which, I venture to hope, will receive increasing
attention in a fresher and broader context.

There is, conceivably, another aspect to this question of
breadth. All approaches to history are interesting to someone.
But do we, in our course offerings, put enough weight on the
history of specific periods, treating these periods from a broad
and varied point of view, with emphasis on their numerous
aspects? And, if we were to do this, should we not see to it that
the aspects of a specific period which have the deepest significance should receive the major attention? I once knew a teacher
who gave a course in the Renaissance and devoted his major
attention to the political rivalries of the Italian city-states. He
might, it seems to me, have better placed the emphasis on the
extraordinary artistic efflorescence of the period and tried to
give to his students a deeper sense of the beautiful. In medieval
history is not the central problem to make vivid the development
of that majestic church of which Macaulay said: "She may still
exist in undiminished vigor when some traveller from New Zea-
land shall, in the midst of a vast solitude, take his stand on a
broken arch of London Bridge to sketch the ruins of Saint
Paul's." Might we not, in general, make more of an effort than
we generally do to seize the spirit of an epoch and come to grips
with the hypotheses and assumptions by which it lived?

One of the major problems of successful teaching, I suspect,
lies in the power with which the teacher is able to portray human
personality. It may well be that there have been writers and
academics who have inordinately stressed the personal. We can
hardly be subscribers, like Carlyle, to the great man theory of
history. Even the largest figures have to be understood in a context which far transcends their individual aspirations, ambitions,
and capacities. But if we must not exaggerate the role of the individual, so we must not minimize it or forget that the decisions

made by presidents and prime ministers and generals may actually alter the historical trend—as very likely did President Truman's decision to go into Korea in 1950. On the whole, as it seems to me, the trend of our modern historical research runs in the direction of depersonalizing history and reducing the role of the central figures. Social history represented—and represents—an immense broadening of our knowledge, and we owe a debt of gratitude to the men who pioneered in the field. But there is always the danger that, in thinking in terms of social forces, the role of the individual will become blurred and that for living, breathing human beings we shall substitute a list of names of the relatively obscure. The peril is equally great in intellectual history. The discovery of a new idea is always worth while, but it is necessary to ask just how much the new idea really mattered. We do not want to spend too much time on the trivial, merely because it happens to be novel. And we do not want the actors on the great stage of the world to be submerged by forces and ideas. The average man is intensely personal; therefore let us be sure that there are people in history. Let us make them live; let us share their triumphs and frustrations; let us *know* them. History is a kind of introduction to more interesting people than we can possibly meet in our restricted lives; let us not neglect the opportunity. Let us get to know Abraham Lincoln or Descartes or Julius Caesar at least as well as we know some of our day-to-day acquaintances.

But there is more to the matter than that. It is not wise to moralize too long or too often in the classroom. There is a sound instinct in undergraduates to react against moral attitudinizing. But is it necessary on that account to ignore the majestic example set by some of the great figures of our history, or all history? Shall we not properly dramatize and honor the burly German who stood before the emperor at the Diet of Worms and, when pressed as to his beliefs, declared: "Here stand I; I cannot otherwise"? Can we properly describe Washington without laying some of the emphasis on the unshakable sense of duty, on the undaunted tenacity with which he faced his problems? Is it not worth while (and encouraging, too) to note of him, as Jefferson said, that, if his mental qualities were decidedly not of the first order, he yet attained enormous wisdom, that he was perhaps, as Lecky said of him, "of all the great men in history the most invariably judicious" because he had the gift of consultation, of weighing and harmonizing conflicting opinions? Is it not possible that some of our students may learn something from his example and that they will order their lives better if they truly catch the feeling of his wisdom? Is it possible to live with Lincoln, as we American historians must live, without underlining and gaining some inspiration from his immense humility? "With malice toward none, with charity for all," run the words of the second inaugural. "I do not allow myself to suppose that either the convention or the League [the National Union] have concluded to decide that I am either the greatest or best man in America, but rather they have concluded that it is not best to swap horses while crossing the river." May we not learn from such expressions as these that humility is not weakness and that pride is not strength? Is it not possible to communicate this feeling to some of those we teach, to their own advantage and to their own growth?

As a matter of fact, our training and, too often, our intellectual habit lead us to analyze away the qualities that have made some of the great figures of the past leaders in their own time. We dissect and criticize—we, the little ones—but too rarely do we strive, in our intepretation of the past, to catch the authentic quality in the lives of the dominating figures of a by-gone era that warmed men's hearts and fired their minds. Let us look for a moment at Woodrow Wilson. He was often obstinate; he was sometimes intoxicated with his own verbosity; his sense of righteousness often became self-righteousness; his moral intensity became cloying; and there is an immense tragedy in the close of his political career. All these things can and must be said. But none of them explains the impact that Woodrow Wilson had on his own generation; none of them helps us to see why it was that so many men followed him, none of them helps us to measure his influence. Only those who lived as adults through the war of 1917–18 can realize just what his leadership meant; and if, in the days ahead, the American people come to take a wider view of their world responsibility than they did in 1919 and 1920, part of the honor and the glory, it can be demonstrated, is due to the Wilsonian example.

I press this point further. It is not only in the assumption of a wider role for America in international affairs that Wilson belongs to the wave of the future. He framed for himself a conception of the presidency that has an abiding vitality and even more relevance today than it had forty years ago; he spoke for the rising nationalities of the world and for a mitigation of the imperial impulse; he set his stamp on the practice of open diplomacy which, whether we like it or not, has become the necessary apparatus of the democratic state; in his views on the tariff and the currency he was one who looked toward our own age. Despite his crotchets, he deserves more admiration than he has usually received and more remembrance than he sometimes commands.

But it is not only through the vivid influence and example of personality that we can make our students see history as an attitude toward life that ought to be fruitful and helpful. Take another matter, the dangerous proneness of the man in the street to form shallow and partisan judgments on current matters on the basis of assumptions that cannot be either proved or wholly disproved. We have suffered in the past from such judgments: "World War I was a great mistake," "we lost China," "we fought the Second World War only to get into a greater mess than ever," and so on. This is the kind of opinion we ought never to permit ourselves to utter, and for reasons closely connected with the

very marrow of our subject. It is to be freely admitted that
the revisionist school of diplomatic historians can perform, and
have performed, a not inconsiderable service. By challenging
conventional assumptions, by demanding new light on the facts,
even by highly subjective interpretations of the facts, they
stimulate discussion and quicken the sense of scholarly responsibility in the rest of us. But it does not seem unfair to say that
in another sense they sometimes perform a fundamental disservice to their profession and to those whom they teach. The
disservice is this. Human events are immensely complicated; the
lines of cause and effect are in many cases very difficult to trace;
and in matters into which so many elements enter, as in foreign
policy, we should beware of that kind of dogmatism which
writes history in terms of hypothesis and which assumes a kind
of prescience with regard to what would have happened if some
other course had been followed than that which was followed.
We should, as the Second World War recedes into the distance,
try—more conscientiously than we have done—to understand the
motives and assumptions of those who described themselves as
isolationists as well as the motives and assumptions of those who
took a contrary view; but we should be careful to make it clear
that no finality can possibly attach to the thesis that we would
have been better off outside the struggle than in. Things were
as they were; they were because the mass of the American people came to believe (not unreasonably) that Hitler and Tojo
posed a definite threat to the future security of the United
States, and of its place in the world; and in this, as in other matters, it is wise to remember that there is some truth in the saying
that "die Weltgeschichte ist das Weltgericht." It is more important to understand the reasons why we acted as we did than
it is to speculate on what might have been if we had acted differently. What a boon it would be if, taking heed from this
principle and instructed by our knowledge, the ordinary man
paid less attention than he sometimes does to the self-interested

interpretations of the past used to promote the fortunes of a party or an individual!

What I have just said with regard to the Second World War raises a larger question. Are we, as teachers, to affirm or to question? Is our function to arouse doubt, to foster the critical attitude; or is it to set some positive standard of thought and action? If one puts the matter in more philosophic terms, is it true that the world suffers more from those who believe too little than from those who believe too much and believe what cannot be proved? Is skepticism corrosive and faith sustaining? Or is skepticism the necessary prelude to clarified thought and action, and is faith sometimes a blinding influence on conduct? The answer to these questions will be given by each individual according to his temperament. But perhaps we can make some little headway in dealing with it. Young people feel the need for affirmation, and yet they should be made to re-examine their own postulates. Can we not, in our teaching, distinguish between the things that can be safely affirmed and things that ought not to be affirmed? We can take positive stands on some matters that admit of prudent generalization. We can say, for example, that the Eighteenth Amendment was a failure, and a ghastly failure at that; we can indicate that much of the New Deal has been right in the sense that it has attained widespread popular acceptance, has been assimilated into the American way of life, and has been accepted—and in some respects even extended—by American conservatives. We can say, to choose an example more remote in time, that the Specie Circular had some very unfortunate consequences. But we cannot make dogmatic judgments on questions which are highly complex and which involve assumptions insusceptible of proof. We cannot, for example, assert that the country would have been ruined if William Jennings Bryan had been elected in 1896, or that the history of the world would have been changed had we entered the League, or that it was a mistake to intervene in Korea. We should illustrate in our teaching the difference between certainty and uncertainty, and the need of both for the well-balanced mind. Let us not shrink from affirmation where affirmation is possible, but let us recognize the limits of affirmation as well.

Closely connected with what I have been trying to say is the matter of seeing many sides. One must remember, however, that there are two sides to the question of seeing many sides. Much of the effective work of the world is done by men of strong feeling who move toward their goals without too much analysis of the pros and cons of conduct. Much is accomplished by men of power who reckon little of the social consequences of their action. But it is, it seems to me, more consistent with the spirit of our profession—indeed fundamental—that we should maintain a kind of intellectual and moral balance in our instruction. The function of the mind is to temper, to direct, to moderate, and to elevate the natural instincts and passions of mankind. If we believe at all in the rule of intelligence, then we must seek to understand divergent points of view and to chasten selfishness and unregulated feeling with reason and some objective criterion of the public good. The spirit of learning was never better described than by Woodrow Wilson in an address delivered to the Harvard Chapter of Phi Beta Kappa in 1909. It consists, to paraphrase him, in a preference for the non-partisan point of view, in the ability to look at the essentials rather than stick to the letter of the reasoning, in the kind of detachment that eliminates from the account personal considerations of mood or class and relates itself to carefully thought-out and disinterested ends. In arriving at some such attitude, it is by no means to be supposed that we come to nothing but a pallid neutrality. It is an error, and a gross one, to imagine that what scholarship demands of us is no opinion at all. As one of the greatest of our past presidents insisted, to come to no conclusion is to come to a very dangerous and antisocial conclusion, to a kind of historical nihilism. Our students do not want this. What they want, and what they will profit by, is to see us turn a question about in our minds, going over its complexities and varied points of view, and then to see us come to a decision informed by knowledge and based on considerations that can be recognized as rational. They want, too, to see us approach a great public question in a spirit of what we deem to be disinterested consideration for the public good. And, if we do this with regard to the problems of the past, we will help them to do the same with regard to the problems of the present.

This kind of intellectual and moral balance can be illustrated in many ways, and with regard to many matters. Take, for example, the operation of our business system. In the course of the last two or three historical generations, workers in the field of American history have been, on the whole, highly critical of the business classes. The fact is understandable. The selfishness and ruthlessness of the business struggle as it unfolded itself in the latter part of the nineteenth century, the resistance of large elements of the business classes to the most necessary reforms, their invocation of legal process to arrest or delay these reforms, the failure of many of the leaders of the business world to understand even the most elementary principles of the economy under which they were operating, and, above all, the dramatic collapse of 1929, all contributed to a very unfavorable view among scholars of the role of the capitalist in American society. But, in reviewing these and other facts of the same kind, our historians have often underrated the essential, the fundamental contribution of the capitalist. The actual management of our vast industrial machine is a task that calls for very high qualities, and they are not the qualities usually associated with the academic mind. The ability to make decisions, the ability to organize a hierarchy of administrative talent, the ability to harness the energies of others in the most productive way, the willingness to take chances, the quality of confidence and faith in the future, these are some of the things that are necessary to the operation of our system; and they are most surely to be found in the higher ranks of business. So long as we have the kind of social and economic order that we have, and so long as we can justly say that this order has played its part in producing the most prosperous society that the world has ever known, we shall do well not to denigrate in generalized terms our business leaders. And there is more than this to be said. In this, as in other matters, we are often the victims of the past which we study. Is it not true that the newer generation in the business field approaches the problems of society with a more enlightened and a broader view than that which prevailed three decades ago? The great depression was a profound educational experience. Its lessons were assimilated, at least in part, not only by academicians but by those who play a more active role in the management of the economy.

Let me make another point. No trained historian can possibly put himself in the position of a thick-and-thin exponent of the static. If there is one thing clearer than another, it is that change is the law of life, one of the deepest and most inevitable of all human phenomena. We shall all of us live more happily if we accept its inevitability. And we ought to help our students to do so, to think of social change not in terms of apprehension or of indignation but coolly and constructively, applying intellectual and not emotional criteria to the problems of social adjustment, weighing the advantages and disadvantages of this or that measure, but recognizing at the same time that it is rarely possible to cling devotedly to the status quo. We have our choice, as all history teaches, between the gradual reconciliation of the old and the new and those more violent processes which destroy much that is good along with much that is evil.

Just as we accept the inevitability of change, so we ought to seek to understand the values of a society that is past. In an increasingly secular age one of the major values of medieval history must lie in a clearer understanding of the great church that flourished in the days of Anselm and Aquinas and still exercises its mighty and pervasive influence over the lives of men. The comfort of faith, the hope of happiness in the world to come, the emphasis on moral rather than on material values, these are all things we should seek to appreciate. For they live on in a world in which preoccupation with social improvement and economic progress often crowds out some of the deepest sources of strength for the individual.

Nor need we uncritically identify change with progress. Take, for instance, a more current problem, the problem of imperialism. In the world of today, the tide runs strongly against the domination of one society by another. Abstractly speaking, this is easy to understand. Does not our own Declaration of Independence declare that "governments derive their just powers from the consent of the governed"? But the question may be looked at differently. Is self-government inevitably—in all cases and in all lands—in the interest, objectively conceived, of the peoples concerned? Are all peoples capable of self-rule; or, on the other hand, does independence, in many parts of the world, mean the domination of the societies concerned by a narrow and selfish oligarchy, less occupied with the welfare of the masses than an external regime might be? Is it not the case that imperialism, now a term of reproach, has provided the basis of order and stability which permitted the importation of foreign capital, put technical abilities at the service of the populations concerned, and provided internal improvement and growth which laid the basis for a more widely diffused prosperity? Was not our forty-odd years' occupation of the Philippines an illustration of this principle? Did not the British rule in India lay the basis for more successful self-government than would have arisen spontaneously in that vast subcontinent? And is it necessarily a gain today if the less mature nations of the world sweat material progress out of the labor of the masses, throw off tutelage, deal harshly with the foreign capital that has made or would make development possible, and insist upon proceeding on their own?

We shall have to wait a long time before we know surely whether this is progress or retrogression.

In judging any age, whether of centuries ago or our own, we need to strike—as scholars—a proper balance between liberalism and conservatism. The essence of the former point of view, as I see it, lies in a humane desire to see the improvement of the social order, in a generous view of the capacities of human nature, in a critical attitude toward authority and dogma, in a wise, though restrained, hope in the possibility of making the world a little better place, in a belief in the dignity of human effort. The essence of conservatism, as it appears to me, lies in the spirit which insists upon a careful and critical examination of any proposal of change, takes account of the intransigence and capacity for evil of the human species, recognizes the difficult tactical problems involved in any project of reform, and understands that there are values to be preserved in any healthy society, as well as new values to be gained. Whatever history we teach, we can give due weight to both these points of view. And, if we do so, we shall produce neither cynics nor visionaries but well-balanced citizens.

And now let me go back to recapitulate what I have been trying to say. I believe that the greatest challenge confronting historians today is the challenge of the classroom. To meet it we shall have to give to teaching a higher place in our scale of values than we do today. We shall have to select our students more definitely with this end in view; we shall have to give them an opportunity to exercise their capacities in this regard; we shall have to reward them adequately for their performance. And—it goes without saying—we shall ourselves have to be the best teachers that we know how to be, the most humane, the most sympathetic, the most dedicated.

And what we teach will be more than knowledge. Knowledge we must have, and have in growing measure—the fruit of an ever-exploring mind, the product of a restlessly inquiring spirit.

But, in addition, we shall be influential in proportion as we think about the *values* that we wish to communicate as well as about the *facts* that we wish to communicate. We must make the past more vivid and the quality of man's adventure more deeply understood; we must interpret the past broadly, in the spirit of a man to whom nothing human is alien; we need not be afraid to speak of moral values, to be sensitive and compassionate, or to exalt wisdom and goodness; we must set the example of a sound intellectual and moral balance, of a broad view of human values; we must make the processes of the mind in seeking truth so fair, so understanding of various opinions, and yet so clear that they will command respect and deserve imitation. And, if we do these things, the classroom will be more than a lecture place, more than a preparation for examinations, and more than the medium for communicating facts that will soon be forgotten; it will be an abiding influence in the life of the great nation to which we belong and a source of light to the generations that sit at our feet. It will be a vital part of life itself.